THE JOURNEY THAT NEVER WAS

AROUND THE WORLD IN A MINI IN THE EARLY 1960s

Jeanne de Ferranti

THE JOURNEY THAT NEVER WAS

AROUND THE WORLD IN A MINI IN THE EARLY 1960s

Jeanne de Ferranti

MEREO
Cirencester

Mereo Books

1A The Wool Market Dyer Street Cirencester Gloucestershire GL7 2PR
An imprint of Memoirs Publishing www.mereobooks.com

The journey that never was: 978-1-86151-370-0

First published in Great Britain in 2014
by Mereo Books, an imprint of Memoirs Publishing

Copyright ©2014

Jeanne de Ferranti has asserted her right under the Copyright Designs and Patents
Act 1988 to be identified as the author of this work.

A CIP catalogue record for this book is available from the British Library.

This book is sold subject to the condition that it shall not by way of trade or otherwise be lent,
resold, hired out or otherwise circulated without the publisher's prior consent in any form of
binding or cover, other than that in which it is published and without a similar condition,
including this condition being imposed on the subsequent purchaser.

The address for Memoirs Publishing Group Limited can be found at
www.memoirspublishing.com

The Memoirs Publishing Group Ltd Reg. No. 7834348

The Memoirs Publishing Group supports both The Forest Stewardship Council® (FSC®) and
the PEFC® leading international forest-certification organisations. Our books carrying both the
FSC label and the PEFC® and are printed on FSC®-certified paper. FSC® is the only
forest-certification scheme supported by the leading environmental organisations including
Greenpeace. Our paper procurement policy can be found at
www.memoirspublishing.com/environment

Typeset in 11/15pt Bembo
by Wiltshire Associates Publisher Services Ltd. Printed and bound in Great Britain by
Printondemand-Worldwide, Peterborough PE2 6XD

CONTENTS

Introduction

Postcript
Appendix – notes on motoring and camping

My appreciation goes to the Writer's Group of Andorra, especially to Clare Allcard, Patricia Grey and Judy Wood, without whose help and encouragement this book would never have reached completion.
Also to Chris Newton for his patient editing.

INTRODUCTION

The Morris Mini-Minor, a British icon of the 1960s, was designed for BMC (the British Motor Corporation) by Sir Alec Issigonis in 1959. It had two doors, tiny wheels (the total diameter was eighteen and a half inches) and front wheel drive, which removed the need for a transmission tunnel and allowed 80% of the floor pan to be used for passengers and luggage. It had brilliant road holding and its revolutionary design took advantage of every inch of interior space.

My father, an electrical engineer, loved it and considered it ideal for the young: economic to buy and to run. And so, on my twenty-first birthday, I became the proud owner of a pale blue Mini. I christened her Honey and proudly wrote her name across the bonnet.

In many ways, she was my passport to freedom. Life in the first three years of the 1960s was still very restricted. Society expected offspring to conform to their parents' wishes. Colour television did not exist; in fact few people had television at all. This meant no documentaries and stunning photos of the

World's Cultural Treasures to tempt you to go and see for yourself. Mass tourism had not yet been invented and few people could afford to travel overseas. My knowledge of geography beyond the confines of Western Europe was limited to the names of countries, oceans, mountain ranges and important rivers. Internet research was a dream somewhere out in the future and it never occurred to me to find out anything very much about any of the places I would eventually visit.

I had a dream; to go to Australia. Rather than go by ship I opted to go 'overland'. I was lucky to have a father who extolled independence, as he himself had travelled widely as a young man. He understood my vision of adventure and rather than stand in the way, encouraged and helped me, even though I was 'only a girl'.

Another English girl, Jane, who I had met briefly in Switzerland where we had been working, was also eager for adventure. She agreed to go with me, providing we included New Zealand and her extended family in our plans.

The Mini, Jane and I eventually reached Australia and New Zealand. After a year of trying to adapt to the culture and earn a living, we headed back home (which had not been the original intention), across the Pacific Ocean, through Mexico, the United States of America and Canada. Our expedition took two years to complete.

It was definitely a first for the indomitable Mini, to travel all the way round the world and home again. The achievement was never released to the press, as it never occurred to me to do so. Besides which, my family shunned publicity. So the story that follows has never been told before.

CHAPTER ONE

FRANCE, SWITZERLAND AND ITALY

The airport at Lydd, in the south of England, was casual and friendly after the turmoil of preparation in the big city. Passengers sat around idly waiting, cups half-full of tasteless coffee on the bare tables in front of them.

The 12.15 flight, No 206, was a quarter of an hour ahead of schedule and the early morning drizzle had finally cleared. With only eight other passengers and minimal fuss, we filed past the customs officer, who eyed us critically as he examined our passports. Three cars were lined up with their bonnets open so that the engine numbers could be checked before being driven, by the airport chauffeurs, up a wide ramp into the gaping mouth of the small plane. Once inside they were secured with heavy chains, the ramp was removed and the great doors were closed.

It was the 5th of September 1961, and at last Jane and I were on our way to Australia, overland in a blue Mini. I had met Jane earlier that year when she came out to Switzerland as a replacement for my job in a finishing school. She was a trained children's nurse, tall, with short dark hair, twenty-eight years old, a no-nonsense sort of girl. I was only twenty-one, ripe for adventure, with a burning ambition to go to Australia.

In those days most people went by passenger liner via the Suez Canal, which took six weeks, but that meant that I would miss all those exciting places on the way. So slowly a plan took shape; to drive overland through Europe, Turkey, Iran, Pakistan and India. The RAC were extremely helpful providing me with a very rough map showing the principal, mostly dirt roads, crossing the region and the necessary triptych, containing all documents and a detailed passport for the car, which guaranteed I would not sell it on the way,

Initially I had planned the expedition with a cousin, but we soon fell out over whose car we should use. That was the first blow. I had already given up my job and preparations were well underway. It was not a journey I could undertake on my own, and no way did I want to back down and go by ship, so I wrote to a friend I had worked with in Switzerland. She suggested I ask Jane, who enthusiastically agreed, provided we postpone the departure date. She felt obliged to give her new employers six months' notice. We also agreed to modify the route to include six months in New Zealand, where she had numerous relatives.

At last we were on our way, belted into rough canvas seats at the rear of the aircraft, which lumbered along the runway, creaking and shuddering as it gathered speed and then finally took off protesting, and oh, so slowly!

"I didn't think we'd make it!" remarked one of the passengers. Neither had I. The sea below looked very close and rough and I began to wish we had crossed the Channel on an old-fashioned steamer instead; that is until only twenty minutes later, we circled over Le Touquet and glided gently down onto the runway in France.

Somehow we had managed to pack all our requirements into the compact and brilliantly-designed little Mini – cooking equipment, clothes, maps and spare parts for the car. A heavy-duty sump guard had been fitted underneath as a precaution on the unmade roads and tracks we would encounter; there was much less clearance than in a normal car, let alone a Jeep. I had had her name proudly painted on the bonnet - Honey.

Instead of a tent, we had a solid six-foot-long roof rack, to which at night we attached a semi-circular canvas top, not unlike those used on the covered wagons by early American explorers. It was an adaptation of something more elaborate exhibited at a recent car show. We slept in sleeping bags on a double air mattress which had to be blown up every night. Our clothes were tucked under the pillow in case someone disturbed us camping in the wild and we had to get up unexpectedly.

It was exhilarating to be on our way, and chatting happily we soon covered the first hundred miles along the then narrow poplar-lined roads of northern France. But just beyond Cambrai, Honey coughed, spluttered and stopped on a steep hill immediately in front of the lorry we had just overtaken. The driver leaned out angrily to swear and shake his fist at us. Dismayed, we got out and peered under the bonnet; nothing was loose. I could find no apparent reason for the breakdown.

"What do we do now?" asked Jane as I extracted a comprehensive car manual from one of the side pockets and started to leaf through the pages. As if on cue, an English couple, returning from their holiday in Italy, noticed our obvious helplessness and kindly stopped to give advice.

"Why don't you check the fuel pump?" suggested the young

man. So I produced the shiny new red jack from the boot. Too flimsy for the job, it buckled like cardboard under the weight of the loaded car. That was not a good start.

They laughed, in disbelief, when we explained that we were driving to Ceylon via Turkey and India.

"Don't worry. Do you have a rope? Good, then we'll tow you back to the nearest garage."

The garage owner, a small, unpleasant man, waved his arms about furiously and refused to have anything to do with the British, whom he obviously disliked intensely. Apparently he had been unable to obtain parts for a baby Austin that had been dumped in the garage a week previously. Unperturbed, we refused to move; to no avail. He just pushed the car back out into the road and left us standing there. Fortunately the English couple had not left and they agreed to tow us back to Cambrai. It was second time lucky, for the charming *patron* himself changed the electric fuel pump and we were soon on our way.

Around four o'clock in the afternoon we started looking for somewhere to spend the night. The towpath of a nearby canal seemed far too remote for slightly nervous inexperienced campers, so we parked the car on the playing fields of Viller Franqueux, a farming community. As the village shop didn't sell milk, we were sent to a farm hidden behind tall green doors in the main street. The picturesque courtyard was ablaze with flowers. A barn was piled high with straw and children played happily among the hens in the dust. A woman came out from the kitchen, wiping her hands on her apron, and took us into the dairy to fill our bottle with milk, still warm from the cow.

While Jane collected wood and built a roaring fire, I rummaged through our goods and chattels in search of cooking pots and camping equipment. Out came a first aid box including never-to-be used malaria tablets, desert rations, a large oil paint box, four suitcases of clothes, sleeping bags, a seemingly unending supply of paraphernalia and a typewriter. All had to be repacked methodically so that things would be easier to find and I wondered how often we would have to repeat this performance.

We feasted on cold chicken brought from England and washed down with hot coffee. I had never thought a picnic could taste so good or that camping could be such fun. Smoke from the fire kept the horrid little midges at bay and the camping light connected to the car battery completed the cosy feeling. Needlessly, I worried whether we would end up with no power.

Finally, after making sure the fire was out, tidying everything away and locking up, we clambered up onto the tented roof rack. This was easily reached by putting one foot on the rear bumper. It began to drizzle Far into the night we lay awake listening to the drops splashing on the canvas above us, to the leaves rustling in the trees, straining anxiously for any unfamiliar sound; an owl hooted, a hedgehog squealed, a scooter buzzed by.

Next morning we were up at seven, having slept surprisingly well. After dismantling the camping equipment, we prepared coffee and porridge on a small butane gas cooker and were en route before nine o'clock.

The drizzle continued all day as we drove across France along straight, narrow, tree-lined roads and on through the picturesque Jura Mountains into Switzerland. Our route flanked the familiar shores of Lac Léman and climbed up into the mountains to Diablerets. Just beyond the village was a cluster of chalets belonging to the posh finishing school, Mon Fertile.

The main building housed the office and dining room. The

chalet where I had lived above the stable had never lost the strong smell of cattle. It was down a narrow, often icy path, facing the freezing air from the glacier tumbling down the mountain opposite. But this was rural Switzerland and I had loved my job. Nothing had changed. This was where we had met briefly eight months previously. Jane had arrived to replace me as secretary cum teacher.

The joint heads gave us a curt reception. What did we expect? We had unwittingly left them with a staffing problem.

"No, you can't possibly stay here overnight, but you may borrow the key to the empty chalet in the village." That was a great blessing as it was warm and dry! None of our former friends seemed to be around, so we treated ourselves to the most delicious *croûte au fromage* at La Couronne, in the village.

It was still drizzling in the morning. One of the tyres had a slow puncture and to make matters worse, the foot pump fell apart and had to be repaired at the local garage. Perhaps our equipment was not as new as it needed to be for the long journey ahead. After all, the Mini already had over 12,000 miles on the clock and had been my runabout in Switzerland the previous year. Unperturbed, we took it in our stride.

Honey managed the long, spectacular climb up a narrow, tortuous road to the top of the 2005-metre-high Simplon Pass without any problem. It was deserted. Trails of damp cloud hung over the surrounding peaks. We parked and raced uphill to look at a monument, a giant stone eagle commemorating the Second Mountain Brigade. They had been responsible for guarding the pass during the Second World War.

The road was built during Napoleonic times to transport artillery over the pass from Switzerland into Italy. Subsequently it was used by the postal carriages and later buses. Ten years previously I had come here with my father squashed in the back of his Bugatti together with the luggage. At that time a lone hospice run by monks had looked bleak looming out of the mist. A couple of friendly St Bernard dogs wandered around. They were used to rescue lost travellers caught in a snowstorm. Attached to their collar was a tiny barrel of supposedly reviving brandy.

On the southern side of the Alps, the road tumbled down a narrow gorge into Italy, where great fortresses, camouflaged by the rocky cliffs, must have daunted many an invading army. Patches of blue sky appeared and grew. The sun came out and at the frontier, the Italian customs greeted us with much playful banter, surprised by my fluency in their language – I had learnt it at school in Firenze.

The field, overlooking Lago Maggiore where we camped that night, was hemmed in by the curve of yet another steep zigzag road behind the town of Verbania. We asked for water at a nearby house and a woman dressed in black came to the door. She was a widow and it was still customary for all widows to be dressed in black whatever their age. She filled our two-gallon plastic can at the outside pump and chatted animatedly about her family; her three sons, one who had died accidentally, her daughter married to a farmer, her meagre pension and even the price of her house. Her life was a constant struggle. The property was extensive, with magnificent views over the lake, but very run down.

Later, when drifting off to sleep, a seductive voice reached us out of the darkness.

"Come out so we can see you… Surely there is room for four up there…Look out of your tent… I am very beautiful."

Italian men are notoriously romantic. Nervous, yet with suppressed amusement, we held our breath and pretended to be asleep, hoping the two men would soon leave. Was I glad to hear their footsteps die away in the distance! Camping wild was such a new experience and without the protective walls of a house, little fears lurked in the mind. I was alert to every new sound, yet again it took me a long time to drift off to sleep.

A luxurious ferry plied across Lago Maggiore from Verbania to Laveno on the other side.

"Let's take the ferry," said Jane, keen to avoid the long slow drive around the lake. On board, perched on the roof rack, we had a grandstand view of the blue waters stretching away to north and south, framed by steep wooded hills. Hidden among the trees were the modern weekend villas of prosperous Milanese people.

I loved shopping in the local markets and the one in Gavirate presented us with a good excuse to buy provisions – spaghetti, oil, tomatoes, aubergines, parmesan cheese and some *mortadella*. We certainly weren't going to starve. It all looked so good and colourful.

"*Prova, Signorina*" (try it), insisted a beaming Italian, his large paunch barely concealed behind a copious apron as he handed Jane a slither of parmesan to taste.

"Come buy my fruit, my vegetables, my baskets..." called the vendors. The baskets were decorated with patterns of flowers and birds worked in raffia. But alas, we had no room for souvenirs in our tiny car.

On through undulating, sparsely treed countryside, stopping briefly for lunch by the lake in Como and again to look at the uninspiring *Lago di Garda*. Jane bought her first-ever bikini, the very latest daring and revealing fashion. Even recently, in Spain, you were expected to wear a short skirt over your swimsuit. Fearful of the slimy weeds she imagined lurked beneath the surface, Jane could not be cajoled into the murky water to christen it. That didn't deter me from having a dip.

It had been a fairly oppressive day but torrential rain soon cleared the air, making the remainder of the journey to Venice hazardous, especially as it was already dark when we joined the new, fast *autostrada*. Italy's link roads were innovative, wide and engineered for speed, but even with comparatively light traffic they had their drawbacks. Skidding was always a possibility on a wet surface. Two motor scooter accidents happened before our very eyes, causing several long delays.

On the Venice camp site, we met the King's College 'Expedition to Greece in search of the lost city of Thrace'. The young men volunteered to help change the tyre that had a slow puncture. Their jack, made for an antiquated Austin shooting brake, was too large and ours was beyond repair. Amid much laughter, these five hefty chaps attempted, working as one, to lift the front end of the Mini off the ground. She was far too heavy. They had not bargained for the solid sump guard.

I then asked a bearded Israeli if he had a jack to lend us, but he misunderstood and pointed to the bank across the road. Realizing that we were talking at cross purposes, he produced a book of 'useless' phrases and we found the word for jack. I ended up borrowing one from the local garage and with the help of the expedition members, we managed to get it under the sump guard and jack up the car. At least the puncture repair outfit came in handy and the tyre was soon as good as new.

The day in Venice, the city of my ancestors, was unforgettable and I was quite convinced that I should return again at a later date. Leaving Honey on the camp site, we took the number 6 bus to the terminus and boarded the steamer ferry to *Piazza San Marco*. The *Gran Canale* was like Oxford Street in the rush hour. Instead of buses, private cars and taxis, steamers, launches and gondolas jostled for space. Palatial buildings, their foundations reaching deep below the surface, with Moorish windows, mushroom shaped and heavily barred, reflected in the sunlit waters of the canal. In the *Piazza* pigeons mingled with the tourists.

The Cathedral appeared more breathtakingly beautiful than we had imagined; its façade of multicoloured marbles and the biblical scenes, depicted in mosaic above the great arches, framed ornately carved doors. An army of marble saints, soldiers and lions strode across the domes. In the cold, dark interior, candles flickered on the altar of the *Madonna,* throwing patterns of light up into the gold mosaic dome above.

The Doge's Palace, once the centre of Venice's political, social and economic life as well as the residence of the Doge, was equally magnificent; a maze of richly-painted rooms with gilded ceilings, priceless murals, glistening marble walls and floors and heavily ornate marble fireplaces. Reading through the engraved list of incumbents, we found the Doge Sebastiano Ziani, my illustrious and perhaps notorious ancestor, who had enlarged and embellished the Palace in 1173.

Back out in the bustling *Piazza,* the numerous cafés were packed with tourists enjoying *gelati* and *pasta.* A newspaper vendor wove his way between the tables. On the quayside tourists bargained with gondoliers, clad in red and white striped shirts and boater, for a trip across the lagoon. The slim, highly-polished craft rode gracefully on the choppy water.

Venice was such a fascinating and vibrant city, full of unexpected vistas and history. I had expected to find it marred by a putrid smell of heat, pollution and crowds, but in September with the main tourist season over, the days were cool and the atmosphere surprisingly pleasant.

Towards evening we made our way back along narrow streets

lined with shops specializing in blown glass and hand-embroidered linen, along alleyways rarely reached by the burning sun, over delicate hump-backed bridges, through a market and across the *Gran Canale* back to the mainland.

A far cry from the speedy *autostrada,* the road south from Venice was narrow, full of potholes and diversions, crossing flat monotonous country. Long queues of cars built up at the numerous railway crossings and at bridges that had to be opened for the passage of laden barges using the canal system.

Somewhere we managed to lose the front number plate and were subsequently stopped several times. Because of all the fuss, we reported the loss at a police station. A lone official, sitting behind a desk at the far end of a large bare room, meticulously recorded all the details in a hefty tome. A letter, in Italian, with all the relevant details was handed to us in case of further questioning, but it was never required even though we travelled across several continents.

South of Ravenna, the road climbed steadily to 900 metres through picturesque countryside. It was Sunday and again progress was slow. It must have been a feast day as the village streets were choked with religious processions. One was the funeral of a child escorted by young children clad in their best, weaving and wobbling all over the road on their bicycles. On the corners of a cart, drawn by two white ponies, sat four little girls with flowing hair and long white dresses holding bouquets of flowers and in the centre lay a white coffin decorated with gold; a touching farewell to a young life.

The road improved and we had a flat-out run into Florence, chasing a nippy little red car which eventually disappeared into the thickening traffic. The campsite, on the banks of the river Arno with a view of the town, was expensive, overcrowded and a hive of activity. But it was a veritable camper's paradise with everything imaginable laid on for civilized comfort. Though we drove round and round we couldn't find flat parking for the Mini. When finally Jane spotted one, someone else nipped in. Luckily there was just room for us behind a tree, as it was already 10 pm when two very tired girls pitched camp.

At six in the morning, the bells rang out from all the city churches and two hours later a loudspeaker greeted all campers to a "good morning" in countless languages. So much for a lie in!

Just to make things worse we were a mere 45 lire (the equivalent of a few shillings) short for paying the bill. The campsite wouldn't change a pound note, nor would a nearby hotel. Fortunately some Australians came to our rescue. Now we just had to find a bank.

Florence had long been a centre of European trade and finance and was considered to be the birthplace of the Renaissance. Even in September, it was seething with tourists and traffic; invisible policemen with shrill whistles kept the jay-walker in his place, should he unwittingly venture across the road on the '*Alto*' sign. Famous churches stood on every corner; the Church of the *Santa Croce* with its Dome painted by Donatello and Luca della Robbia and inside the Pietà, a breathtakingly beautiful sculpture by Michelangelo. The *Duomo* with its striped marble façade, a massive building conveying grandeur and awe, the magnificent murals of the Baptistery and the Gates of Paradise intricately worked in bronze. The Church *of Santa Maria Novela*… all, so ornate and different from English places of worship.

"Surely not another church," complained Jane, "Italy is nothing but churches!" But they fascinated me, and I wanted to see them all.

Typically two Italian students tried to pick us up, but by this time we were too overwhelmed with sightseeing to be able to cope with them. Zigzagging through the crowd to throw them off our tracks we found ourselves on the *Ponte Vecchio*. The original stone pillars supporting the three arches dated from Roman era, though the bridge had been rebuilt several times due to flooding. It spanned the sluggish brown waters of the River Arno at its narrowest point. Jewellery was on sale in the open air shops which have always been a structural part of the bridge. Legend has it that the concept of bankruptcy originated here. When the merchant couldn't pay his debts, his *banco* or table was physically broken or *rotto* by the soldiers. *Bancorotto* meant that he no longer had a table and he couldn't sell his wares – hence the English word 'bankrupt'.

As a thirteen-year-old schoolgirl, I had been sent to live with a family in Florence to learn Italian. Through the years I had lost touch and felt I should like to meet them again. The *Viale dei Mille* along which I had trudged each day to school was still the same tree-lined avenue I remembered. The corner café where the coffee beans were ground was still there, but *Via Marchetti*, the street where we had lived, was transformed. The road was up, the apartment building was covered in scaffolding and under repair and nobody remembered the family who strangely bore the same name as the street.

Travelling through Italy was more like a holiday than the beginning of a long journey into the unknown. It was easy to cover the two to three hundred miles a day planned into our schedule. We had time to get to know one another and get used to life on the road. Little did we realize what lay ahead.

After a morning spent in a quiet spot among the olive trees lazing in the sunshine, sketching, talking, writing letters and enjoying doing nothing, we stopped off briefly in Siena to look at the cathedral. It was similar in style to the *Duomo* in Florence, yet smaller and richer in design, built in the form of a Greek cross, its façade and interior striped with horizontal black and white marble. The sun on its daily round lit up, one by one, the heads of the eight saints that embellished the inside of the main dome. Amethysts and rubies adorned the countless crosses and shields of the warrior statues and parts of the marble floor. Normally hidden beneath protective wooden boards, these were uncovered and allowing glimpses of the vibrant Italian marble used to portray some sixty Biblical scenes.

Looking for a suitable place to camp wild where we would remain undisturbed was never easy. After a couple of disappointing attempts, we headed wearily south towards Rome, finally turning off near the town of Ansedonia. Here at last was the perfect spot near an abandoned primitive restaurant, overlooking a stony beach and the sea. We parked Honey under the palm trees, collected driftwood and made use of the fireplace left by previous campers. It was a wonderfully balmy night and so good to be out of the turmoil of cities; to sit under the stars, watching the twinkling lights of the fishing boats, with the rich scent of burning pine from the thin curl of smoke rising lazily from the wood fire, teasing our nostrils.

Awake early, I inched myself out of my sleeping bag and without disturbing Jane, who was still asleep, I climbed down from our roof top tent. Seeing no one about, I undressed, leaving my clothes in a neat pile on the beach, and slipped into the soft, caressing sea water. This was bliss. I could have gone on swimming forever, towards the distant horizon savouring the solitude of the dawn.

Suddenly, the spell was broken. A man was standing near my

discarded clothes, his arms folded, waiting. For nearly half an hour I swam backwards and forwards until at last Jane, still half asleep and disapproving, appeared with a towel. After threatening to leave me to my own devices, she condescended to walk some way up the beach so as to shield me from that odious Italian. As I emerged from the sea, he turned and walked away, but managed to startle us by reappearing, to explain in sign language and a torrent of words that it was not customary to swim in the altogether. I pretended not to understand and silently we continued to eat our breakfast bowl of porridge.

One night we tried to camp in among the *macchia*, a prickly scrub found on the sand dunes. Just as we had found a suitable flat place for the car, an enormous woman appeared on the dune above us.

"You can't stay there" she called out. "The *carabinieri* [the police] will come and move you." Oh no! That meant we'd have to move on and find somewhere else. But then she surprised us. "Come into my garden" she said. "You can park under the lean-to. Here, it has a corrugated roof for shelter."

Jane looked at me dubiously. "Do you think we ought to? What about rats? We could be badly bitten by mosquitoes during the night."

"Oh, don't worry, it'll be fine."

It was, except for the oppressive heat given off by the tin roof that kept us awake most of the night and as from daybreak, the endless pitter-patter of pigeon's feet just above. At least we felt quite safe.

Grandma turned out to be quite a character with her large brown eyes, loud cheerful voice and a generous heart. She shared her home with her son and daughter-in-law and their tiny child. They stood watching in amazement as the roof-rack tent was prepared for the night, with a light, connected to the car battery, hanging ready for use inside. They had no electricity and used candles to light the two small rooms they lived in at the back of a seaside villa, of which they were the guardians. There was a bedroom and kitchen-cum-sitting room; Grandma slept in a hut at the bottom of the garden. After supper we shared a chocolate bar with our new-found friends.

In the morning, the whole family insisted on changing into their best clothes and then stood rigidly to attention to have their photograph taken before we left. Mother presented us with two brown eggs, plucked all the flowers she could muster and burst into tears as she affectionately hugged us goodbye. They had so little, yet gave so much.

Travelling through Italy was great. We easily covered three hundred miles a day without feeling tired and spent the remaining daylight hours lazing on a beach or in the countryside somewhere. The weather was perfect and the temperature around 80° Fahrenheit.

Next day we arrived in the capital. Rome is considered to be the birthplace of western civilization and in the first century became the seat of the papacy. After the Middle-Ages, like Florence, it became a major centre of Italian Renaissance. St Peter's Basilica was one of those marvels.

Visitors to St Peter's were expected to be decently clad; ladies must have their arms and heads covered, men their legs, and cameras had to be deposited for safe keeping at the door as photography was forbidden. Jane, as usual, disappeared in search of tombstones and plaques commemorating the great of the past, leaving me in the nave enthralled by the sheer magnificence of design achieved by Michelangelo; for me the splendour of St Peter's lay in its simplicity.

As one by one I explored the side chapels, I pretended not to notice the beautiful young Italian, with flashing black eyes, following me about. He was coming towards me at every turn, until in the end I could not resist returning his disarming smile. His name was Pietro, and when I explained that I was not alone but accompanied by Jane, his cousin Angelo materialized at his side. They took us to see the cathedral treasure of most delicately hand-embroidered vestments, bejewelled crosses and golden vessels, and then invited us out to lunch on chicken and spaghetti, washed down with plenty of wine at a typical Roman bistro. It was below street level; legs of all shapes and sizes strolled past the narrow windows just under the ceiling.

At four o'clock we collected our mail from the main post office. It had been sent 'poste restante', the only form of communication we would have with our families for the next six months. Telephone calls would have been too expensive and connections to the UK not only unreliable but often entailed hours of hanging around waiting, so we had agreed to write regularly and arranged to pick up mail at strategic stops along the way, usually every three weeks; somehow we nearly always managed to arrive at these places on a Sunday or Friday, the Moslem holiday. Rome was the first, and only ten days from home.

Tempers frayed as Jane, who was map reading, continually misdirected me along one-way streets leading nowhere in an attempt to find the official camp site situated on one of Rome's seven hills, overlooking the city. I had arranged a rendezvous with Pietro on the camp site and never expected him to roll up, but he did, together with Angelo. Jane was tired and had had enough of the Italians for one day, so she opted to stay put. Besides she had met an English couple and was keen to exchange experiences with them. Angelo conveniently disappeared, leaving Pietro and myself to enjoy the evening.

Next morning, after hanging the washing out on a line strung between two trees, we lifted the tented roof rack off the car and placed it on the ground to reserve our place. Then off we drove to look for the catacombs. They were not, as we had expected, beneath the cathedral, as this area was reserved for the tombs of popes, but out along the *Via Appia Antica*. Disappointed to find them closed, we visited the Coliseum instead. What a dreadful way to die, even for the bravest, to be fed to the hungry lions while the crowds looked on cheering or jeering.

I had the Mini serviced and the jack repaired by the BMC agents in Rome in a large, stuffy subterranean garage, while Jane went out shopping. We couldn't really leave Honey unattended as she was stuffed full of all our belongings.

Jane soon returned with a young man, tall and blond. That was great, as then I did not need to feel guilty about spending another evening with Pietro, who took me out dancing. He was an awful dancer, but we had fun together, laughing with Angelo, who was serving drinks behind the bar. When he tried flirting with me, Pietro ended up getting temporarily annoyed, so it was back to the dance floor.

It was well past midnight when I arrived back at the camp to find the gates closed and locked. I was just wondering what to do when another car turned up, driven by a German. He assessed the situation and announced, "I'm going to park here and sleep in the back of my car."

I didn't fancy that as there was not much room in the back of the Mini. "Maybe I'll climb over the gate" I said. At that moment the guardian appeared with the keys and let us in.

Jane awoke with 'travelitis', her first dose of an upset stomach, and had to resort to the Sulpha G we carried in the first-aid kit for this problem. It recurred several times until we reached India, where a chance remark in a chemist was overheard by a doctor, who prescribed the remedy that cured her for good. At the time we wondered whether the intense heat in the city, which she was not used to, had caused it, or something she had eaten.

In spite of this, we set off for the Catacombs of S. Sebastiano, S. Pietro and S. Paulo. A Monk accompanied a small group of us into the cool interior, down underground, to visit the chapel where S.Pietro and S.Paulo were originally buried. Forty-two catacombs had been carved out of the volcanic rock in and around Rome and used by the early Christians to meet secretly during the time of persecution. They were so extensive it would have been easy to get lost.

Neither of us really appreciated the wonders of Rome. Perhaps Hollywood films had over-emphasized its charm. Besides, it was unusually hot and stuffy for September.

Once out in the country, we found a suitable field near Colleferro for a rest, only to be disturbed by a couple of scruffy youngsters on a motor scooter. When we finally managed to get rid of them, I lay down, my thoughts with Pietro, and dozed off, exhausted by lack of sleep. But they returned.

Jane's angry voice penetrated my slumber declaring "Jeanne, I'm leaving." I pretended not to hear her, until one of them came near me, his melting ice cream splashing onto my clothes. He pulled my long hair. That was too much. I sat up, picked up a book and to Jane's amazement, I slapped him hard. Stunned at my reaction, the young men slouched sheepishly away.

My brother Nigel had been sent to Colleferro when he was sixteen to live with the Rognini family, to learn Italian and to work as an apprentice in their factory for six months. They had been very kind to him and he had enjoyed his stay. Their daughter Ornella had then spent a summer with us in England. She was now married and expecting twins.

We arrived unannounced – and found the family had gone to the country for the weekend. All we could do was await their return, so we parked Honey in a peach grove nearby. The owner enquired what we were doing and then insisted we move to the courtyard in front of the farm building. His caretaker, delighted to have company, fed us on fresh eggs, filled our glasses with wine and told us all about his family.

The Rogninis thoroughly spoilt us with copious Italian meals. Ornellla's brother Bruno drove us to Segni to see the stupendous view of the surrounding countryside. The incredible number of donkeys everywhere surprised me. Jane didn't speak Italian, but she and Sr. Rognini found a common interest in stamp collecting. Even Nigel's rather dishy-looking friend, Santino, came round to meet us and take us out for an ice cream.

They had reserved us a room at the local hotel for the night, but the bliss of sleeping in a bed was shattered at 5.30 am by the noise of traffic speeding by just below our window. It would have been great to stay longer – we had so enjoyed all the attention – but we were already booked on the ferry sailing from Brindisi, on the toe of Italy, the following day.

We arrived in Brindisi on the 20th September. Eagerly we picked up a pile of letters from the post office, with news from home and friends we hoped to visit on the way. We were on schedule and had driven 2027 miles. This first part of our journey had been easy-going, a gentle introduction to life on the move.

One of the brakes was sticking, no doubt caused by dust, and as I was unable to remove the wheel to clean it we had to find a garage, where they loosened all the bolts. I insisted they had to be hand tight or we would be in trouble in the event of having a puncture.

To use up the few remaining Italian lira, we shared a piece of tasteless pizza and an ice cream for supper, then strolled along the streets until sailing time, as is the custom on hot evenings in Latin countries. The town was awash with sailors from all over the world, sitting in groups at tables in open air cafes or rolling along in pairs, whistling at the girls in tight black dresses, tottering along on stiletto heels.

I was sad to be leaving the familiarity of Italy behind, but beyond lay Greece and a whole new world.

CHAPTER TWO

GREECE

The *Appia*, a ferry built in 1960 to accommodate 750 passengers and 300 cars, was ultra-modern and extremely luxurious; classless, yet catering for those requiring cabins and for others like us, who could only afford a Pullman seat to sleep on. We were amazed to find it equipped with a swimming pool, sundeck, television sets galore, a comfortable lounge, bar and dining room – so different from our dreary cross-channel steamers.

It was yet another short night, as the clocks went forward an hour and we were rudely woken by the ship's siren at dawn, in time to witness our arrival in mist-shrouded Corfu. Later that morning we reached our destination, Igoumentsa on the Greek mainland. The sun was shining out of a brilliant blue sky; flowers adorned the quayside, the air was hot and dry and the surrounding hills looked bare and lifeless, except for the dried-up scrub covered in white dust. Greece was for both of us a country unexplored, with an incomprehensible language and a strange alphabet.

After disembarkation and completion of customs, a young man, oozing Greek charm, handed us some general tourist information about the country and directed us to the local market. Amid laughter and hand signs we bought hot, oven-fresh bread, grapes, melon and cheese for a picnic lunch. Jane had been exasperated in Italy because I spoke fluent Italian and chatted with everyone. Now we were both reduced to sign language, guesswork and a three-word vocabulary, though French, was helpful.

The Pull Inn, on the sea front, had a beach and changing room especially reserved for foreigners where we could sit unmolested by the locals. Here we met a highly intelligent thirteen-year-old boy, working as waiter and interpreter during his holidays, who explained that he was learning English in high school. We also chatted with a German family who were waiting for the evening ferry. They told us all about the bad roads we were to encounter on our way down to Patras.

Some of the Greek roads turned out to be excellent, though not as well engineered as in Italy. The one we travelled along to Ioamenina (pronounced Yanena) was atrocious: under reconstruction, it wound its way across the arid hills, in places almost impassable for the Mini with barely four inches clearance. The uneven surface was littered with spiky stones. Mounds of gravel, placed in neat and regular piles along one side of the road, towered above us. We had to drive really slowly and it took three hours to cover one hundred kilometres. We met very few cars, as donkeys were still the main mode of transport in rural Greece, their saddlebags filled with shopping and live hens, or buried under piles of greenery harvested for use as fodder.

On the outskirts of Ioamenina, large roadside advertisements lured tourists to the cave of Perama, discovered by a peasant boy during the war and used as a shelter for refugees. This seemed like an interesting diversion and a good excuse to stretch our legs. A narrow track led through an untidy village. Men sat idly in doorways, absentmindedly fingering their worry beads, an essential accessory to their life style.

Strung beads first appeared in Saudi Arabia over a thousand years ago. They were made of amber and believed to help relieve rheumatism. The prophet Mohamed adapted them as prayer beads and Christians copied the idea using tiny coloured beads, creating a rosary of Hail Marys and Our Fathers. Only the men in Greece carry worry beads. These have nothing to do with prayers and are not necessarily made of amber. They are used to run the fingers along and fiddle with, showing that men have the time and money for leisure, whereas women are always busy with domestic affairs.

In a wayside café, an Orthodox priest with a long grey beard and flowing cassock sat deep in conversation with another man, on the table two glasses and a bottle of wine. A donkey ambled down the street flicking flies with his tail, heavily-laden baskets strung across his back, followed by a small boy brandishing a stick to keep him moving. Children scampered in all directions pointing towards the cave.

The guide, who spoke only Greek, led us rapidly along a kilometre of cold, dank underground passages, occasionally stopping to draw our attention to a particularly unusual stalactite. Suddenly we found ourselves standing on a natural platform overlooking an enormous cavern. It was far larger than those I had seen in Derbyshire, with incredible stalactites and stalagmites intricately sculpted by the unrelenting drip of water.

The cave plunged into darkness, and then slowly, very slowly, a faint red light lit background figures, casting shadows and highlighting strange forms. As it grew brighter a battlefield emerged, knights and their ladies, castles, Buddhas, even a mundane cauliflower.

A vertical climb brought us back out into the warm fresh air and to another platform overlooking the valley. Surrounded by mountains, the town of Ioannina, famous for its silverwork, hugged the shoreline of Lake Pamvotis. Tobacco and grapes filled the fertile slopes. Just offshore lay the island of Niss.

"Do you see the monastery over there?" asked our guide. "That is the monastery of Pandelimonos where Ali Pasha, the despotic ruler of the Ottoman Empire's European territory, was murdered in 1822. He was known as the Lion of Ioannina. His court at the time was superior in wealth, refinement and learning to any other Greek town."

In Ioannina, an old man who knew a smattering of Italian sold us some tomatoes and grapes and smilingly filled our can with drinking water. On the other side of the lake, a sandy track crossed a flat stretch of pasture land and as it continued on into the distance with no sign of habitation, we bravely parked Honey for the night, just there in the middle of nowhere, without any shelter.

As we prepared our sleeping quarters and started to cook the evening meal, distant, tinkling sheep bells grew louder and forms in capes eerily loomed out of the darkness, silent but watching. We felt surrounded. Two shepherd girls approached to make our acquaintance, but as any attempt at conversation was in vain, they returned to their own kin, now gathered round a large fire some distance away. They were nomadic people, living way up in the mountains during the summer months, descending to the plains near the villages with the approach of autumn and the colder weather.

The nearby presence of the shepherds meant that we had to dress in bed the following morning, quite a feat in the cramped space of our wagon-top tent. In daylight, the girls returned and we somehow managed to exchange a few comprehensible words. They were so pretty and to my surprise many had natural blond or red hair, which they wore in two long plaits, their heads covered by large black scarves. Dressed in black, the women rode side-saddle on donkeys, often in the middle of the road. The men did not seem to work much, but the women's hands were never idle. While tending the sheep or riding, they spun crude wool or cotton into fine thread.

The road south to Amphilokia was also under reconstruction with diversions through fields and over rubble. Honey took it in her stride. It was a hot dry day and the nearby lake looked enticing despite the jellyfish lurking near the surface. We took it in turn to stand on a rock high above to observe the enemy and alert the swimmer. While we were thus occupied, two small boys, who had been watching us, managed to prise open the sliding windows of the Mini. The simple locking devices proved to be unreliable. They made off with the only things they could reach, Jane's small leather writing case and a travelling first aid kit. She was very upset, and worried that a child might swallow the contents of a codeine bottle. With the help of an interpreter who spoke a little Italian, we managed to convey our tale of woe and concern to the local policeman plus a fast growing, intensely curious crowd. There was nothing more we could do, so we continued on our way.

A complete lack of knowledge of a language can be

embarrassing. We had to wait for the ferry to cross over the Corinth Gulf Straits from Antirion to Rion. A policeman kept insisting that the Mini should be parked facing away from the ramp. No other cars were waiting.

"That's ridiculous. We'll lose our place in the queue to board the ferry," I grumbled, so every time the policeman looked away, I turned the car around. This little game continued until the arrival of the ferry and the trucks were instructed to board in front of us – stern first.

"You see. The policeman was right all the time," taunted Jane triumphantly.

It was after seven in the evening when, at last, we arrived in Patras, a few miles from Rion. Everything was closed. We had no food and no drachmas left to pay for a meal in a restaurant. We wondered what to do and whether we would have to dig into our desert rations.

"Do you need any help?" asked a man out for an evening stroll with his family. We explained that we had been trying to find a restaurant and somewhere to change money.

"Here, I'll exchange a pound for 72 drachmas and on the corner of the square you'll find a cheap restaurant where the food is good".

And it was. We ordered meat, tomato salad and rice and were confronted with four huge plates of food which we devoured hungrily.

Darkness had fallen by the time we left the restaurant. On the outskirts of Mansolawe we turned off the main road down a sandy lane, intending to camp by the sea. The sea remained elusive and the track started to deteriorate. We had gone far enough. This would have to do. While turning around so as to be facing in the right direction for a quick getaway, should it be necessary, the Mini came to a grinding halt in the soft sand.

At that very moment, a man and a boy, curious to know where we were going, appeared just in time to help push us out. The man spoke some German and a little Italian and tried hard to persuade us that it would be safer for two lone girls to stay in a hotel. At last he said goodnight and left, but soon returned with Antonio, who he proudly introduced with a sweeping gesture, as 'Australian'. Antonio, a shy, slim young Greek with the inevitable moustache, had spent two years in Australia with his parents, sisters and brothers, but his father had developed a mysterious illness, and they had had to return to Greece.

"If you remain here in this wild place overnight, the village boys will disturb you. You must come back with me to my home," Antonio insisted. "My mother and sisters will welcome you," he added by way of assurance.

In the end, dying to get some sleep and not wishing to offend, we agreed and followed Antonio back through the village to the farmstead, where he woke his mother, who spoke excellent English, and asked her to prepare some Turkish coffee. Leaving us in the company of his sisters, he returned to the village to fetch his brothers. Even father came home, an apparently unusual occurrence. Mother, once she had accepted us, became cheerfully conversational, proudly displaying the rug she was weaving in bright colours for her daughter Dimitria's dowry. We ate grapes, drank coffee and sat talking on the veranda until long past midnight. I could hardly keep my eyes open. Meanwhile, from inside the house, came sounds of intense activity and sweeping, presumably cleaning up for our benefit. When at last somebody suggested it was bedtime, the women led Jane and me into the backyard, where under an olive tree, heavily laden with sleeping turkeys, we squatted in a row. Jane was bewildered. Apparently there were no sanitary arrangements in the house.

No way would they allow us to sleep on top of the Mini. Exhausted, we climbed into a double bed especially vacated for us. At dawn, the uncouth gobbles of turkeys, strutting in the yard outside the bedroom window, disturbed us. Everyone else was already up and in the kitchen-living cum bedroom. There was a sink in front of the window, above which hung a bucket full of water and fitted with a tap. The waste water disappeared through a hole in the wall which was large enough for us to see the chickens scratching in the yard, and in the middle of the room, under a sort of canapé, a pot of water was boiling on an open fire, ready for the scrawny chicken mother had just caught, killed and plucked in our honour.

Breakfast was a strange meal of coffee, dry bread, rather tough chicken and resinated wine (retsina); all very indigestible at that time of the morning. The resin was used to preserve and flavour the wine. A fresh bottle and the remains of the chicken were wrapped up for our lunch, which we later fried with onions and ate with rice. Such wonderful hospitality was quite overwhelming. Before we left, Mother, Antonio and his two younger sisters stood in line for a photograph.

After filling up with petrol, which was much cheaper in Greece, we made a hurried detour to Olympia, the home of international sport. There were no entrance fees to pay or wardens to be seen, so we wandered freely across the whole area, just a large field surrounded by rubble and trees. In my mind's eye I saw the highly-trained athletes and imagined the quadrennial games taking place. Beautifully-carved pillars lay strewn among the foundations of nearby temples and courtyards. The stadium was still being excavated and in the nearby museum

I spent ages gazing at the truly beautiful statue of Hermes, the God of frontiers and travellers, as well as of poets, thieves and athletes; one of the Seven Wonders of the World. Jane, however, was more interested in helmets and graves, so whenever we visited anything connecting art and history, we wandered around separately. The remains of the shrine at Olympia, in the middle of nowhere, were impressive and we marvelled that such a great civilization could have existed in the remote past.

Tired and hot, after a short night and sightseeing, we headed for the Olympic beach, but the road deteriorated so much we decided to give it a miss and stopped under some shady trees for lunch, a sleep and diary writing. Then in the cool of the late afternoon we drove on to Patras across the Peloponnese. The fields were cultivated with neat rows of cotton plants, their flowers like white balls of fluff, which when harvested are used for spinning thread and making cloth.

Next day we almost missed the Corinth canal linking the Aegean to the Adriatic. It is cut deep down into the rock; so narrow, it is only 25 meters wide. We drove across the bridge without realizing it was there and had to turn back. The water was a vivid blue, quite unlike the meandering murky waters of the French canals, with their shade trees, locks and towpaths.

Before its excavation, ships circumnavigating the Peloponnese added about 185 nautical miles to their journey as well as having to contend with notoriously rough seas. Periander, known as the tyrant of Corinth, first envisaged the canal in 602 BCE, but such a project was technically impossible in those days, so instead he linked the two seas with a stone road called the *diolkos* or slipway, along which ships could be moved on wheeled platforms. Centuries later and with great foresight, the Emperor Nero acquired 6,000 slaves for the job and started work himself, by digging with a golden hoe to the strains of music. But the venture died with him three months later, so it wasn't until in 1882 that work started again on the 6.3 kilometre canal. Plagued by insufficient funds, it was finally completed for regular use on the 28th of October, 1893.

Mauve tints from the flowers were reflected in the sea water along the coastal road into Athens. A profusion of ultra-modern homes of varied design were under construction on the arid hillside. Nearer to the city, attractive, more mature villas with large gardens and bungalows were squashed onto a postage stamp of land; intermittent farmsteads remained, retaining only enough land to feed a couple of goats and some hens.

At a viewpoint, we were accosted by a man who tried to sell us pistachio nuts; two packets for ten dirham. We agreed to buy one, expecting five in change for our note. He just pocketed it and departed at high speed, but we called him back and made him return the ten dirham. We returned the pistachios and refused to have anything more to do with him, even though he tried vainly to explain away his mistake.

After driving along numerous streets, we eventually found the office of my father's friend, Mr Pawson, and were redirected to his home in a smart residential area. The maid opened the door. She spoke only Greek and told us to return at six o'clock, which we did. Mrs Pawson was writing letters and didn't seem exactly pleased to see us. She had not received our letter and must have had a hectic week and was tired. When her husband, a kindly man, arrived we were given a quick supper and dispatched to see the Acropolis, open after dark during the three nights of the full moon.

We couldn't have timed our arrival in Athens better. Since time immemorial, this has been a sacred site. Remains from the

Neolithic era have been discovered; a palace-temple used by the Mycenaean priest-kings and successive temples dedicated to the Goddess Athena. She is the patroness of Athens and represents the highest order of spiritual development. In the 5th century, the temple was appropriated by the Christians as a church and later by the Turks as a mosque. The latter kept a store of gunpowder there, causing an explosion which destroyed the central area.

Steep steps led up to the Parthenon, and what remains of this enduring shrine to the Goddess Athena keeps watch over the twinkling lights of the city. An old man, dragging his gammy right leg, pointed out the deep grooves worn into the rock by the passing of countless chariots. We marvelled at how such massive blocks of stone, now strewn on the ground, could ever have been hauled up one on top of the other. The brilliant white marble pillars tapered upwards towards the sky and the soft light of the moon mellowed the harshness of centuries of damage and destruction. It was quiet, peaceful and timeless.

Next morning we revelled in the luxury of a glorious bath, hot water to do the washing and breakfast of ham and eggs. Despite Mrs Pawson's initial unenthusiastic greeting, the Pawsons really made us feel at home and thoroughly spoilt us; the maids helped with our ironing and the chauffeur gave the car a perfunctory wash.

Athens was a city of contrasts. We explored the clean, cool squares and wide tree-lined avenues and modern shops and later discovered the narrow, dirty back streets. Outside the palace gates, the royal guards dressed immaculately in white skirts similar to Scottish kilts, stood at ease like statues and whiled away the monotony out-staring a few idle onlookers.

The port area of Piraeus was quite different; approached along a bumpy road, it smelt strongly of sewers. Dilapidated ships lined the quays. As usual, we had great difficulty finding a toilet, and concluded that the Greeks probably didn't use them.

I dragged Jane into a small round Orthodox church, so old that it had sunk several feet below street level. Inside a christening ceremony was taking place. The priest, surrounded by a family at the font, his black robes protected by a long red waterproof apron, was officiating. The naked child, already about a year old, remained quite calm throughout the ceremony while the priest covered him with symbolic crosses, muttered prayers and submerged him in the holy water of the font three times. The baby was then clad in pristine white clothes befitting one reborn in Christ. Meanwhile, his older brother proudly held a ceremonial candle twice his size.

Religious pictures hung from the walls, lit by numerous chandeliers. I watched a businessman come briskly into the church, carrying a briefcase. He marched purposefully up to one of the Icons hanging on the wall, bent to kiss the sacred image, murmured a prayer and left.

That evening the Pawsons took us out to dinner at the local tavern; a romantic setting in an enclosed garden. Climbing plants cast shadows on the tablecloth and twinkling stars shone in the sky above. It felt quite strange to dress up and make an effort to look pretty for the first time since leaving home.

Dinner was followed by a disturbed night, not because of the food, but because a cat climbed up into our tent and curled itself around Jane's neck. She just couldn't settle. Tossing and turning, she rocked the Mini and kept waking me up. I was not pleased. It was like trying to sleep on a rough sea.

We wasted an hour travelling south through Athens towards

Daphni, instead of north to Delphi. The strange letters of the Greek alphabet can be extremely confusing. Eventually, after struggling yet again through the city traffic, we found the correct road and as we drove over the first range of mountains, the frustrations of the morning quickly dissipated. The river Asopos lay stunningly beautiful in the valley below, meandering its way between fields clad in autumnal gold and red; the green *macchia*, a prickly Mediterranean bush and natural ground cover, took away the harshness of the grey volcanic rock strewn across the surrounding mountain slopes.

The road was good and the Mini hummed along. By late afternoon we arrived in Delphi, perched high on the edge of Mt Parnassus and overlooking the bay of Itea. In ancient times, Delphi was considered to be the centre of the world, the place where heaven and earth met, where man was closest to the gods and where many came to consult the oracle. It was also the centre of worship for the god Apollo, who embodied moral discipline and spiritual clarity. We drank from the cold, clear and heavenly-tasting water of the Castalian Spring, said to be the fountain of knowledge. Poets had come here for inspiration. This too, was where contestants in the Pythian Games and suppliants ritually cleansed themselves by washing their hair before consulting the Delphic Oracle. Ancient traditions say the source was named after a local lady.

We explored the remains of temples, the theatre and stadium and marvelled at the genius of the stonemasons who had constructed the walls, shaping and fitting the stones like crazy paving to defeat the ravages of time and earthquakes. The glow of the setting sun lit the orange fissures in the volcanic rock and slowly the shadows lengthened, blotting out the valley of olive trees. The braying of a donkey echoed in the silence and the tiny bell of a grazing goat tinkled monotonously. Together with a few other tourists we sat in awe on the steps of the amphitheatre, transported back in time, until dusk fell and we spectators slowly drifted away.

That night we froze; a bitter cold wind penetrated below the flaps of our canvas roof tent. Our sleeping bags were quite inadequate at that altitude. Dawn, breakfast of hot coffee and porridge cooked on our tiny butane gas ring and the first rays of the morning sun soon brightened our spirits.

I was not used to such a sedentary life, sitting in car most of the day, and needed more exercise, so off I went down the hill for a good run until Jane, who was less energetic, arrived with Honey. The road was appalling; full of potholes and ruts. The Mini's small wheels and minimal clearance meant slow progress. But it gave us time to appreciate the rolling hills and wave to the shepherds tending their sheep or goats, until we re-joined the main road, an exceptionally good one by Greek standards.

Together with lorries and buses, we hurtled along towards Kardhiza, arriving on the outskirts around midday. An enormous market was in full swing. Men, women and children with sheep, cattle and donkeys were picnicking, bargaining their livestock and enjoying reunions with friends. Stalls displayed farm implements and produce, leather goods and vividly-dyed long-haired rugs; so very tempting and we desperately wanted to buy one, but didn't really have room and would perhaps eventually fight for ownership. This was a town bustling with trade. The people were still dressed in national costume; the women in long skirts, wide-sleeved frilly blouses and brightly-coloured scarves and the men in black suits with fancy shirts. Buggies drawn by smartly-groomed horses clattered over the cobblestones.

The Greek language remained a mystery to us, but at least we had learnt to decipher the script and read the road signs. Imagine our delight when the manager of the local bank spoke English and after cashing a traveller's cheque was happy to answer many of our questions.

Back on the highway, large roadside posters lured us onto another diversion, this time to Meteora (which means 'suspended in the air') and there, rising out of the plains of Thessaly, a quite unexpected treat awaited us. Dozens of smooth pinnacles of rock, sculpted by wind and water, sprouted like mushrooms. Crowned by ancient monasteries, these were once genuine retreats from a wicked world; small villages with cells, refectory, square, church, well and garden. Their isolation helped to keep Greek orthodox religious traditions and Hellenic culture alive during the turbulent Middle-Ages. Only good climbers were able to gain access. A pulley system of baskets and nets were used to draw up supplies and less able monks. Later, steps were tunnelled up inside and a drawbridge made life easier. The monasteries, mostly deserted and left to decay, had recently been acquired by the Ministry for Tourism, which was renovating them for the benefit of the fledgling tourist industry.

We wandered around inside the main monastery through unfurnished rooms, peering out of small open windows at rocks that rose like skyscrapers. In a mixture of Greek words and hand signs we asked an old monk who was shuffling around if he would kindly unlock the church, which was famous for its paintings. He beamed his assent and turned the large key in the heavy wooden door to let us in. But to our dismay, it was impossible to appreciate fully the deep blues and gold that shone in the dim interior because of his wandering hands. Unable to speak English, he grabbed us by the wrist to point out and explain details of the pictures. I kept dodging out his way. He became quite irreverent as he grew bolder, grabbing Jane around the waist and pulling her over to the door to look at an enormous plank, used as a gong and worn with age and use.

"Jeanne! We must leave. I don't trust the gleam in his eye," Jane said.

"Let's go then." We beat a hasty, yet reluctant retreat. There was so much to see.

Later, when we had finished eating supper and were quietly relaxing by the dying embers of a small fire, an unexpected visitor arrived. A tall gangling teenage shepherd squatted down beside us, holding out his hands to the dying embers, smiling contentedly, as we tried to communicate in sign language. After a while he wandered off, reappearing with a friend and some curious-looking oversized apples which he indicated should be cooked, as well as some sweetcorn. These he buried in the remains of the smouldering ashes; they tasted delicious, even though we had already had enough to eat. Wondering how to explain that it was bed time, Jane started to clean her teeth. The youngsters took the hint and disappeared into the night without even saying *kalinichte*, Greek for goodnight.

'Kalimera', called the peasants early the following morning; riding donkeys, a couple of pack horses in tow, they passed by with their sheep, sows, piglets and goats, all on their way to market. An old woman with twinkling eyes and hollow cheeks, her wispy grey hair covered by a headscarf, stopped to talk to us and beckoned to me to follow her and there I was, running to keep up with her white horse until she came to a place where the corn grew. She dismounted, thrust the reins into my hands and went to pick six fat cobs; these she gave to me with a toothless cackle, before following me back to our camp to explain how to cook them. When we offered her some coffee as a thank you for her kindness, she made her excuses and rode off quickly.

Jane lazed, tucked up in her sleeping bag, while I mended Honey's horn. Then I tried to clean the carburettor, but had to give up as the nuts were too tight. In fact all sorts of little things seemed to go wrong that morning. First I had to rummage for a screw I had dropped somewhere in the engine, then the plastic plates stuck in the saucepan of warm water I was using for the washing up and I couldn't get them out. In desperation, I went off for a walk.

Greece has a hot arid climate; most rivers run dry in summer and only spring to life during the rainy season, so we were delighted that day to find a beautiful cool spot for our picnic lunch beside a river bed, with a trickle of water flowing in it. But the peace was soon shattered by the arrival of a gaggle of school kids, curious and wanting to touch everything.

Hurriedly we packed up and set off towards to the spacious modern town of Thessaloniki, best remembered for its attractive waterfront. On the way we overtook dozens of army vehicles out on manoeuvre, and began to feel uneasy about the movement of troops in the area. We were getting close to Turkey. Could there be unrest in the region? Would the border be closed? We hadn't seen a newspaper in days and had no idea what was happening in the big wide world. What made it worse was overtaking them all over again after we got hopelessly lost in the sprawling, un-signposted suburbs.

Our last night in Greece was spent beside the sea; an idyllic spot just off the main road. A gallant young man with dark curly hair and a beaming smile helped fill our water can from the village pump and splashed extra water for a face wash. We then took a bar of soap into the warm sea for the first wash we had

had in two days, only to discover that it didn't lather in salt water. It didn't really matter as we felt refreshed.

We collected driftwood to make a fire, and cooked a delicious dinner of onions, tomatoes and spaghetti followed by corn on the cob and a couple of glasses of local *retsina* wine. We finished the meal with a small glass of *ouzo*. By this time we felt quite light-headed and beautifully warm as we watched an almost full, bright orange harvest moon rise from behind the cliffs. The sound of crickets filled the air. The traffic roared dully in the background and the occasional thud of a large wave crashed onto the beach. This was the life of gypsies. We had stepped out of time; an experience to be savoured and remembered.

A narrow strip of Greece stretches north between the mountains of Bulgaria and the fast-flowing River Euros on Turkey's frontier. The only bridge was further north at Edirne. In this region there is an obvious mingling of races and culture; women in Moslem dress, their faces veiled; women with pretty scarves and brightly coloured, long pleated skirts swirling around their legs; others wore pantaloons or European dress and the widows were draped drably in black. The donkeys were being replaced by slow-moving, creaking bullock carts, heavily laden with an abundant harvest of corn cobs. The land was markedly greener and more fertile than it had been in the South.

Orestia, the last town in Greece, was entirely different to anywhere we had been so far. The streets were seething with people going in all directions. Women sat or crouched down on the pavements chatting, nursing their babies at the breast. What a culture shock! After all, this was before television or documentaries, and we had no idea that people could live so differently and have such diverse customs.

As we approached the Turkish border, the narrow tree-lined

road began to deteriorate. The gravel surface slowed us down to about 40 miles an hour. Everything rattled and a cloud of dust followed us like the wake of a ship. The change of environment was stimulating and exciting. It was the last day of September and we had already covered three thousand, four hundred and sixty-seven miles. We had now been on the road for three weeks. Jane and I were no longer strangers and had become comfortable with our individual views and foibles. Honey so far had only given us minor problems.

CHAPTER THREE

TURKEY

Customs formalities were brief, and after chatting with a young English couple who had been travelling by Land Rover from Syria, we drove on into Edirne to change a traveller's cheque, as we now needed Turkish lira. It was Saturday afternoon and the bank clerk politely but firmly said we would have to wait until Monday, as they were closed for such transactions during the weekend. Hoping everything would turn out all right, we motored on.

By the time we reached Çorlu, (pronounced Chorlu) a larger town, the petrol tank was nearly empty. In sign language we asked a policeman where there was a large hotel. He escorted us on foot through the back streets to a building near the market, up some rickety stairs into a room full of beds. Though the sheets looked reasonably clean, we were glad of our tent. This was not exactly what we were looking for.

"Hotel" he announced with a smile.

"No," we explained feeling rather despondent, "No sleep. Change money – lira."

Sensing my obvious disappointment, he patted me on the back and led us downstairs again where we met another policeman, who was better educated and spoke a smattering of English. To add urgency to the situation, we told him that we must be in Istanbul that evening and needed petrol. He took out his notebook and started writing, then changed his mind, tore up the page and said with a smile, "You visitors to Turkey. Police pay for the petrol." He climbed into his jeep and indicated we follow him to the petrol station, but the tank ran dry half way there.

"No worry," the policeman said and leaving us in the middle of the street surrounded by curious onlookers, he drove off to collect a can of petrol and insisted on making sure the tank was topped up before escorting us out of town. To thank him for his kindness, we gave him a packet of English cigarettes that we carried for just such an occasion. He seemed delighted.

The Hilton, the largest, most modern and luxurious hotel in Istanbul, stood high on a hill in the centre of the city and was easy to find; this was our first port of call. The Mini looked small and travel-stained parked among the large shining American limousines. Jane and I felt too scruffy to mingle with the chic international clientele in the lobby, but we desperately needed Turkish liras and some other general information, which is most easily obtained from a hotel of this stature. Without blinking an eye the receptionist changed the traveller's cheque and gave us a map. We then headed out of town back to the main road to find the camp site, just seven miles due west in the suburb of Filoria.

The camp site was officially closed in October, but roughly two hundred tourists and overlanders were still making use of the facilities provided, free of charge; Land Rovers, Bedford vans, Volkswagens and motor cycles, with their owners of diverse nationalities, all on their way to India. Another five Land Rovers and two Indiaman buses arrived the following evening with a complement of eighty passengers, among them a lively octogenarian, who we were told withstood the journey better than many of the younger women. We had never expected to see so many other travellers. Jane's father had predicted traffic lights in the desert; perhaps he was going to be right after all.

Airplanes revving up for take-off woke us early next morning. The campsite was too close to the runway, but the setting was great. There was a large swimming pool, reasonable facilities and so many interesting people to talk to; Americans who had been travelling through Russia, two Germans who had been hitch-hiking in Turkey for their holiday, and another English couple we had met previously in Greece. It was such fun to exchange travel stories and find out more about places not to miss. A German travelling with his tall, good-looking wife, a squirrel, two dogs and their caravan were very helpful in teaching us about the Mini's tappets, which constantly burned out in the heat, and how to file them down.

Istanbul was fascinating; so different from the western civilization we had grown up in. It was a fusion of East and West with narrow winding streets. Men sat in the shade smoking hubble-bubble pipes and women shuffled along with large shopping baskets past dingy shops. Tall modern buildings, hotels and ramshackle restaurants competed for space with numerous mosques, their slender minarets and domes etched sharply against the glow of the evening sky. The *dolmus* was a great way to get about; a shared taxi that ran from end to end of a particular street or area, always stuffed with passengers who after paying the appropriate fare embarked and disembarked at will.

In the refreshingly cool, dim atmosphere of the covered bazaar, a maze of stalls sold everything from junk, curios and everyday items, such as household utensils and clothes to colourful carpets, brass coffeepots and gold and silver jewellery. Each trade had its designated area. Men were fashioning brass trays or sitting behind their sewing machines in dark corners. A rich odour of spices hung in the air. People of all nationalities jostled side by side, bargaining with vendors who expected to haggle and were surprised by those stupid foreigners who accepted the asking price. Shopping was an experience. You were invited to sit down and have tiny glass of strong sweet tea or coffee while you admired your prospective purchase, spent time haggling and making a decision, finally agreeing an acceptable price and parting all smiles.

The Blue Mosque was stunningly beautiful. In the courtyard, special stone wash basins were provided for the faithful to wash their feet as everyone had to leave their shoes at the entrance. A myriad of luxurious red Turkish carpets covered the floor from wall to wall, wonderfully soft to walk on. Heavy wrought iron chandeliers with naked electric light bulbs hung low. The walls, thick pillars and domes were faced with delicate blue mosaic tiles, inscribed with verses from the Koran.

An elderly man ushered us into a corner from where, astonished, we could watch the men doing strange exercises, holding out their hands, bowing down, kneeling and standing again. The women, segregated from the men, sat cross-legged on the carpet listening to the incantations of the *Hoja* or priest. No ornaments or images filled the focal point. It was just an empty niche. An intense feeling of prayer, reverence and peace pervaded the mosque.

A few tourists, wearing carpet slippers over their shoes,

shuffled in and stood behind us, talking in stage whispers. Jane and I sat cross-legged on the carpet for a long time, soaking in the atmosphere, unknowingly privileged to be there without today's prejudice or special hours and barriers for tour groups.

Santa Sophia, more renowned than the Blue Mosque, was now a museum. It was used by both Christians and Moslems at different times and was once the most important cathedral of Christendom; architecturally a fine building, majestic with spectacular stained glass windows, through which light beams, filled with swirling dust, streamed down. The once marble clad walls were faded. The Christian Virgin Mary and child remained behind the high altar which, in deference to the Moslem Mecca, had been placed just to the side of east. However, all the crosses had been painted over. In spite of its grandeur, I was so disappointed. The building seemed unloved and without the rich carpets and people at prayer, lacked the atmosphere and peacefulness it had been designed for.

Next morning the car battery was flat and I learnt that in warmer climates it needed topping up with water fairly frequently. A few friendly campers helped push, so that we could give the car a jump start. At a nearby Shell garage, the Mini was oiled and greased and the exhaust pipe secured where the rear bushing had broken loose. Now we had done all we could to make ready for the journey across Turkey. And then, as it was Monday morning, we could finally go to the post office, hoping to have news from home. Jane was lucky, but sadly no letters for me, only a post card from Pietro in Rome. Well, that was better than nothing and I missed his enchanting smile.

Back at the campsite we ate supper with a few of our new friends, including Raymond who we had met on the way into Istanbul and a tall bearded Austrian we nicknamed the Vicar, because his pride and joy was a beautifully kept 1935 Austin 7 which he called 'the Vicar'.

Turkey's European territories are separated from the Asian side by the Bosphorus, a narrow stretch of water linking the Black Sea to the north and the Sea of Marmara to the south. This we crossed on one of the many ferries plying to and fro. The bridge had not yet been constructed.

We continued along the coastal road around the Sea of Marmara, through picturesque fishing villages. Small boats lay drawn up on the beaches and nets were spread out to dry. The area around the town of Izmit at the western extremity reminded me of Lake Geneva; both the distance across the water and similar shape of the high mountains. Further on and despite some threatening clouds, the startling blue freshwater Lake Sapanca glistened in the sunshine.

We were making good progress, especially as the road to the capital, Ankara, had recently been resurfaced. This made travelling on diminutive wheels much more comfortable. It was wide and straight, climbing imperceptibly through the hilly countryside.

The lowlands were more fertile than in Greece, more trees and more cultivation. Nature was donning her autumnal colours; small red-leaved trees contrasted with yellows and various shades of green. In stark contrast upon the plateau, it was arid and a cold, penetrating wind was blowing. Villages consisting of small wooden houses, the summer homes of shepherds, nestled in shallow valleys. It was the cemeteries that fascinated us most. Tall, narrow tombstones stood drunkenly, like miniature towers of Pisa, in unkempt fields of tall grass. Each was engraved with Arabic script and crowned with a carved round knob, symbol of a stylised turban.

During the course of the afternoon we ran into Raymond again. He was travelling to Morocco via Syria and the Aswan dam, providing the ongoing political crisis allowed it. On arrival, he hoped to spend three weeks taking photographs and writing. He was such a serious young man, interested in remote Indian tribes, mythology, theology and art and so well read. I felt quite ignorant and uneducated and vowed to rectify the matter.

We pitched camp together in a sheltered grove so as to arrive in the capital city, Ankara, early in the morning. We were all up by 6.30 am collecting wood to build a fire. It had been a bitterly cold night. A deaf and dumb man stopped to stare and uttering strange noises, pointed with astonishment at Ray's beard. Before long an audience of four young peasant boys in colourful clothes gathered around. They wanted to look at everything and were especially delighted with Jane's smalls hanging on the roof rack to dry, but the giggles provoked by the photographs of Polynesian women in the book 'Aku Aku', which I was reading at the time, were quite funny. Most Turkish women were still in purdah, even though it had been forbidden by government decree during the time of the revolutionary president, Ataturk. Pictures of almost naked girls must have been a revelation. As a parting gift, the young boys presented us with two delicious melons taken from the basket strung across the back of their donkey. Then amid roars of laughter, we had to push the car. The battery was flat again!

We drove in convoy into the centre of Ankara, parked the cars at *Ulus*, in the old quarter and went in search of the tourist office. We all needed some general information about Turkey. We trudged along a wide avenue, three miles long and endlessly uphill, past numerous embassies and other large residences until at last, after an hour and a half, we arrived at the British Embassy.

It certainly had a superb view over Ankara and was in a position where it could benefit from the breeze during the hot summer months. Though Ankara had always been a major urban centre, it only became the capital at the birth of the Republic of Turkey. It seemed like a backwater compared to Istanbul. The population was still less than a million in the early 1960s.

We enquired about the best route to take to Erzerum, which turned out to be the coast road along the Black Sea. Jane also wanted to find out about cholera injections. They suggested we go and ask in the BEA office, where they told her that it was advisable further east. Completely unaware of conditions in India, she hadn't wanted to believe me. After that we visited the Maritime office to check on sailings in the Mediterranean for Ray.

By this time we were starving, so we found a roadside eating house where instead of selecting food from a menu, we followed the waiter into a narrow, dark, yet spotlessly clean kitchen; on the hob several large cauldrons of meat and rice concoctions were bubbling in spicy, colourful sauces. The waiter dished up and brought the chosen dishes to our table. The food was excellent and cheap, though not very substantial. Here too, Ray's beard caused some consternation. One of the waiters spoke a little English, and when we returned to the same restaurant a few days later he remembered the dish we had ordered.

After lunch we said goodbye to Ray and took Honey to have her battery tested. The Austin agents were unable to help and sent us to the Chevrolet garage. They said it contained no acid at all, but they couldn't find any leaks. While they presumably filled it with acid and water and recharged it, we took a taxi to the UNICEF hospital for Jane's first cholera jab.

Tired from so much walking around during the morning, we

decided to catch a bus back. Every time one stopped, we asked if it was going to *Ulus*. People nodded their heads vigorously from side to side in a sort of circular movement, which we thought meant 'no' and so we let many buses go by before realizing that it was an affirmative nod.

One of the most difficult things to find in Ankara was a public convenience. Eventually, in desperation, we asked a policeman. He looked aghast at such a request from two girls, and reluctantly directed us to a very sordid place.

When we picked up the car, the petrol gauge was showing empty. That seemed strange, so we put in ten litres. Still the gauge showed empty. Concerned that we had been diddled and worried by a gathering crowd, we decided to move on. As we drove along the bumpy road, the gauge sprang back to life and showed the tank to be three quarters full. The garage attendant had been honest after all.

It was getting late in the day. We were both overtired and irritable, and it seemed to take forever to find the official campsite. This turned out to be a few wooden tables and benches under the pine trees, rather too close to a military camp for our liking. The two guards on duty had eyed us up and down with a sneer and had surreptitiously started to exchange money when we had asked them for directions. 'Why did they do that?' I wondered, feeling uneasy. Perhaps they thought us fair game. They gave us the creeps. We moved on and had better luck at a nearby house, where seven children came to the door and excitedly showed us the way down a steep track. Here we felt safe.

Early next morning, the eldest, a blonde girl, came to enquire if we had slept well. She was carrying a tray with two tiny glasses of strongly stewed black tea. The glasses were barely taller than egg cups, with narrow necks and bowl-shaped bases. 'Chai' was

Turkish for tea and always served in this way with rectangular lumps of brown sugar. I found it bitter and drank it that first time out of politeness, but soon grew to welcome its appearance.

One of the hillside guards stopped by to talk to us while the girl was with us, and we learnt that three buses had just passed on their way to India, as well as another party of English who were also on their way East.

Before heading north for Çorum (pronounced Chorum), we drove back into town via the Embassy, where we bumped into a few fellow travellers, including Ray. Amazingly, most of them had spent the night under the pine trees on the same hillside.

The suburbs of Ankara consisted of primitive dwellings built on terraces hewn out of the hillside. People lived in dire poverty and squalor; women and girls were veiled and the young boys, who never went to school, learnt their father's trades as soon as they were able. Continuous roadworks impeded progress along the now un-metalled surface of the road to the coast. The bitter cold wind continued to blow across the plateau. Large clouds scudded across the sky, casting dark shadows on the parched hills, which stretched away to infinity, a blaze of ochre and green, the typical background scenery used for a Cinerama western.

Suddenly a lorry travelling at high speed overtook, sending loose pebbles flying and practically pushing the Mini off the dirt road. Instinctively I felt nervous, due no doubt to the reckless way it was being driven. A few miles further on, we passed the same lorry, as it had stopped to pick up a load of passengers. Jane was driving at the time and accelerated to prevent him overtaking again. The lorry was bearing down on us from behind. The car skidded and Jane began to lose control as she drove round a corner and over the brow of a hill into a steep winding descent. The Mini lurched violently in zigzag fashion across the road. I clung tightly to my seat, praying that we would avoid going over the edge (in those days seat belts didn't exist). At the bottom of the hill, the road took a tight left turn on a narrow bridge. It spanned a stream some ten feet below. Instinctively, as taught from a young age, I braced myself for the impact with my hands on the dashboard. Travelling at roughly 40 mph, we hit the low protective wall head on, with a deafening thud. We stopped dead.

The impact smashed part of the engine and damaged the framework. The roof rack had gone sailing off into the ditch below. Shaken yet unhurt, we clambered out to look at the damage and the ten-foot drop we had so narrowly escaped. The heavy sump guard made of a metal sheet and coated with fibre glass had miraculously saved the engine from greater destruction.

So many thoughts flashed through my mind: what would happen now? How would we get to Australia? How degrading to arrive home so soon, after only one month, with a wrecked car and an uncompleted mission! I was too stunned to utter any words of recrimination.

Within moments the lorry that had been the initial cause of the disaster arrived on the scene. The driver and his passengers were most sympathetic and helpful and even offered to drive their lorry into a field and back it up level with the road, so that they could load Honey on board and take us to the nearest town. In the ensuing chaos, somebody swiped my transistor radio and Jane's lace nylon petticoat, which she had left lying on the back seat. The driver chose to ignore my complaint. After all, in his opinion, we were fortunate enough to have a lift.

In nearby Songorlu, they unloaded the Mini onto a high bank at the side of the road. We then had to do some hard bargaining, as the driver insisted on being paid 300 liras for his trouble. This was unfair as we felt he was partly to blame for the accident. To put an end to the argument, Jane suggested we all go to the police station where an interpreter, who spoke German, was found to translate. The driver duly received 50 lira.

The car could not be repaired in Songorlu, so the interpreter kindly managed to persuade another driver and his mate to take us back to Ankara; the agreed price was 150 lira, very reasonable as we had expected to pay between 200 and 250 lira. This lorry, already fully loaded with bags of cement, was backed up to the bank and the Mini pushed on board and secured with a stout rope. The lorry now had its rear wheels stuck in the ditch and a tractor was needed to tow it back onto the road.

Meanwhile the interpreter took us off to a nearby restaurant for much needed schnapps and a meal. It was a dark, dingy place with the usual soiled table cloths, though the food on display in the kitchen, laid out in enormous dishes, looked inviting. A short diversion, caused by the proprietor wrestling with a drunkard who had been sitting at a corner table and refusing to go home, helped to lift our spirits.

At last it was time to go. We thanked our interpreter and piled into the cab of the lorry beside the driver and his mate. I found myself sitting first on the gear stick and then on Jane's knee. Four people squashed into a space for two is extremely uncomfortable on a long journey. How our backs and bottoms ached after only two hours, so that during a short stop at a petrol station, Jane and I decided to take refuge on the cement sacks, sheltering from the biting wind behind the Mini and huddled in a blanket.

Two hours later, we stopped again at a wayside café for a reviving glass of *chai*. A man sat hidden behind some wooden trestles brewing tea, while another, who occupied one of the few chairs in the bare room, greeted us. A large urn containing water, topped with a pewter plate and a jug, stood in the corner and an oil lamp hung above the window, giving a dim light and warmth to the room. We handed round a bag of sweets, while the men smoked and we managed some sort of conversation with a dozen shared English and Turkish words. The driver, a large fat man with a mop of curly black hair, took good care of us in a kind and thoughtful way. He was the father of twelve children.

It was already 10.30 pm and dark. We had only covered 40 kilometres in four hours, with 108 more to Ankara. Because of the cold, we were not allowed to return to our refuge on the cement bags. The mate took over the driving and the driver somehow managed to squeeze himself onto the floor in front of the passenger seat, leaving room for us to sit more comfortably. Poor man, he puffed and panted so much that I felt it most unfair that he should suffer such distress and when the drivers next changed places, I sat on the floor. That would have been fine except for being molested by the wandering hands of the driver's mate. I tried scratching him to show my irritation, but was rewarded with pinches! That was enough. I turned round and snapped, "Stop it!"

Fortunately it was time for a break and another glass of *chai*. Jane and I had mentioned that we never saw any women in Turkey, so the owner of the tea shop dragged an old hag, draped in a drab brown robe, out of bed in the dead of night and with chuckles of delight and sweep of his arm, proudly announced, "Turkish woman".

At last we arrived in Ankara in the early hours of the morning, with sore bottoms from sitting so long and hardly able to keep our eyes open. It was 3 am. A flock of sheep were being shepherded along the dark, deserted streets and kept in a close huddle by three vigilant dogs. We flatly refused to go to a hotel for the few remaining hours of the night, preferring to stay near the car and our belongings. The lorry was parked at the foot of Ottoman Ataturk hill, not far from where we had camped the previous night. That seemed so long ago. Appreciatively, we snuggled into our sleeping bags on top of the cement and in spite of the night chill slept soundly until daybreak, which wasn't long. One of the men slept in the cab and the other beside us under the stars.

CHAPTER FOUR

ANKARA AND ERZERUM

Somewhere a cock crowed. Dogs started to bark and slowly dawn broke, promising a bright, clear day. By six o'clock the lorry was parked in the industrial, panel-beating, engine-repair and scrap-collection part of town. Already people were in the streets on the way to work. Small, grubby boys played in the dirt and vendors strolled past touting their wares as loudly as they possibly could. As there was nowhere in this particular district to have the Mini repaired, Jane opted to stay behind with the driver's mate to keep an eye on the car. Meanwhile the lorry driver and I went to look for the Chevrolet garage, where we had had the battery seen to the day before, to see if they could help in any way. We walked through the poorer suburbs, past smithies and stalls that lined the hard-packed dirt road. Enormous cabbages grew in tiny back gardens. Women filled their water jugs at the fountains they shared with the cattle and sheep roaming and rummaging at will.

At *Ulus,* while waiting for the Chevrolet Garage to open, we breakfasted on hot milk, freshly-baked bread and syrupy rose petal jam which swam all over the plate and tasted heavenly; such a simple meal, but oh so good.

Jane was not so lucky. However, eventually a man stopped by the lorry for a chat. He spoke some English and offered her a cup of tea. This prompted the driver's mate to top up her glass and give her a couple of scones to eat. By this time she was ravenous. Food was frequently uppermost in her mind, and her diary was full of descriptions of all the new things she had tasted.

We returned with good news and all piled into the cab and set off for a small market place.

The staff at the Chevrolet garage were most supportive and when the manager arrived half an hour later, he made arrangements to have the car unloaded from the lorry onto a bank in a nearby marketplace and pushed into the garage. The men, who had helped, stood around hopefully, until we realized what they were waiting for. They seemed satisfied with the five lira we gave them. The proprietor helped too, by writing a receipt to say we had paid for the transport back to Ankara, and our friendly driver left delighted with the agreed cash and the few cigarettes we offered him.

The head of the Chevrolet Agency was kindness itself and explained that though they couldn't do the actual repairs at their garage, he would see that it was done by the people they normally used and who he trusted to do a good job.

The mechanics could not believe their eyes as they saw more and more stuff come out of the boot and from the rear seat. This was then stored away in boxes in the spare parts storeroom in the safety of the basement, and Honey was towed away to a workshop in a back street; yet another maze of garages, similar to those in a London mews, where we left her to have the engine taken out. We arranged to return in the afternoon to agree on a price and to find out what spare parts to order and have sent out from England.

Somebody offered to drive us to the British Consulate so that we could report the accident and ask for help in finding suitable accommodation. Conscious that it would be sometime before we could leave, we also wanted to advertise ourselves as babysitters, in the hope of earning a few extra liras.

The Consulate gave us a list of addresses, but advised us to go to the Bureau of Tourism first. An engaging young Turk knew just the place and insisted on accompanying us to a hostel for female students attending university. Best of all, he negotiated a price of only two and half lira (the equivalent of two shillings) a night. Fortunately for us, the new semester hadn't yet started and several spare rooms were available. That was good news. Even so this did not lift our spirits. Feeling tired and dejected, we ate a picnic lunch in the park. The reality of what had happened hit home. All the excitement and anticipation of reaching our goal had suddenly gone up in smoke. But it was no good bemoaning our fate. We just had to pick ourselves up and do the best we could.

Back at the garage by four o'clock and over a glass of *chai* we discussed the necessary repairs to the car. The engine was already hanging from a pulley; miraculously it had suffered little serious damage. The radiator was all right but a new clutch plate, flywheel housing, dynamo, starter and distributor were required. Unobtainable in Turkey, they would have to be imported. A price of eight hundred lira was agreed for straightening the bent chassis, reshaping and spraying the panelling and reconstructing the engine. No-one had ever seen a mini before, but with the aid of the production manual we carried with us, they eventually managed an excellent job.

Honey was moved to a large field and put among rows of damaged cars, where young men and boys patiently beat out the panelling ready for spraying. The Chevrolet agent typed up the list of required items, and made all the arrangements for a telegram to be sent to my parents. While waiting, we sipped yet another glass of *chai*. Then, armed with the cooking stove, some stores, typewriter and clothing, we took a taxi to our new home. It was just like being back at boarding school. We shared a room with a Turkish student from the south who couldn't speak English. Hot water was strictly limited and all residents had to be in by 8 pm.

Next day we returned to the British Consulate, to inform them of our whereabouts, and to the Chevrolet garage to collect an official piece of paper, indicating that certain spare parts were unavailable in Turkey.

There was still no hot water in the hostel at any time during the morning as it had been turned off, so we wrote letters and went to the post office. Jane asked a man which of three boxes was the appropriate one for overseas mail. She correctly assumed that as he was wearing a suit, he was more likely to speak English. He introduced himself as Hikmet, a civil servant busy compiling a snow chart of Turkey. He seemed keen to engage us in conversation.

"May I invite you for a cup of tea?" he asked politely. We looked at one another.

"Shall we?" Glad of a diversion, we readily agreed and he took us to a chic continental tea room. This was just the man to explain what sort of weather to expect as we drove east. Jane launched into a barrage of questions. Because of this unexpected delay, we had been worried about meeting snow on the pass into Iran. He assured us that we should have no problem.

'Turk' he explained means 'strong' and is the origin of the country's name. As the conversation became more animated, he started to insist that he was 'always available'. We decided that it was high time to return to the hostel and afterwards always referred to him as 'Always Available'.

Seven pm. The water was hot at last and the bathroom free. This was just large enough to contain a bath without a plug, into which had been placed a marble bowl and a stool. Hot water poured unchecked from a big old-fashioned tap. Jane sat on the stool while I sat on the edge of the bath with my feet in the bowl. Our dirty clothes soaked in the water between us, onto which we poured detergent so as to wash them at the same time.

Somebody knocked at the door and handed in a bucket to be filled from the tap. In return we were given a copper dish with a long handle to slop water over our bodies. The water was soft and caressing; never before had I appreciated the sheer luxury of hot water. The allotted half hour was over all too soon and we emerged wrapped in towels, with dripping hair, carrying bundles of clean wet clothes.

The hostel was a six-storey building in Kizilay, set in a quiet suburban street with attractive houses and well-tended gardens. The rooms were sparsely furnished with narrow brown cupboards and iron bedsteads. Red stone tiles covered the floors. Our room faced onto the street; several times a day, fruit vendors passed by, calling noisily and invariably making sales to the hostel girls. Each floor had a wash room with cold running water and Eastern toilets, without locks on the door, so we had to remember to knock first. The director, a young woman with abundant black hair and big brown eyes, spoke little English, but was extremely kind to us. Her adorable four-year-old son always greeted us with a big smile before burying his head in his mother's skirt. As we were tourists, she granted us special dispensation from the eight o'clock curfew. That didn't stop the guardian signifying his disapproval; young girls ought not to be out unchaperoned in the evening. To qualify for admission to the hostel, we explained that we had just left university; just a small white lie.

No doubt worn out from the journey and our recent experiences, we slept long hours, rested and tried to fill the days of waiting by getting out and about. Being centrally placed, we had a two-mile walk one way to the garage to check on the repairs and a two-mile walk the other way to the Consulate to see if there were any telegrams. The staff were always helpful, and more so because we hadn't arrived with a hard-luck tale, but rather with a *fait accompli*. We had made all the necessary arrangements ourselves.

One morning we called at the Customs and Excise for permission to import spare parts to repair the car. While we were waiting for the Director to condescend to see us and sign the necessary documents, a man in his early thirties came over to talk with us. He walked with a slight limp and peered short-sightedly through thick glasses. He seized the opportunity to converse at length about ballet and the opera, suggesting we take advantage of the present superb programme; we didn't tell him that we were saving every penny towards completing our trip out to Australia. As it was, we hadn't bargained with a long stay in Ankara.

'Always Available' rang to tell me that when travelling East, Mt Ararat could be seen from the main highway, and that even during winter the road was passable. This was a great relief. I thanked him and assured him everything was fine. A few minutes later he rang again, this time to invite Jane and myself to join him and a friend for dinner the following evening.

He arrived in a large American Plymouth with Mehmet, a short, stickily-built man with a round Mongolian face. His tribe were descendants of Genghis Khan's invasion in the 13th century, who had settled in Eastern Turkey. He had studied in America, where he had fallen in love with an American girl, who had sadly refused to marry him. His English was excellent.

Keen for us to understand that Turkey was a modern country, every bit as modern as the West, they took us to the State Farm Restaurant on the hill of Ottoman Atatürk, near where we had camped on arrival in Ankara. It was more or less empty. An orchestra played loud Turkish and European music in a dimly blue-lit alcove, almost drowning out any attempts at conversation. This was irritating, as both men were well educated and extremely proud of their country. They were Government employees with first-hand knowledge of Turkey's rich natural resources and the difficulties in exploiting them. We learnt about the challenge to increase educational opportunities, the promotion of industry in Eastern Turkey to stop the population drain to the more developed West and the plan to send students abroad to learn new ways, methods and science from the Western world. Interestingly, Mehmet deplored the new ruling that allowed only one wife, even though the Moslem faith, of which he was a strict adherent, accepted informal wives.

One afternoon walking back from the clinic, where Jane had gone for her second cholera jab, we passed a lot of little boys coming out of school. We stopped to talk to Jocelyn, their teacher, an English girl, who invited us to call by for some English coffee.

"I came to Ankara with my father, to teach English on a three-year contract at the State College," she explained while putting kettle on the hob. "We had difficulty importing our car as we lacked the necessary documents. I find the children hard to put up with and I can't stand the Turkish food and the language is so difficult to learn. I doubt it will be much use later on." Her litany of woes continued. She seemed bitter and regretted her decision, not having found anything out about the country beforehand.

I found her attitude hard to understand as I considered working in a foreign country, learning a new language and meeting the people an exciting opportunity.

Returning to the hostel, we stumbled on a market. The young porters with large baskets attached to their backs, used for carrying purchases home for their customers, pestered us for work. It had been raining earlier that afternoon and now the town looked freshly washed and clean, and Atatürk's monument stood out majestically against a patch of blue sky. The remaining clouds, tinged by the setting sun, lifted our spirits.

Wednesday night was bath night; once again I revelled in the abundant hot water, flowing from a single tap, this time into a large marble basin on the floor. The only light came through a tiny window near the ceiling. In semi darkness, I knelt on the floor, already swimming in water. I washed all my clothes, myself and my hair. Hot water was still the same delightful luxury, especially as I had the bathroom to myself and could splash to my heart's content.

When we called at the garage next morning we found Honey had been pushed away into a corner to await the arrival of the spare parts many weeks hence. Devastated, we explained that they would arrive within a few days and that we did not want to be in Ankara any longer than necessary.

Two days later the chassis had been straightened and the body work was beginning to take shape. At last something positive was happening. We smiled, rubbed our hands together to express satisfaction and over steaming cups of *chai*, we repeatedly chanted, "*tamam, tamam*", Turkish for good.

Mehmet must have had a soft spot for Jane, as he arranged to take us out for another good meal. I had so hoped that he wouldn't bring Hikmet along - he was too pushy and I didn't trust him — but he did. Conversation was more strained this time and afterwards they took us for a drive to a lake ten kilometres out of town. Hikmet ushered Jane into the front of the car, refusing to let her sit in the back, and climbed in beside me. I huddled into the corner, assuring him that I wasn't cold, and in every way trying to make him realize that I was not as available as his 'availabilitiness' thought I should be. On the way back from the lake, which we could barely see in the darkness, he expounded on the laws of nature and laws of man and how I should forgive him such advances, from which I shrank further and further almost falling off the seat. We insisted on returning to the hostel early on the pretext of feeling tired. I had a strong impression that Mehmet had been roped into taking us on this jaunt against his will. He didn't approve of his friend's behaviour, especially as he was always very correct and respectful in the way he treated us.

It was already nine days since the accident. Mehmet drove us out to the airport in his oversized Plymouth to collect the spare parts. We were kept hanging about most of the day sitting in one office and then another, while seven different officials grudgingly added their signatures of approval to a permit, granting us a duty free import.

We teased Mehmet unmercifully about what we thought of

the customs regulations in Turkey and how we would explain all this in a book we planned to write. However he grinned happily when we relented and promised to write only about how kind and considerate the Turkish people had been to us.

To our utter dismay, when the parcel was finally produced and opened, two essential parts were missing. The whole procedure would have to be endured all over again; another telegram, as well as a letter of explanation, to my father, who couldn't believe that the actual engine had suffered some damage in spite of the hefty sump guard.

To raise our spirits Mehmet invited us out to dinner once again, this time bringing with him his tall slim friend, Dürsün, an irrigation engineer, who was very correct, but shy. In a small, noisy restaurant we ate *Göl Gazinasi*, a form of *Siç Kebab*, with which we drank *raki*, similar in taste to Greek Ouzo – take a sip of *raki*, chase it down with water, followed by a morsel of cheese and a slice of cold melon; a delectable combination. Afterwards they took us to a night club in the Kültur Park, attractively lit with soft twinkling yellow and blue lights, mirrored in ornamental lakes. The club was patronized mainly by groups of men, though there were a few women present. At first Dürsün was rather embarrassed to look at the scantily-clad blonde dancers but he soon settled down to enjoy the excellent cabaret: Spanish and Indian numbers, followed by Italians playing the fool. Everybody clapped enthusiastically. Reluctantly we had to leave early; we didn't feel we could keep the guardian up beyond midnight and face further disapproval.

We set off early on the Sunday morning to go to church at the American club, but ended up attending mass at the Italian Embassy instead, because we didn't want to hang around until 11 am. It was election day and Jane expected riots and disruption. She seemed quite disappointed to find that everywhere was quiet and orderly. The Turks, who had been under military rule since the 1920s, were about to adopt the American system of a senate. We shopped for lunch and while buying cheese, the proprietor suddenly dropped everything, rushed to the door and barricaded it. The police were on patrol. Apparently grocers' shops were supposed to be closed on Sundays. Chairs were found and we were asked to sit as quiet as mice and wait for the danger to pass. Meanwhile the men stood around nonchalantly smoking. When eventually we were allowed to leave, the police were engrossed in the next door shop looking at accounts and did not notice our departure.

Later, Mehmet and Dürsün drove us out to the old town, which appeared to be surrounded by two different fortifying walls, from where we could see modern Ankara spread out across the plateau. Directly below, a flourishing market was in full swing and people swarmed like ants between the stalls. We spent the afternoon at the dam site and reservoir built about thirty years previously to provide water for the burgeoning city. We climbed a hill to a flag staff from where we could get a bird's eye view of the reservoir, which was well below the high level mark as it rarely rained during the long hot summer months. Young trees had been planted on the arid banks, with provision for further planting. Below the main dam was a smaller lake set in a garden of poplar trees, pines and small colourful shrubs; vivid blues, greens yellows and browns were reflected in the water, a haven for city dwellers who came to picnic and relax in the shade.

We crossed a bridge to admire the gardens and have tea in a café in front of a roaring log fire. Jane and Mehmet had a great time discussing the views and customs of their different cultures. Dürsün was very charming, quiet and unassuming. Apparently he was a successful man and well read, yet even in the company of his native Turks, he tended to silence. Not that I minded, as I was happy to observe those around me.

Due to some remark of Jane's, they decided to take us to the theatre. It had started raining and I secretly feared for our safety as we sped along so as not to be late; late comers would have to wait until the second act before being admitted. Mehmet was a competent driver and we were all seated comfortably as the curtain was about to rise. The play, *Korella*, had a legendary theme similar to Robin Hood and was both enjoyable and apparently amusing. Dürsün had difficulty explaining the action to me, but Jane seemed to have a much clearer idea of the plot.

Jane was not very good at getting up in the morning, so I would prepare and bring her breakfast in bed, but that morning she made breakfast for a change. She had had another call from Mehmet to say he would call for her at 9 o'clock. He arrived with four other men, who all emerged from his car to greet her, and after introductions she was driven away to the government offices to start work. Jane had landed a job for a week, typing a report on soil erosion in Turkish, on a Turkish typewriter – the letter distribution was quite different, only two keys corresponded to the English keyboard, and most of them had squiggles above or below the characters – for which she earned the princely sum of 1. This was enough to pay a week's rent. It kept her occupied and she enjoyed the attention, as the men, attracted by her twinkling eyes and quick sense of humour, took it in turns to bring her glasses of steaming hot *chai*.

Meanwhile I filled the days going for long walks, and armed with a dictionary, learning Turkish. I had ten teachers, all students in the hostel. I thought they were no more than eighteen years old, but soon discovered that they were in their mid-twenties; older than me. It was a great way to make friends and my new language skills would stand me in good stead during the coming weeks.

During the lunch hour, Mehmet took us out again, this time to Atatürk's Mausoleum; an imposing monument to the leader and hero of the Turkish national liberation struggle, Kemel Atatürk. He had driven the Greek army out of Asia Minor in September 1922 and assumed virtual dictatorship in 1923, as the creator of the new Republic of Turkey. He implemented many of the necessary cultural and socio-political reforms, including economic development and agricultural expansion. He also abolished the Arabic script and since then the Latin alphabet has been used. His style of government reflected the wishes of the people through the Parliament. Primary school became compulsory and women's education was given great importance. He was a defender of peace at home and in the world and is not only revered by the Turks, but has been honoured by UESCO and the United Nations on the centenary of his birth in 1881. He was president for 15 years until his death in 1938; altogether a remarkable man.

One of my favourite haunts was the second-hand bookshop in the bazaar on Atatürk *Boulvari*, where for a few coins two books were given in exchange for three. The shop catered mainly to Americans stationed in Ankara at that time and was the only place where English books were obtainable. The walls of the tiny room were lined, two deep, to the ceiling with books. A table in the centre of the room groaned under still more books overflowing onto the floor beneath. Reading was a good antidote to the mounting depression I was experiencing, despite this unplanned opportunity to get to know Ankara, Turkey and its people so much better.

Fortunately, when I was feeling down, Jane would be on a

high. This helped us get through our troubles on many occasions. I was just finishing a nauseating autobiography written by Errol Flynn, the Australian-born Hollywood actor, known for his romantic swashbuckler roles, when Jane burst into the room and announced,

"Come on, hurry up, we are going to cook Mehmet's supper this evening."

We rushed out to buy spaghetti, tomatoes and cheese in the market. Mehmet's one-room home was built in the traditional way of dried mud blocks. It had a bed on either side, a couple of tables, several chairs, a minute kitchen with cold running water, a stone slab bench and a home-made gas ring. The outside toilet was a hole in the ground, oriental style. In spite of the grime and chaos, we managed to produce an edible meal with just a few too many red hot chilli peppers.

The following morning, Mehmet turned up an hour late to pick Jane up for work. She was beginning to wonder what had happened to him, as he was always punctual. The electrics had failed on his car. He was most apologetic.

As it was a clear crisp day, I decided to walk up to the Consulate to let them know that I was expecting another telegram from home. It was rather disconcerting to walk alone in Ankara; the men put down whatever they were doing to turn around and stare. The drivers of large cars and taxis slowed down and hooted their horns. Young women just didn't walk around unchaperoned.

All of a sudden, diverting everyone's attention, several fire engines came hurtling along the main boulevard, preceded by a small red vehicle, sirens wailing, on which two men dressed as if for outer space stood balanced like charioteers. Two larger fire engines followed behind, the firemen sitting poised, with hose ready to extinguish the fire wherever it was and yet another larger, red support vehicle was bringing up the rear.

On the way back to the hostel, I saw a VW with 'New Zealand' written boldly across the front windscreen. I stopped to talk to the occupants, four young Kiwis who were on their way home via Syria, Teheran and Calcutta having toured round Europe for four months. They too had had their difficulties and had to have a camshaft repaired. It was good to know that other people had troubles too.

The hours and days dragged by; the waiting and killing time was beginning to weigh heavily. At last, I was summoned to the Consulate for two letters from home and a telegram announcing the imminent arrival of the missing spare parts. I sang all the way along the road on my way to meet Jane for lunch and tell her the good news.

As we walked along the *Boulvari* together, she spotted a VW, this time with UK number plates, heading up the road towards the Consulate. Our bearded friend Ray was back in town. We jumped on a bus to catch up with him. He was just leaving for Izmir. He had left Ankara the same day as us, crossing the border straight into Syria, where he bumped into several of our Istanbul acquaintances. He had driven through Jordan and back to Damascus and here he was back in Ankara, to get his car serviced, before heading off for Cyprus. It was great to meet him again and hear about his adventures.

I returned to the customs office that afternoon to do battle. I needed another letter allowing the duty-free import of the remaining spare parts, Once more, the director, a small man, peered at me through his 3D glasses. He was again far too busy to be bothered with my request as he had already signed the necessary papers the previous week. Finally through an interpreter, I asked him if he spoke French, and amazingly he melted. The stern mask fell from his face and he was all smiles, assuring me that everything would be ready within half an hour. And it was. Meanwhile I had a long and interesting conversation with my interpreter, who ended up inviting me to the ballet, should there be a performance that evening or the following one. I thought it was a great idea and he suggested I bring Jane along as well.

Over supper we had a good laugh about all the invitations coming our way. As it turned out, there was no ballet; we went to the opera instead. Jane was horrified, as she definitely didn't like opera. *The Pearl Divers*, though sung in Turkish, was colourful with a pleasant lilt and an amusing story. It was my first and unexpectedly pleasant experience of the opera. Even Jane had to admit she enjoyed it.

The strident call to prayer at 5 am, echoing across the city from the loud speakers of the minarets, woke me as usual, along with all the other early morning noises; a crowing cockerel and sheep being herded along the street by barking dogs. It seemed strange to hear so many animal sounds in the centre of a capital city.

It was Jane's birthday, but as it was Friday she had to go to work and I had to be at the airport by eight o'clock. When I arrived, the weigh bill was missing, because the BEA plane from London to Zurich had been delayed and my parcel had missed the connection. What a birthday present! It was unbelievable that so much could go wrong. The next flight would be on Sunday evening; another two more days to kill. I idly watched a Turkish flight take off, followed by the American Air force and the arrival of the most beautiful BEA airplane, so clean and streamlined in comparison with the few other aircraft in local circulation. Jane was extremely upset by the latest setback, so we stayed in and drowned our sorrows with a bottle of *raki,* a popular Turkish alcoholic drink similar to Greek *ouzo.*

Ankara, at that time, was not the place to spend a prolonged holiday and we were running out of things to do to fill the long wait. We were both desperate to be on the road again. That Saturday we decided to visit the newly-built mosque that Mehmet had proudly told us about. The main door was barricaded but we eventually found an entrance round the back. The colourful, thick-piled carpets were soft under our bare feet as we took in the stained glass windows and twirling patterns of the blue ceramics framing the high dome. The quiet atmosphere was awesome and refreshing after an energetic walk. The men were at prayer and someone suggested, in Turkish, we go up to the overhanging balconies reserved especially for women. A dapper young major stepped forward to translate, escorted us upstairs, explaining as we went that since in prayer it was necessary to kneel and touch the ground with one's forehead, women who wear skirts needed to be behind so as not to distract the men.

When the *Hoja* (priest) appeared, the major rejoined the faithful as they lined up neatly for prayer. Watching from above, Jane's barely suppressed giggle very nearly disgraced us, as in unison, the men knelt and bent forward to touch their foreheads to the ground. After the ceremony, the major returned bringing the *Hoja* with him, a youngish man of medium height with a strong handshake, flashing black eyes and the inevitable moustache.

The *Hoja* is willing to explain everything about the Moslem faith," translated the Major.

"We believe in one God and Mohamed is our prophet who gave us the teaching of the Koran. Friday is a holy day, when women come to the Mosque too. Normally they are busy taking care of the cooking and the children. Women may not pray during menstruation. They are, however, expected to pray five times a day at home. The ritual exercises are to keep the mind continually centred upon God. Face, hands and feet must be washed before prayer, otherwise the worshipper is not acceptable in God's sight." There seemed to be no acceptance ceremony into the faith or baptism, though sometimes the *Hoja* would be called into the home to give a new child God's blessing. And as we were well aware, the first call to prayer was at 5 am; the time for making special requests.

When we finally emerged into bright sunshine, my feet were numb with cold. The Major, an unassuming man, perhaps a little anxious, invited us to lunch at the officer's club. He spoke excellent but rusty English. He had been a pilot, but due to an accident had subsequently joined the army and travelled widely. He told us that he suffered from homesickness when abroad, but as he never mentioned his family, we didn't know whether he was married or not.

After lunch we strolled in the Symmetrical Park: weeping willows hung low over an artificial lake and the walkways were lined with tall poplars already clad in their autumn yellows, another of Ankara's pleasant surprises. The Major was too polite to mention the football match he was longing to see, and was visibly happy to escape when we finally announced that we had to be back at the hostel at five o'clock for a phone call.

Things in the hostel were not always easy. It was Sunday morning and bath day. I had to fight for the right to have the bathroom at the time requested and paid for. Not only that, I was kept busy filling a constant stream of buckets which were handed in to me and by the end of my allotted half hour, I had become pretty fractious.

It was one of those days. The bus was behind schedule, so I had trouble persuading Jane, who didn't like to arrive late for church, to go inside with me. Then we listened to an interminable sermon on the creed to prepare the congregation to answer any questions they might be asked about their faith. What's more, the singing was appalling. As we filed out, Jane first, the imposing and bearded Vicar shook hands. Now it was my turn. He raised his bushy eyebrows and asked, "Are you new here?"

Completely taken by surprise, I stammered in reply, "Oh no, only passing" and quickly moved on. At times quite shy, I wasn't used to being spoken to after church. It had caught me off my guard.

Walking back through the almost deserted streets of the bazaar, I felt someone dig a large hand into my behind. I let out an involuntary scream and turned to catch a glimpse of the offending youth bounding round the corner and out of sight. Bottom pinching was a normal occurrence in Italy, but not in Turkey, besides we were always conservatively dressed to avoid offence; short sleeved blouses, slacks or voluminous, three-quarter length skirts, nipped in at the waist, as was the fashion.

On Monday morning the weigh bill had arrived at the Swiss air office. That was good news, but still we had to hang around for another two hours before we could pick up the parcels. An official, a big man called Umet, greeted us, playfully announcing that the papers hadn't arrived. He couldn't fool us though, because we already knew that they had. He accompanied us over to the customs office and helped complete the formalities at great speed. But a wrong number appeared on the weigh bill. My heart sank. Both Jane and I were petrified that another wrong part had been sent. What a relief to open the parcel and find all was exactly as requested.

At the bus stop, Umet introduced us to a co-worker, Adana; a tall slim man with a jaunty moustache and always joking. The two men invited us to a night club later that evening. Meanwhile, Umet accompanied us on the bus, making sure that we could alight near the Chevrolet garage to deliver the parts.

Amazingly, a lot of work had been done since the last visit. The car sparkled like new. The panel beaters had done a good job and the bonnet had been sprayed light blue. The workmanship was excellent. Even the mechanics shared our joy. All being well we could be on our way by Wednesday midday. We chatted with the owner for a while and he thoughtfully enquired after our well-being and whether we were short of money.

Adana and Umet took us to the Majestic in Genflick Park, a pavilion with a large hall and a restaurant with a tiny dance square in the middle. The black wall behind the bar sparkled with coloured lights. Blonde dancers mingled freely with the men before and after the floor show. This was supposed to be a real night club. It wasn't enthralling, but the entertainment eased the flagging conversation. The best part was watching the goggle-eyed spectators.

During the evening a telepathist handed out four envelopes: one for Jane to write her birth date on and a question pertaining to her future. She asked if we would reach Australia and to her astonishment, he replied "Bon Voyage".

Adana was an excellent dance partner, especially when it came to the cha-cha. We were having fun and didn't notice the time pass. Suddenly it was two o'clock in the morning; time to face the disapproval of the hostel guardian. It was a good thing that soon we would be back on the road and free of restrictions.

Oh no, I thought, that wretched room-mate of ours is as usual making a terrible din. I stretched and idly looked at my watch.

It couldn't be… It was eleven o'clock. Jane was reading. She too had overslept and only just woken. The day passed quietly, with a last visit to the bookshop to stock up for the journey and a couple of hours at the cinema to see a film in French.

Back at the hostel, we cooked supper. The guardian appeared at the door of our room to ask me to go downstairs. "Telephone?" I asked. He nodded up and down. That meant no. He mimed glasses. I was horrified when I realized it was Izmet, the man at the airport who had kept me hanging about for hours. Jane insisted I go down to meet him. After all, he too had promised to take us to a night club. I told him I was very sorry, but as we were leaving in the morning I didn't think we could possibly accept. We had to pack up all our things. I called Jane, who was very cool, and when asked for a positive answer, replied that it was 'positively no'. Looking abashed, Izmet left. Jane said he lacked the courage to even look at her. A faint smile flickered across the guardian's face as we sped upstairs trying hard to suppress our giggles. He obviously thought the whole episode highly amusing.

We had to wait until late morning to go to the garage, so for the last time, we made the most of the abundant fresh water. Once back on the road we would once again have to make do with a saucepan of tepid water for our ablutions. Of course the car wasn't ready. To our surprise, Mehmet, who had been away in Adana, in the South, for a week, turned up. He was quite convinced that by now we would be well on the way to Erzerum. To help pass the time, he invited us out for lunch. The traffic in Ankara was reduced to a snail's pace, as the army and scouts were preparing for the Anniversary of the Republic; battalions paraded to the accompaniment of brass bands and the scouts blew bugles with little musical success.

The Mini was still not ready at four o'clock. We started to check the car and found that in removing the petrol tank to do the body repair work they had damaged the fuel pump. The mechanic wouldn't believe that it wasn't an electric fault, but something wrong with the pump itself. Mehmet stayed late, translating when necessary, but I suspect he often didn't because he didn't think we had a clue. After all, girls were not supposed to understand how cars work.

Resigned to another night in Ankara, we returned to the hostel. That night it started raining, the first rain we had seen since leaving Switzerland. It had been getting steadily colder; weather for thick sweaters, and what a treat when the central heating came on.

Next day, when I opened Honey's bonnet, I discovered that the electrical contacts were loose. They had also broken the electric pump on removing the petrol tank to bash out a dented corner in the rear. That mended, they found the petrol was overflowing into the engine. When I took the mechanic for a drive we didn't get far. The gears weren't engaging into their sockets properly, so the gearbox had to be dismantled; something was incorrectly aligned. The petrol wasn't flowing freely, so off with the fuel pump and the carburettor. Meantime Jane and I sat on chairs in front of the garage getting sunburned, watching the passers-by and drinking *chai*, which appeared at regular intervals to appease our disappointment. They even brought us *Siç kebab* at lunch time; half a loaf of bread, with the middle taken out and filled with meat, tomato and peppers followed by grapes.

At long last the car was ready. We paid the bill, purchased a new, more solid jack, shook hands all round, everyone smiling cheerfully, glad to see us on our way. We climbed into the car and drove off. To our horror the dynamo wasn't charging. We returned to the garage to find an electrician to replace the faulty coil in the new dynamo with one from the old dynamo. They were dismayed to see us back so soon.

Finally, back at the hostel, we paid the bill, said goodbye to the guardian and struggled to pack the car. The boot had been strained in the accident and the suitcases wouldn't fit in as before. It would take a day or two before things would once again have their allotted place.

It was Thursday, 26th October and well into autumn. The days were already cooler. We had been in Ankara, the capital, for three long weeks. At least it had given us a wonderful opportunity to meet so many delightful people and learn much more about the Turkish culture. Now, finally, we were on our way, heading north in the late afternoon traffic: along the broad boulevards, past strings of small shops, their wares spilling out onto the pavements, on past cafes and workshops, ultimately leaving the last straggling habitation of the city behind. The Mini felt strange to drive, but at least she was in one piece and roadworthy again. From that point on, without either of us ever mentioning it, desperate to avoid another mishap, I became the sole driver.

Our spirits rose. We were travelling again and thought we should be lucky enough to make it through the mountains and over the border into Iran before the snows came. But we didn't get as far as planned for that evening. All of a sudden the lights dimmed. There was a smell of burning. Quickly I pulled off the road onto a fortuitous lay-by and there, Honey stopped dead. It was already dark, so we were stuck until daylight and couldn't even seek safe shelter for the night. That was that.

Nothing seemed to be going our way. Depression set in. We had eaten our sandwiches earlier on, so we couldn't even console ourselves with food.

Jane slept badly, cold and anxious about being so close to the busy road, but she needn't have worried. In the morning we discovered that some large fuel tanks had given sufficient protection from the passing traffic and the truck drivers, taking the turnoff to the nearby quarry, had not even noticed us. Two women passed by, one riding a donkey. They stopped to watch us eat a bowl of porridge and offered some unleavened bread. It looked like cold pancakes but tasted good rolled up and stuffed with honey.

As so often happened in this part of the world, two men materialized out of nowhere and stood at a respectful distance until the women moved on. They then seated themselves nearby while we ate the remains of our breakfast.

We push-started the Mini with a little help from our spectators, and as the dynamo wasn't working headed back to the nearest town, Kirikkale, where we hoped to get it repaired. We explained the problem to the men at the Mobil petrol station . A welcoming glass of *chai* promptly appeared. They then sent us to the electrician, whose workshop opened onto the main street. Here the inevitable crowd of curious little boys and grown men gathered ever closer around us, pushing and shoving to get better view, until a benevolent and bespectacled policeman, his bushy moustache set at a jaunty upturned angle, came to our rescue and shooed them away. But in spite of his efforts, they kept coming back.

The electrician had a graphic sign above his shop depicting a dynamo. Ours was burnt out and the new spare one, though reacting well to most of the tests, proved to be faulty. We bought a replacement for 125 lira. He would have charged us 30 lira less for rewinding the coil on the old dynamo, but this meant waiting twenty-four hours for him to do so. The electrician was teaching his young son the skills of the trade and gave him the easy part of re-assembling the dynamo, watching carefully all the time. While making numerous checks, he discovered that the cut-out motor was working excessively in the minus. This too had to be repaired. Another cup of steaming *chai* appeared.

It was a pleasantly warm, sunny morning and by 11 o'clock we were on our way once again. The scenery seemed less splendid than I remembered it three weeks previously. Perhaps the autumn colours had been exceptional on that fateful day. I drove unhurriedly down the steep winding dirt road, with the loose pebbled surface, where the accident had occurred; the low protection wall on bridge at the bottom had been cracked by our impact. We stopped to have a look. We were so lucky not to have gone sailing over the top to land a couple of meters down into the ditch.

We drove on past Songorlu, where they had loaded the Mini onto the truck for the return journey to Ankara, and into new territory. In Çorum, a traffic policeman pulled up alongside in his Jeep and because we couldn't remember the word for grapes, he offered to show us where we could buy the best apples. We left the vehicles, parked side by side in the central car park, and walked to a shop of his choice. He helped with the purchases, all at great speed. He then escorted us to the town perimeter and wished us '*gülegüle*' (goodbye). Were foreigners unwelcome in town we wondered? As soon as possible, we stopped again, this time to wash the grapes and to recover from the whirlwind round of the shops, normally a relaxing, leisurely occupation and a good excuse to get out of the car.

The road snaked endlessly on through the hills. Night fell and the lights of slow-moving trucks could be seen either high above or far below. We had been trying to cover as much ground as possible. I was tired. In vain we looked for somewhere suitable to camp, until we found ourselves in Samsun, a large, rambling town with no signposts. We took a wrong turning and got hopelessly lost, irritated and bad tempered. Finally, after driving up and down numerous, tortuous, semi-lit streets and making enquiries, we emerged onto the coastal, tarmac road. An oil refinery cast soothing reflections on the calm water. The road turned inland.

We would have to get used to camping wild once again. Finding somewhere secluded enough was a continual problem. After a couple of abortive stops, we found a pleasant grassy spot with trees to provide cover from the lights of passing lorries. It had been a long day and we were not happy when two men stopped to stare. We just wished they would go away and leave us in peace. We put out the lantern and climbed up onto the roof rack. The men wandered off, but were soon back to tickle Jane's toes, which must have been peeping out under the canvas curtains.

"Go away" she hissed, "Leave us alone".

They did, but were soon back again whispering "*tamam, tamam*" (good, it's all right). How I longed for sleep. Jane, who had an African knobkerry tucked into bed with her for just such occasions, menaced them with her weapon when they tried to touch the car. It was all too much and we didn't feel safe. There was no alternative other than to scramble down, get into the car and move on. The men ran off, gleefully clutching Jane's tights, which had been dangling off the roof rack, and two extension pieces we used for providing shade during daytime stops. When they realized we didn't want anything to do with them and were leaving, they signalled to us to stay, but we didn't want to risk it. It was close to midnight and we were both worn out.

The main road was lined with houses and farmsteads. There

was nowhere to turn off. At last we came across a canal. Here we pulled out onto a tow road, hoping that this time no one would see us, parked the car and climbed into bed exhausted. Poor Jane was too worried to sleep and had another bad night.

Even though we got up at the crack of dawn, an inquisitive audience soon gathered, egged on by one daring young woman who came over to talk to us. The men and children kept their distance. Once again our privacy had been invaded. Though they meant no harm, their curiosity made us nervous. Hurriedly we packed up and left.

The newly-surfaced road was excellent, despite occasional lapses where a bridge had not been constructed or had collapsed. There was very little traffic apart from the queues of slow-moving bullock carts creaking along the verge. The countryside was flat and wet. Mud houses were mainly perched on stilts. The wetlands gave way to gently undulating pasture. Herds of sheep hungrily cropped the meagre grass, watched over by young boys clad in grubby lengths of cloth to keep out the chill; their only entertainment waving to the passing vehicles. Scruffy dogs scampered around keeping an eye on their charges. Soon we were back in the coastal hills. Stalks of corn were stored up in the trees ready for winter and out of reach of greedy goats and other animals.

Down to the last ten lira in cash, we tried to change a traveller's cheque in Ordu. The first bank was unable to do it, but the second bank did so as a favour, even though they weren't sure what to do with it. Perhaps it wasn't surprising as even the shops were very rundown and uninviting. Foreign travellers rarely stopped in Ordu.

We ate lunch sitting on the black sandy beach. I had never seen black sand before. No wonder it was called the Black Sea. The usual crowd gathered to stare. Two young girls travelling on their own was certainly not part of their culture and the little blue Mini an added attraction. Still unsettled, Jane wanted to move on, but I had found that when you take no notice people eventually disperse, hitching a lift on a passing lorry or walking on their way. Some friendly women and children stopped briefly to talk, offering hazel nuts.

Leaving the town of Ordu behind, the road deteriorated and became narrow and tortuous once again. However each new corner revealed sweeping views of the sea, black beaches and rugged cliffs. The region was rich in abundant vegetation. Everything was so green. In a hamlet along the way, we bought swordfish from a fisherman bringing in the fresh catch; cooked on an open fire, sitting on the sandy beach with the sea water lapping at our feet, it tasted heavenly, so much better than anything bought in a fish shop.

October 29th was Atatürk's Day; a national holiday to commemorate the creator of modern Turkey, whose mausoleum we had recently visited in Ankara. The sun sparkled on the sea and surf broke on the black beach. Brightly-coloured fishing vessels bobbed in the coves. In all the villages, the school children were on parade; flags and bunting were everywhere. People streamed into the towns and villages. Men outnumbered the colourfully-dressed women wearing red and white striped aprons and wrapped in red rugs covering their heads and shoulders to keep out the cold. In some places the women were confined to sitting on the roof or hanging out of windows to see the festivities and dancing. Men were all over the place and it was difficult to steer clear of them.

While we were filling up with petrol, a Mercedes with German number plates pulled in. It was driven by a Persian whose name was Carem, on his way home to Tabriz in Persia.

We decided to travel on together. He spoke good German, though he seemed to understand a little English. Escorted by our new friend, we took a break in a village, to watch the dancing; four young men in a row, dressed in crisp white shirts, black trousers and red scarf wrapped around the waist, hopped energetically from one foot to the other, twirling and crouching to the accompaniment of a drum and fiddle.

Someone spotted us three foreigners peering over the heads of an impenetrable crowd and ushered us to the front. Chairs were produced to sit on and permission given to take photographs. To enthusiastic clapping, the show started all over again. Our host, who offered us sweet Turkish coffee, sat and had his shoes polished, perhaps to indicate his importance in the community. The dancers shook hands with us. We felt very honoured, being the only women present.

The road suddenly improved for the last ten miles into Trabzon, a large and busy port. In top gear, the Mini managed to speed up to an amazing sixty miles an hour, but that was the best she could do since the accident. We stayed just long enough to buy food. Turning inland and leaving the Black Sea behind, we drove on to search yet again for somewhere to camp.

For once we found the perfect spot, in a clearing by a water pump, near to a bridge and river. The usual crowd collected, but were more interested in talking to Carem, who had learnt some Turkish while studying in Istanbul. After supper Carem and I spent half an hour strolling back and forth across the bridge chatting in German, much to Jane's disgust, as I got to bed later than she did. Knowledge of German had stood me in good stead in Turkey, as this was the language of the educated people. Many had studied at German universities.

During the night, Carem's car rolled halfway down the river

bank and was firmly wedged against a tree stump. I awoke to find him wandering about helplessly wondering what to do. We set about jacking up one side, inserting stones under the wheel and removing the earth from underneath. We tried sitting on the bonnet, but the wheel just spun in the air. Just then, a gang of men on the way to work came to the rescue with a pick axe, muscle power and good humour. The Mercedes was soon back on the road. Carem was really lucky that it had not rolled further down the hill, as it would have been much more difficult to recover the car. Everyone gathered round warming their hands on mugs of steaming coffee.

It was one of those days. First we had to push Honey uphill so that we could give her a push start. She stalled frequently for no apparent reason. Carem was a hopeless mechanic, but thoughtfully stopped and waited each time. The scenery was wild and rugged. Sturdy stone houses, their mud roofs laden with the winter's stock of corn, huddled together in the fertile valleys. The people looked desperately poor, their clothes mere rags. It was a long winding way up the 9,000 ft/2,743 m pass. Progress was depressingly slow. It was getting colder. Each time the car ground to a halt, we cleaned the points on the distributor, which seemed to help temporarily. Near the top it started to rain and then hail. Seeing our predicament, the drivers of two lorries stopped to help, as once again, this time crouched under an umbrella, I had the distributor head off. One of the men, dark and gorgeous looking with a neatly-trimmed black beard and long, curling eyelashes, filed the points and helped to restart the engine. Later in the day, an Englishman working for NATO in Erzerum explained that cars are often affected this way at altitude.

Erzerum, at over 5,000 ft/1,500 m above sea level, served as

NATO's south-eastern air force post during the cold war. In NATO code, it was known as the 'Rock'. Here, a Turkish student attached himself to us. Speaking a mixture of languages and with the aid of a dictionary, we soon managed to make a few necessary purchases, but then spent ages looking for the Dutchman to whom Carem had promised a lift into Teheran. Eventually, after enquiring at the police station, we found him walking along the street looking for us. His name was Hans, a tall blond guy with an impressively detailed knowledge of the countries he was travelling through.

"This is a military zone, but we don't need to have a special permit," he told us. At least that was good news.

On the way out of town, we had the first puncture since leaving home. By then we had suffered enough setbacks. We just drove off the road and stopped. What a day!

Some youths woke us at dawn, chattering noisily, walking around and peering at everything. It had been raining and was bitterly cold, so we ran around to warm up while the water was heating for coffee. Hans complained of an upset stomach, which 'Nurse Jane' treated with bicarbonate of soda. We then set off across the apparently flat dusty plain with the car heater on full blast, climbing imperceptibly as we zigzagged through a maze of bare stony hills. The sparse villages consisted of mud houses surrounded by mud walls. The people were mostly clad in rags and the women, covered from head to foot, stared at us vacantly.

Halfway up the pass we met a large crowd of campers; a minibus and two motor bikes, two girls and five men, a mixture of English and Kiwis. They had all met en route and were having a riotous time, though unlike us, they had apparently found the local people unfriendly.

During the morning, Carem and Hans managed to get lost.

They took a wrong turning, reversed, and ended up with the rear wheel stuck in a ditch. While waiting for them to extricate the car and catch up, we splashed around in the cold water of a secluded stream.

In Agri, a small dusty town, we had the damaged tyre repaired. I soon dismissed the unpleasant character who had offered to do the job, paying him just 2 lira so he would go away. After that a kinder, better educated man, surrounded by a large audience, who obviously took pride in his work, mended the tyre beautifully. He refused to accept any payment. The inner tube was beyond repair. Luckily we still had a spare.

Brightly-clad women stared at us dumbly in the local shop; it was just a small dark room opening onto the street, lined by dusty shelves containing a few rusty tins and drab, torn cardboard boxes containing biscuits, matches and candles. Among the many strange foods was a delicious chocolate spread, cut from a slab like cream cheese. The honeycomb and nuts were cheap. Grains, flour, lentils, rice and spices were displayed in large sacks, stacked one against the other and sold to the customer by weight in recycled newspaper bags. There were no vegetables or fruit, and no eggs because the hens were 'sleeping'.

That night Hans opted for the local hotel as he was still feeling queasy. We chose to park in the lee of a deserted prison on the windswept plain. Moonless, it was another bitterly cold night. Even the spaghetti froze when lifted out of the boiling water.

The main road continued to climb steadily towards the frontier at the very top of the pass, across the desolate, rust-coloured sloping plain bordered by bare, rugged mountains. In the distance, Mount Ararat stood sentinel, floating above the haze between Armenia, Turkey and Persia. The flat, snow-covered summit was reputed to be the resting place of Noah's Ark, where he finally found land as the great flood retreated.

It was the 1st of November. We had covered 5,152 miles from London and we had made it over the pass before the winter snow. This outlandish place was surprisingly alive with tourists. Two Bernese were on their way west, after a flying two-month visit to India and the Taj Mahal. Iranian men, speaking fluent French, returning home from Paris, and suggested we join them. They were good for a laugh but they appeared to think we were fair game, so we declined their invitation. A German, in a dilapidated Mercedes, who drank coffee with us...And many others.

We said goodbye to Hans. He had accepted another lift to Teheran, as Carem was having trouble processing his car through the customs. We changed our remaining Turkish lira for Persian toman; each toman consisted of ten rials. We were at a loss to understand the strange signs that represented the numerals but Carem helpfully taught us how to read the numbers. He explained that the spoken language was Farsi and that they used an Arabic script.

Now we were ready to explore the fabled land of Persia; a new country and a new challenge lay ahead.

CHAPTER FIVE

PERSIA

After completing police formalities, we crossed the border into Iran, which in those days was still known as Persia; a different and exciting new world. The road descended steeply towards a fertile, intensely cultivated valley irrigated by the intelligent and ancient use of man-made conduits. These were known as *qanats*, a series of underground canals linked to wells covering immense distances, providing 75% of water used in the home and for irrigation. Everything was so incredibly green in comparison with Turkey. The villages and dwellings were softened by shady trees, the vivid browns of the distant mountains framing the horizon in striking contrast. The valley widened out and once again we started to climb gradually.

Petrol stations were non-existent. Increasingly worried and not knowing what to do and with the tank running low, we finally asked for '*Benzin*', in one of the villages. This was produced from a backyard stock of eighteen-litre cans and was incredibly cheap; eight toman the can, the equivalent of only two shillings a gallon.

Buying bread was a problem, as we had no small change. The baker sat on the floor of his shop, enveloped in a floury haze, fashioning little round loaves out of dough. Once baked, they were neatly stacked on a bench out in the street. His father, elderly and grizzled, sold the bread by weight, using stones of varying size as a measure, and tearing pieces off other loaves to bring the bread up to the required amount. No other food was available in this village of mud huts and flat roofs, so, waving goodbye to the hordes of little boys who had been trailing us, we headed out into the countryside, where a large herd of camels ambled about grazing peacefully.

Carem caught up with us later in the day, having finally managed to wrangle his way through customs. His arrival was fortunate. A sudden spray of oil covered Honey's windscreen; the copper piping leading to the pressure gauge had severed. Of course we were in the middle of nowhere. Several people stopped to help, but no one could offer any constructive advice and we were unable to unscrew the bolt that appeared to be causing the trouble.

Carem came to the rescue and volunteered to tow the Mini to Hoy, the nearest town, fifty-six kilometres away. It took four hours, mainly in the dark, along the narrow, uneven dirt road, with numerous stops to repair the rope; though made of tough nylon, it could not withstand the strain of slowing down into corners and accelerating out of them. Carem had had no previous experience of towing another car. What a nightmare!

During one stop a distraught shepherd approached us, tearing his hair out, asking if we had seen his sister. She had disappeared, run away, probably with a man. His eyes were wild with anger. Menacingly, he brandished a large stick as he vanished into the dark.

When we finally reached a garage in Hoy, the damage was easily repaired, by disconnecting the pressure gauge; all we had actually needed to do was to bend the copper piping back to stem the flow of oil and in so doing avoid four hours of hell. In the corner was an abandoned Jeep with a broken piston and a large notice hanging on the back door advertising 'Bed and Breakfast'. Realizing that others had setbacks was a terrific boost to our morale.

By this time we were all hungry, so we treated ourselves to a large plate of *Silö Kebab,* lamb skewered and cooked over embers, usually served with rice. Tradition has it that medieval Persian soldiers invented the dish by skewering the meat on their swords to cook it over an open fire.

Next morning, Carem suddenly became visibly nervous and was impatient to be on his way home to Tabriz. We broke camp in record time, including changing a wheel, as one of the tyres had a slow puncture. We had covered only a few miles along the bumpy road when there was a ghastly grating noise. Jane and I looked at one another horrified. What now? We stopped and looked under the car to find that the sump guard had come loose. One of the bolts had broken and the heavy metal plate was dragging along the ground. The only solution was to undo the remaining three bolts and store it on the roof rack.

Then, for no apparent reason, Carem was no longer in a hurry. He suggested we take it easy and park among the trees, beside the crystal clear water of a lazy stream, to take photographs and idle away a few hours in the tepid sunshine.

Towards midday, dozens of cars came streaming out of Tabriz in a dusty haze, across the now stony flat plain. They had come to welcome Carem and a doctor, also returning home after a long sojourn in Europe and who we had met previously at the customs. There was great rejoicing with hugs all round. We joined the convoy of cars heading back to Tabriz.

It was just our luck that only six miles from town, the Mini ran out of petrol. Despite the excitement of being together with family and friends, Carem promised to return with a canfull as soon as possible. In the meantime two men in a VW volunteered just enough fuel to take us into town.

At the town gate we met a very happy Carem surrounded by friends. He introduced us to two students, Mahmud and Javot, who led the way to a garage so that we could give Honey a much-needed service. For a pre-arranged price the engine was thoroughly washed with oil, air and water to rid it of sand residue. All the nuts and bolts were tightened by an apprentice under my supervision. The sump guard was bolted on again. The distributor timing was checked. The plugs were changed, which was good as one had not been working at all, and all the joints were thoroughly greased.

Three more students joined us: Mehrmud, Jashmid, and Nusrat. They invited us to dinner and to overnight in their student accommodation. We parked the Mini in Javot's garage and walked to their home.

A gate led into a courtyard, with an outside toilet in one corner. It was very clean; the only inconvenience was the need to fetch a pail of water from the tap to flush it. The house consisted of one main living room and another that was more like a large walk-in cupboard, a tiny kitchen and a bedroom with two beds and some shelves. The floors were covered in beautiful Persian rugs making their home cosy and inviting.

The men changed out of their street clothes into comfortable, loose, cotton pyjama bottoms. We all left our shoes at the door and sat cross-legged on the floor in a circle, to eat dinner that had been ordered from a take-away in town. A large flat cooking pan, laden with *Silö kebab*, rice and fried eggs, was placed in the centre, on a green plastic cloth. There were no plates or utensils, only sheets of unleavened bread to scoop up the tasty food from the communal dish. What a great way to enjoy a feast. We had a choice of Pepsi, Canada Dry, *Chahani* (a local beverage) and cognac to drink.

The evening passed quickly teaching each other card tricks. The men were a mixed bunch. Mehrmud, a medical student, spoke excellent English and acted as interpreter. He was short and stocky with kind, dark eyes and seemed to take a fancy to me. Nusrat, his best friend, was tall, his hair thin and wispy. As he spoke, he jerked his head to one side and in halting English explained his love of music. Javot was a great character with a wonderful sense of humour. He had a VW and worked for Simca. He insisted that had his mother been at home, we would have stayed there for the night, which would have been more appropriate. Jashmid, another medical student, short with crinkly hair, also spoke good English. He was smartly dressed. Mahmud was a tile salesman, blond, very quiet and a devout Muslim, who retired into the cupboard room to say his prayers aloud. At five the following morning he rose briefly for more prayers.

That night we slept on the two beds in great comfort while the five young men lay in a row on the floor, under a large blanket, laughing and whispering until we all fell asleep.

Early next morning Javot and Mahmud accompanied me to collect the car and buy a bowl of butter mixed with honey to eat with the sheet bread for breakfast, which we ate again sitting in a circle on the floor. This time we drank *chai*. We then drove out of town, in convoy, to Shiral along a dreadfully dusty road full of diversions, to see an artificial lake; a favourite picnic place for the people of Shiraz, surrounded by terraces and trees. It was out of season and disappointingly, the lake was dry. A deserted restaurant stood high and dry on an island in the centre. We walked all around it, taking lots of photographs in the warm autumn sun.

Javot cooked eggs, tomatoes and peppers for lunch, which we again ate from a communal dish sitting on the floor. This time we had spoons as well as sheet bread. I declined the *chahani*as because I had to drive; it is swallowed in one fair swoop like the *raki* in Turkey and chased down with Canada Dry or Pepsi, according to taste. We clinked glasses, exclaiming '*Bisalamati'*, Persian for 'cheers'.

The young men followed us out of town in Javot's VW as far as the first village, singing away happily in their car, weaving all over the road. It was a good thing there wasn't much traffic. Here we exchanged addresses and waved goodbye. The generosity we encountered was fantastic. Everyone was so helpful, insisting that it was their duty to do so; that it was an honour to invite us for a meal or to give us accommodation. Unable to thank them enough, we gave them our home addresses and invited them to visit us in England, should they ever travel to our country.

Progress was slow and tiring, bumping along the ridged dirt road and trailed by a cloud of dust. Time no longer seemed to matter. It was impossible to hurry and we barely managed to cover more than 150 miles per day.

Just past Mianeh, the shock absorber rubbers disintegrated. No wonder, after driving so far on such rough roads. The passing of countless cars and lorries had left it corrugated, just as the receding tide leaves ripples in the sand. To avoid further damage we slowed to a mere 20–25 mph, bumping more gently along until we got to the next town, Zanjan. A tousle-headed youngster who spoke limited English directed us to the Fiat garage. There, like a guardian angel, a man materialized out of the blue and helped me to buy the necessary rubber pieces and then organized everything. He gave the mechanic, who refused payment, 10 toman and took us off to have a meal with some friends who had invited him to lunch. Their house was hidden away behind a high wall and accessed from the dusty street through a wooden door. It also had a courtyard with an outside toilet and main water tap.

The lady of the house spoke a little German; two army officers spoke French and our benefactor spoke English. So we all managed to communicate, as we ate a wholesome meal of rice, chicken, meat and vegetables, followed by melon and sweets. Again such unbelievable hospitality. The living room was simply furnished; beautiful carpets covered the floor and lots of embroidered cushions were scattered about. I especially loved the intricately-worked silver boxes they had on display.

The deep ruts in the gravel road out of town made it almost impossible to negotiate. Alongside ran a slip road, the surface more like a heavy swell, which was kinder to the springs. Even travelling slowly a sudden unexpected dip would send us lurching out of our seats. Seat belts were non-existent in those days.

It was spotting with rain, which did nothing to improve the scenery; an endless, wide, flat valley, flanked by distant colourless mountains. Here and there was an oasis, a few mud houses or palm trees. A railway line ran parallel with the road.

At a remote railway station we found the New Zealanders, the mad crowd we had met previously in Turkey; two weary-looking girls and five men. They were unpacking their gear and getting ready to camp. We decided to stay with them. They brought one of the motorbikes into the waiting room and rigged up a light. This was a treat. Not only did we have shelter from the rain, but somewhere to cook, sleep and relax in relative warmth and swap stories.

When the alarm went off at 6.30 in the morning, nobody stirred except Jane and me. It had been a disturbed night: coughing in one corner, whispering in another, and somebody was up twice.

On examination we found that the joint which holds the shock absorber onto the wheel had snapped off and was hanging loose. No wonder there had been a loud bang whenever we went over a bump. Dejected, we motored on at snail's pace until we reached a settlement. The local motor bike mechanic dismantled the arm which holds the wheel in place, drilled a hole and fitted a new piece of metal to secure the shock absorber. It was a sloppy job. He failed to tighten the screws properly and forgot one of the bolts. A villager sauntered up, wearing a trilby and sporting a cigarette and holder. He proceeded to make a mess of the brakes and then had the audacity to ask an outrageously high price for the job. We gave him twenty toman and left in a hurry.

The village was typical of many, consisting of an extended, tree-lined street, along which ran *dupes*, narrow conduits supplying water for the trees and for squatting women to wash their dishes and clothes. They say that water flowing over stones is purified by the sun. An unshaven, kindly-looking man sat at the door of his home smoking a long handled pipe and talking to two little girls. Through the door, we could see a raised platform on one side of the room. It was covered in carpets and served as a bed. Every five or ten minutes a bus came hurtling through the village, scattering the children, men, donkeys and sheep. The women looked old before their time, sad and despondent compared to their Turkish sisters. The men wandered aimlessly, fingering their beads or huddling in small groups to gossip at the tea house door. An old hag, dressed in long black trousers and several layers of frilly skirt, her hair dyed red and covered with a scarf, advanced towards us, her hips swaying provocatively, I wondered who for. She wanted a lift. The bus wouldn't accept her. The men thought she was a huge joke.

The New Zealanders drove past waving. Soon after, we followed them on the newly-asphalted road; no more bumps or dust. We sped along comfortably towards Teheran and through Gasvin, a small town, as crowded with motorcars as with horse-drawn carriages. Camels sauntered along, tied together in a long line, heads held proud and high, unperturbed by the traffic. Donkeys ambled unwillingly, carrying incredible loads, prodded along by their impatient owners. Pedestrians crossed the road blindly, unthinkingly. Traffic lights flashed red and green at every crossroads. Suddenly we were surrounded by the buzz of civilization.

More and more traffic filled the highway, thundering across the endless, monotonous plain. Snow-bedecked mountains framed the factory chimneys and smoke of Teheran, now looming on the horizon.

We soon reached the impressive Shahrezza Avenue and stopped outside the Teheran Palace, a chic, modern hotel with sliding glass doors that opened miraculously on approach. Jane acquired a map of the town and some tourist information about Persepolis and Isfahan. A member of staff directed us to the central post office, where we collected a bundle of post, including a message for Hans, the German, who had not yet arrived. The clerk took a great interest in all the tourists passing through town and promised to help us find a hotel, should we need one.

Teheran was a modern vibrant city, such a contrast to the rest of the country. This was the first time since crossing the border that we saw women walking in the streets unveiled and wearing the latest western fashions, though the majority wore the chador. Cars galore filled the streets and the standard of driving was appalling; accidents were happening everywhere and driving was more petrifying than in London or Paris.

Back at the Teheran Palace, the bell boy helped us to locate the home of the Keshvari, who were surprised that we hadn't arrived several weeks earlier. Their son was studying textiles in Manchester and shared a flat with my brother Nigel. He often spent the weekend with us at home. We felt rather embarrassed to be invited into their stately sitting room in our scruffy, dusty state. Fruit and cakes were offered, and when at last they realized we weren't booked into the Teheran Palace, they invited us to stay with them. What a relief, especially, as in our naïve way, we had expected this. Honey was duly parked alongside their VW in the small garden.

Mrs Keshvari was horrified when we asked if we could possibly have a bath or a shower. "We never use the shower during the six winter months" she said.

We changed into clean clothes, enjoyed a delicious supper and an early night snuggled into soft, comfy beds.

It was a great surprise to find that the family kept their sitting room locked up and only used it for special and formal occasions. Apart from some priceless Persian carpets and several attractive pieces of pottery, it was a show room and not at all homely.

In the morning Mr Keshvari drove us to the VW service station, which redirected us to the Austin agent. Eventually, in a run-down district of town, we found an ultra-modern garage, complete with an assembly line for new cars. Apparently two other English girls, driving a van, had had their shock absorbers replaced two weeks previously. The agent, looking very Oxford in his winkle-pickers and skin-tight trousers, wearing a blazer and smoking a pipe, was extremely helpful, though lacking in charm until we completely ignored him.

The mechanics meticulously tightened up all the nuts and bolts, while Mr Keshvari disappeared to buy new shock absorbers for the rear, which he very kindly paid for. They were the sort used for motor bikes, and proved to be extremely durable. The brakes were re-adjusted and the hand brake repaired. In the meantime, we were taken home for lunch and then sent out with Feresthe, the secretary, to accompany us as interpreter. He escorted us briskly around the bustling Bazaar with its many different industries, copper beating and silverware predominating.

On the second day of our stay with the Keshvaris, they took us to visit the Golestan Palace, set in a garden of pine trees. Bowls of light hung in sprays over small pools of cool water. Known as the Palace of Flowers, it belonged to a group of royal buildings and was used for state receptions during the era of the Pahlavi reign. This was where Queen Elizabeth stayed during her visit to Persia. It was fabulous. The walls of the entrance hall and throne rooms were covered in glass, carved in intricate patterns that shimmered in the light; the perfect setting for the 'Peacock Throne', decorated in painted enamel and said to have originated from India. Exquisitely hand-painted enamel urns from Sèvres, in France, lined the elegant and richly-carpeted staircase; massive coloured chandeliers hung from the ceiling in the imposing state room. A mosaic tiled floor lay hidden beneath priceless carpets, over 150 years old, which surprisingly showed no sign of wear. All the alcoves contained precious treasures from around the world: ivory from India; intricately carved chairs and tables from Kashmir, decorated with little birds and animals; gifts from England; paintings from Holland. The last room we saw was quite plain, displaying some sturdy oak furniture.

We ate lunch in the comfortable Vanak hotel, out of town and rather deserted at that time of the year. It was so enjoyable after all the snack meals and camping. The barman, sporting large ears and compelling blue eyes asked my name. I didn't really want to strike up a conversation, so I didn't reply.

"I'm a Christian," he said, "My name is Simon."

"Mine is Jeanne", I replied, so as not to be rude.

We ate *Chelö Kebab*, a speciality of rice and two kinds of meat, topped with a raw egg.

Later we drove out to Shemiran, a mountain suburb, where soldiers were training to scale rocks with ropes. It was a quiet, peaceful place. A woman washing her clothes in a stream nearby was so absorbed she never noticed us watching her.

It was luxury to live in a house for a couple of days. The Keshvaris were extremely kind and hospitable and when we left they provided a box of bread, nuts and raisins for the onward journey and as a memento of our stay, gave us each a small bowl and plate, hand-crafted in Isfahan.

The road south from Teheran across an endless brown desert with few signs of habitation was asphalt. It was almost too good to be true. Gleefully, we sailed past the Waltzing Matilda, a VW bus full of Australians. Honey was so much more comfortable and a delight to ride in now she had new shock absorbers, and for once we made great progress.

In the holy city of Gom, not even a glimpse of the beautifully-tiled courtyard of the mosque was permitted. Soon the car was surrounded by men in turbans and brown cloaks. They gaped, bemused to see two unveiled women in short skirts. We felt menaced. This was certainly not a good place to be. Unbeknown to us, the holy city was out of bounds to the infidel.

The mountains we hoped to reach by nightfall remained tantalizingly distant as we continued eternally on across the open plain. Late in the evening we came across the now disabled Waltzing Matilda. She had sped past us during our lunch stop, but a bearing in the back axel had broken. Seven men and two girls emerged to exchange news. Before long, five of them managed to hitch a lift on the trailer of a lorry for a dusty four-and-a-half-hour journey on to Isfahan.

We opted to stay and cook supper for Peter and Duncan, the two who remained on guard. We bought food in a nearby village, assisted by numerous villagers who were all eager to help and managed to create an edible stew out of onions, potatoes and tins of this and that. Peter had a strong Cockney accent; he was tall and blond, a lazy individual, full of nervous energy, who liked to be in control of the situation. He entertained us with his guitar, the music soothingly breaking the uncanny silence of the desert. Duncan was quite different; a Scot from Aberdeen, he was a freelance photographer who had travelled widely on cruise ships. He kept us enthralled with accounts of his adventures. He had joined the Waltzing Matilda on a whim, at two days' notice on his return from Canada.

During the bitterly cold and disturbed night, Jane was unwell with an attack of recurrent dysentery. Before leaving, I drove back to the village to buy food for Duncan and Peter. The bread shop was a dark little room, below street level, where a couple of men and a boy worked all day kneading dough and making flat loaves to cook on the rounded sides of the mud oven, heated by a small gas flame. Then in exchange for a handful of nuts, a delightful youngster from the gas station accompanied me in the car to the well and helped me fill our water can.

The freshly-paved road into Isfahan was as yet unfinished. We hit two bad stretches of dusty corrugations which annoyingly slowed us down. The Masjid-i-Shah Mosque dominated the Imperial Square in the centre of town, its striking turquoise tiled dome framed by the deep blue of the sky. We had planned a visit but found it closed. As we turned to walk away, we bumped into Val and Christine, passengers on the Waltzing Matilda, also doing the sight-seeing thing. They had survived the rough trip into Isfahan. The men had returned with help for the ailing bus.

The bazaar, compared to the more dignified one in Teheran, was bustling with life, colour and smells. Each section had a different trade. Copper trays were beaten into shape with tiny hammers and patterns scratched onto them with a sharp pointed tool. There were silver jars and bowls, tables decorated with patterns of birds and animals, gold and silver jewellery, food, spices, pots and pans, carpets and colourful bales of cloth. Everything imaginable was available if you knew where to look. Men and boys learning their trade sat or knelt on rugs beavering away in little alcoves. Old men smoked long-stemmed pipes or shared a hubble-bubble pipe with a friend. Youths carrying trays of *chai* were much in demand. Unfortunately many of the items on sale seemed rather shoddy, due perhaps to mass production for the American tourists who visited in droves during the summer.

Viewed from the circular platform that tops one of the tall and slender minarets of Masjid-i-Shah Mosque, which we explored later in the day, Isfahan was an enchanting city: mud houses, each with their own tiny garden, a rectangular square, the sprawling bazaar, the entrance to the Hasht Behesht Palace and water gardens; innumerable mosques covered in delicate blue and turquoise tiles glistening in the sunshine, decorated with stylized motives and Arabic script.

To reach the viewing platform, we had had to climb on all fours up the steep, worn and winding stone stairs in the dark. Only part of the mosque and theological school seemed to be in use. We stood beneath the main dome and stamped our feet to hear an echo come whispering back at us. Walking back through the ladies' courtyard, a group of women sat reading the Koran and smiled at us, until they realized that they were unveiled and we were strangers. Embarrassed, they shyly hid their faces.

It started to drizzle. Against my better judgement, Jane insisted we find a hotel room for the night as she was still feeling unwell. Most were too expensive, or too dingy, dirty and uninviting. The proprietors gave me the creeps. Finally we settled on the Tooz, which turned out to be reasonably pleasant, though lacking washing facilities. We parked the Mini in the grounds of the largest hotel in town, where we felt she and our few belongings would be safe, and carried the little gas cooker upstairs so as to prepare some food. Our friends from the Waltzing Matilda were staying in a superior hotel nearby and offered us use of their shower; the first we'd had in three weeks. What bliss.

We continued to explore Isfahan. The Jamé Mosque was fascinating; a combination of styles left by the conquerors who ruled Isfahan through the ages, dating from 771 to the twentieth century. Carved mud pillars were still standing propped up by concrete beams and intricate stone carvings, once used as altars, were hidden away in a side room.

In the Christian quarter women walked unveiled. An elderly woman showed us around the richly-carpeted Gregorian church with its quiet courtyard, built in the style of a mosque. Holy pictures hung on the tiled walls and the simple altar was made of solid silver. On the outskirts of town buses and cars were being washed on the shore of the shallow River Serarood.

Looking back across the desert, we could see the palm trees and minarets of Isfahan, an oasis of beauty and industry, sinking below the horizon and melting into the glow of the setting sun. Ahead of us lay an endless desert. The so-called road was marked by telegraph poles striding towards infinity. Insignificant mud villages that merged with the landscape became fewer and further apart and it grew dark.

Nobody discovered our camp in a ghost hamlet of crumbling mud huts until we were ready to leave. It had been eerie in the moonlight, but the walls had given protection from the wind and we had felt safe. When houses grow old, or the elderly die, they are deserted and left to disintegrate with the ravages of time, while new homes are built nearby.

The Dasht–e Kavir and the Dasht–e Lut stretch from Teheran as far as Baluchistan and into Pakistan. Seen from the sky years later, it is a vast inhospitable expanse of brown desert, a daunting prospect for a little Mini. But this we didn't know at the time.

Saturday passed and Sunday too, driving slowly and steadily, on and on along the rusty-brown dirt road, sometimes on tracks on either side offering a more comfortable ride. The shock absorbers had to be tightened frequently as they continually worked loose due to the corrugations. The desert grew more and more monotonous and empty: no villages, no trees, no horizon, just a desolate waste. We felt very alone and vulnerable to the elements. The land and sky fused in a shimmering mirage. Distant mountains loomed like islands out of the dust. Layers of flat-bottomed clouds imitated sailing ships on the high seas, scudding across the pale blue heavens, occasionally blotting out the sun and relieving the glare.

A lone American on a motor scooter passed us, bumping rhythmically on his way west. A bus rumbled by, covering the Mini in a cloud of dust. Then an Austrian, bearded and tanned, driving an amphibious vehicle and accompanied by his large dog, stopped to have lunch with us; a strange character, full of fun. He had been on the road for eight years. We had met him before in Teheran travelling with his beautiful blonde Nordic wife, whom he had sadly sent home because she had fallen ill and was unable to rough it any longer. His vehicle was fitted with a burglar alarm and he carried among his belongings an enormous round cheese. Much to our amusement, he had lost all notion of time and was an hour and several days out.

The day closed with the most spectacular sunset: a mushroom-shaped cloud, like an exploding atom bomb, rose high in the sky. Glowing pink flames leapt from the ground, painting the distant mountains crimson, and slowly as light faded they became dark shadows against a turquoise sky. The clouds shielding the sun turned from crimson to gold to orange and blue-grey. Suddenly it was dark, for there is no twilight so far south.

On the third day, beyond Kerman where we had topped up with petrol, bread and water, the Waltzing Matilda went flying by, riding the corrugations with gusto. We tried, in vain, to catch up but had to cope with recurring petrol pump trouble. I spent a lot of time grovelling in the sand under the car, either tapping the petrol pump or tightening up the nuts and bolts that secured the squeaking shock absorbers in place.

Another trail of dust heralded an oncoming vehicle. It was a lorry. The driver and his mate, seeing our plight, slowed and stopped, and came to the rescue by blowing the petrol feed pipe clean with compressed air. It never ceased to amaze me how people in outlandish places are always so willing to help anyone in trouble.

The desert stretched away to an elusive horizon. We had given the small settlement of Bam up as non-existent and kept on driving, worried about running out of petrol. On cue, out of nowhere, an army officer appeared to escort us to a fuel depot and see us on our way again.

Occasionally an oasis of palm trees and a few peaceful dwellings loomed up and disappeared behind us. Drifting sands often obliterated the road and half buried the crumbling ghost towns. Tall rocks stood like sentinels on the flat infertile soil. The road started to climb, twisting round a bare hillside onto another plateau that continued incessantly on and on. A tower appeared, standing solitary in the middle of nowhere. At least we knew we were still on track; discarded tins of Heinz beans testified to the passage of other overlanders.

A VW arriving from the East broke the monotony. We stopped to exchange news about the road conditions and shared cakes with an Austrian and his delightful Indonesian wife. It had taken them eight hours to come from Zahedan, where we were heading. The road was appalling and there were floods in the canyon.

We eventually reached the mountain pass. On either side, rocks tinted red and green towered above us. It looked impassable. We just had to keep going and set off up a barely visible track, almost obliterated by the recent torrential rain that had turned the canyon into a veritable river bed.

Round the first bend, deep lorry tracks marked the way, but they were too wide for the Mini, so we had to ride abreast of them. Large stones, loose earth and sharp pebbles hampered progress. It was a wonder we didn't have a puncture. We had to switch constantly from one side of the track to the other.

It was while crossing over that Honey slid sideways and stuck firmly in the mud. We just didn't have the strength to push her out. Resigned, we waited for the arrival of a guardian angel, who came only ten minutes later. The driver put his cheerful passengers to work and soon the Mini was once more on firm ground. They insisted we drive on ahead in case we should get stuck again and need further help. It took another hour of deep concentration before we finally emerged from the canyon. There, at a military control post, we were asked to sign our names and write our destination in a book.

In the middle of nowhere, on another long straight road heading towards the ever distant mountains, we once again ran out of petrol. There had been no villages in which to refuel. This was one thing we had feared all along and here we were, completely stranded. To whittle away the time, we spread a rug on the shady side of the car and settled down to play chess, one of our favourite pastimes.

Scanning the empty desert, Jane excitedly saw, in the far distance, a plume of dust slowly travelling towards us. Four men jumped down from the lorry and offered to siphon off some fuel. To do this, they needed a bottle. Jane produced the only one we had, a cider bottle with a porcelain cap attached. The simpleton among them was delegated to do the job and he transferred four litres from the fuel tank and a further litre, when we again ran dry near Zahedan. The driver refused payment. All he wanted was the empty cider bottle.

Dimitri, a short fat Greek garage proprietor who serviced the cars of most overlanders on their way through, did an excellent job and even got rid of the squeak. He spoke a little English and showed us his scrapbook full of letters from former clients relating tales from their onward journey and even a photograph of a 1926 Rolls Royce. He was impressed that the Mini was in such good condition, as most vehicles were extremely battered by the time they arrived.

After lunch in a local hotel with some stranded Australians, we changed some money, stocked up on food and water and went through customs. It was the 14th of November. We had been in Persia for two weeks.

CHAPTER SIX

PAKISTAN

No-man's land linked Persia to Pakistan with a road and railway line. Eighty miles of flat emptiness stretched to infinity. It was worse than anything we had seen so far, the monotony broken only by a small group of men repairing the road. Dressed in brightly-coloured garments and wearing turbans, they waved cheerfully as we bumped past. A diversion, marked by a line of stones, led us to an isolated bungalow where a tethered camel sat smugly watching us with his beady eye. We presumed this to be the customs post, but no; it was a little game played by bored outpost men to brighten their day but they were nowhere to be seen.

At last, three hours later we reached the Pakistan customs and went through the usual formalities. Petrol was available, though more expensive than in Persia. The frontier made little difference to the scenery, except for a large notice announcing "From Here on Metallic Road". Wonderful, and it was true. A great relief as neither of us was feeling very well; we were exhausted from the constant bumping and shaking of the past few days.

It was only a single track, but our speed increased to 45 mph on the undulating asphalt. Unlike in Persia, comforting signposts, written both in English and Urdu, popped up frequently as well as numbered posts every kilometre.

Nomads roamed the desert, clad in billowing robes and baggy trousers, their long shirt tails hanging out. They wore turbans, with a length of material trailing to wrap around their faces to keep out the sand. The young girls dressed in vivid red embroidered garments, complemented by ear and nose rings. Their camels were bedecked with necklaces made with blue stone baubles and long chains of clanging bells, so they could be located when they wandered off among the stony dunes at night.

Nature treated us to a crimson sunset resplendent against the gathering storm clouds. The stony ground glistened from the recent rain and a cold sand-filled blustery wind rose sending swirls of sand across the darkening road, until it meant driving from post to post. It reminded me of following the cat's eyes in England on a foggy night.

We changed direction and headed towards an outcrop of barren hills, where thankfully we found a place to stop that afforded some measure of protection. Both of us were too tired to contemplate driving another 200 miles to the nearest big town. Jane was apprehensive though. She could see a distant light twinkling in the darkness, but when we put out our light, it too disappeared for good.

Each day as we travelled further east, it had grown light earlier until on the last morning in Persia we had woken at 5.30 am; now the clocks had been put forward and dawn came at 7 am. It made little difference. We lived from dawn to dusk.

Unbelievably, out of the infinity and silence of the desert, a man materialized to watch us break camp; his beautiful face was bronzed and weathered by the sun and framed by a neat beard tinged with grey. He remained at a respectable distance and didn't disturb us in any way. The world was waking up and coming alive: A Jeep, a camel, a donkey and even a cyclist pedalled by. We were no longer alone.

We drove on past an occasional hamlet or a solitary tree. Road workers brushed the sand from the road, stopped to watch and wave, smiling, revealing beautiful strong white teeth. Cows with curved humps grazed peacefully on the sparse scrub.

Parallel with the railway line, we climbed yet another mountain pass and again began to fret as to whether we had enough petrol in the tank. But we need not have worried as before long an army post hove into sight, where we signed the visitor's book and filled up with fuel. (The Waltzing Matilda had passed through the previous afternoon.)

We found what we thought was a secluded place for lunch and a rest among the dunes, but after a while, a man and his camel loaded with his few belongings stopped to stare. It was strange how hard it was to get away from people, especially as the desert was so empty. He was accompanied by a small boy herding their shoats (a cross between sheep and goats) and a pet lamb. The boy came hesitantly to talk to us, to finger my typewriter and peer into the Mini. His curiosity satisfied, he ran gleefully back to his father with a handful of nuts and sweets.

The Khojak pass reaches an altitude of 6,500 ft. /1981m. It was a long slow climb. On the other side a train of camels was slowly rocking its way across the plateau towards an oasis on the distant horizon. This was Quetta, the legendary stronghold of the western frontier and once occupied by the British, the capital city and an important trade centre of the province of Baluchistan.

It lies at 5,500 ft. /1676 m above sea level. A renowned hill station, it was strikingly beautiful after the tedium of the desert. This was how I had always imagined Paradise to be.

Sheep grazed beneath the tall birch trees that lined long, wide avenues, occasionally straining to reach and nibble golden leaves that hung temptingly low. English-style bungalows graced well-tended gardens. The post office, surrounded by pretty flower beds, had plenty of parking space and even a water pump; somewhere to top up our water can. It was prayer time and the faithful were praying in the courtyard of a pure white mosque, its delicate pinnacles reaching for the vivid blue sky. In the busy market, men smoked strange long-handled pipes, with veritable fires burning in small bowls. Stalls were laden with fruit and vegetables. I just couldn't resist purchasing some maggoty apples from one of the most handsome men I had ever laid eyes upon. His broad smile quite melted my heart.

The Mini had been losing oil. As this required removing the sump guard, something impossible for me to do, we took her to Mr. Davis of Julius Bros to have the flywheel housing tightened. The garage had been recommended by the Australians. The mechanics did an excellent job.

That night we experienced frost for the first time since leaving home. Though warm and cosy in our sleeping bags, I awoke with my toes numb with cold, which didn't warm up until the first rays of morning sun peeped over the mountain at 8.15 am. Even the surface of our drinking water had frozen lightly. Up in the mountains, winter was definitely on the way.

We set off into the brown barren hills, following the course of cascading water. The road still ran parallel with the railway line built in 1894 and still in use. It disappeared frequently into tunnels bearing names such as 'Mary Ann' and 'Windy Corner'. Just round the first bend, we passed through a village of mud houses, all painted white. Dogs lazed in the sun, twitching their ears to ward off the flies. The children gaped at Honey as we went by and started to run after us with whoops of joy.

Nomadic people had camped for the night on the outskirts and were making ready to migrate down to the Indus valley to spend winter on the plains, where there is abundant tall grass for the animals and work for the women in the nearby town of Sibi; returning to Quetta and the summer pastures in March. Groups of travellers straggled over several miles.

The camels were decorated with red and black tassels, bells around their necks and knees. The women, dressed in red and gold, walked or rode perched on the camel's hump, surrounded by chickens and lambs too young to walk. Some had babies in their arms, others hanging in a bag from their heads or shoulders. Men carried the younger children and proudly held them up high for us to see, waving and smiling as we passed. Once I saw a baby donkey slung across the back of its mother and firmly secured. The older men rode plump, healthy-looking cows with humps and children flitted hither and thither in charge of the shoats. Pet lambs were led on a piece of string. Dogs chased each other under the camel's legs and ran alongside the Mini barking excitedly.

Down in the valley at Sukkur, a fabulous new bridge-cum-barrage spanned the slow-moving River Indus. We crossed over and sat on the other side soaking in the sun and admiring the panoramic view of the town. It felt really good to be warm again. We camped on a picnic ground with a sign that said 'LUNCHING TABLES'. Despite the dense habitation all around, the night was undisturbed, except for the occasional diesel train thundering by or a lorry speeding along the main road. A half-moon filtered through the rich foliage of the shade trees. It was the first really balmy night since leaving Greece; the sort of weather I had expected to find all the way south of Italy.

Incredibly early in the morning, the world came alive with bullock carts, horses, camels and people hurrying in every direction. Gone was the emptiness and uncanny quiet of the desert. More women wore purdah than in Turkey. They peered through tiny holes in their heavy white veils. We felt sorry for them and grateful for the freedom we enjoyed wearing jeans and tee shirts, though we were careful to cover ourselves adequately, so as not to offend. After all in Pakistan, it was considered risky for two girls to travel unaccompanied. The men wore long white skirts called 'dhoti', their shirt tails hanging loosely outside.

The River Indus wound its way across flat fertile plains. Camels were used to draw the plough and enormous cartloads of recently harvested cotton. Further north they were replaced by oxen that seemed to grow in stature, towering above Honey, until she looked a mere toy.

We arrived in Lahore around lunch time, having covered a record 158 miles in the morning, the last 30 miles on a road wide enough to carry two lanes of traffic. To celebrate, we treated ourselves to lunch in a restaurant. The upper balcony was reserved for women with curtained-off cubicles, overlooking the lower floor where the men ate.

A young Pakistani we met outside was especially helpful in suggesting what we should eat; two sorts of meat cooked in a hot spicy sauce and scooped from plate to mouth with chapattis – knives and forks were not provided. Customers could wash their sticky fingers, before and after eating, in a small basin conveniently placed in the corner. The proprietor ceremoniously bounced the coins we gave him in payment, to ascertain they were genuine. With a broad smile, the young man presented Jane with a bunch of red roses as a parting gift. She was quite overcome.

Lahore remains a confusion of impressions: the congested, dirty streets thronged with an overwhelming number of flamboyantly dressed people; yellow and black mini cabs; decrepit buildings; the smell of incense, spices and cow dung and loud sub-continental music wailing from loud speakers.

We marvelled at the magnificence of the Badshahi Masjid, a three-hundred-year-old mosque built by the Mogul Aurangzeb, the largest at that time in both Pakistan and India. A fountain played in the main courtyard; paved with chequered marble tiles and surrounded by galleries with pure white marble arches, delicate pillars and prayer niches. The partly-decaying domes were decorated with exquisite floral designs painted on wet clay, using vivid natural colours made from the dye of skins and plants.

As I sat in quiet contemplation soaking in the peaceful atmosphere, a young man and his three sisters approached me and introduced themselves, pointing out the four-hundred-year old Red Fort across the road. He just wanted to talk and was a mine of information.

"Did you know that the Moti Masjid at Shalimar, just across the Indus, is the tomb of the Emperor Anarkalli? He fell in love with a commoner and consequently was bricked up in the wall."

I was horrified. The tomb comprised three courtyards surrounded by cool green gardens, where children came to play and families to picnic. A modern shrine clad in marble and inlaid with precious stones was used to lay the deceased Emperor out in state. To visit we had to take our shoes off, as the site was sacred.

The transition from desert to the hustle and bustle of the city was too sudden. After a short drive around the residential area, we couldn't stand it anymore and decided to head for the frontier, perhaps complete customs and cross into India before nightfall. But a traffic jam caused by the visiting Japanese Prime Minister delayed us considerably and by the time we arrived, an hour after sunset, the customs had closed.

Hotels didn't exist in the outlying villages of Pakistan and India. Travellers stayed at rest houses or bungalows that provided cheap and simple accommodation; a bare room, trestle beds, blankets and a meal; not exactly comfortable, but adequate. We were both tired and desperately wanted an undisturbed night, but that was not to be.

We made enquiries at the police station and were redirected back the way we had come and told to take the first turning to the left.

The rest house attendant, a squat, dirty-looking little man, his friend hovering in the background, welcomed us with a leer and offhandedly showed us two rooms; the tiled floors were unswept and furnished only with a wooden bed. There were no blankets, nowhere to wash and no locks on the doors! It was rather sinister and not at all what we had expected, and we quickly agreed that camping would be infinitely preferable.

Finally we found the perfect spot some 200 yards away from the main road, beside a canal in a small clearing hidden among the giant reeds. As a customary precaution and as my father had always taught us, I parked facing the towpath in case we needed to leave in a hurry. It was a glorious night. The moon, nearly full, cast long shadows across the dank water. The reeds whispered in the gentle breeze and our small fire crackled comfortingly. We cooked supper, a plate of steaming spaghetti with spicy tomato sauce, laughing a little at our unnecessary nervousness. Surely this spot was secluded and safe.

We were clearing up, stowing everything into the car and making ready for the night, when a policeman arrived, the one that had redirected us to the rest house earlier in the evening. We acknowledged his arrival and went on with our preparations. He told us that he had never seen such a small car and was intrigued to see us fit the semi-circular metal frame onto the roof rack.

"You can't stay here," he announced once we had finished. "Bad men and smugglers! It's not safe for two girls to sleep alone. You had better return to the rest house." That we just couldn't do. The very thought of that squat, dirty-looking little man and those bare unwelcoming rooms made us shudder with apprehension. Surely no one else knew of our whereabouts. We thanked him for coming and airily told him that we were not afraid. After all we had been travelling for over two months, all the way from England, camping wild every night with no disturbances. Why should it be any different tonight? Eventually, reminding us that we had been warned, he walked away.

To me this deserted clearing in among the reeds, under a clear moonlit sky, seemed infinitely safer than the rest house with doors that didn't lock and that unsavoury man prowling around. We fastened the car doors, checked as usual that we had left nothing lying about, and taking blue jeans with us in case of an audience in the morning, we climbed up into bed, exhausted. In spite of a nagging unease, we soon slept soundly.

It must have been close on midnight when I awoke, disturbed by somebody tampering with the car door.

"What's that?" I whispered, suddenly alert and tense. Jane was awake too and peered through the end curtain.

"There are two men standing at the back," she said. "There must be another by the car, but I can't see him."

It was my turn to look. There they stood, very tall and thin, wearing lengths of white cloth wrapped around their loins, falling to the ground like a skirt; a rug hung loosely over the shoulder, protection against the chill of the November night. Both men carried long curved knives. They looked menacing and evil, though stunningly beautiful, standing motionless in the moonlight.

The man we couldn't see went round to the back of the car and tweaked one of Jane's toes, which though protected by her sleeping bag, hung over the edge.

"Stop it! Go away!" She screamed hysterically. I laughed nervously. It all seemed so funny, so unreal, yet so terrifying. What did these men want? Did they intend us harm? How did they find us, unless the policeman had told them? Thank goodness we were on top of the car. At least we were at an advantage up there and they couldn't spring on us with those curved knives. I had heard stories of campers in Europe having their tents slashed while asleep – such thoughts flashed through my mind.

"Bad men! Smugglers. You go away. No good to stay here. Bad men! It's dangerous."

How could we go away without climbing out of the tent and getting into the car? What should we do? We lay still, feeling more and more uneasy, wishing they would go away and leave us in peace. The third man was trying to prise open the doors. The other two were coming closer.

"Go away. Leave us alone!" Jane's voice was tense. But they

held their ground. Time stood still. We were so tired. It was long past midnight and it seemed we'd never get any sleep that night.

At last, unable to stand the tension any longer, we made the decision and somehow slid into our blue jeans, always a difficult operation in such a confined space.

"Stand back by the canal," called Jane, "then we will come down and drive away." To our surprise, the three men stood back on the tow path, a small threatening gang, while we clambered quickly out and down from the tent to make a dash for the car doors. I fumbled too long with the key, but managed to open the door before one of the tall men leapt forward and took hold of me by my collar.

I turned angrily to face him and grabbed the shining blade he was waving in front of my nose. I started screaming piercingly, my voice tearing the tissues of my throat. "Jeeeesus! Jesus!" A hand covered my mouth to stifle the cries that continued to come, now somewhat muffled.

Suddenly, I felt savage and strong. I bit deep into the man's thumb, glad that I had learnt to fight with my brothers. Abruptly, I found myself on the ground, crouching over the knife, trying to dig it into the earth. Still I screamed, but I no longer felt any fear, only strong, very strong. All my energies were directed into keeping the point of that knife against the ground. Another man was prising the knife from my hand. I was no match for the two of them.

Voices and dogs barking broke the silence of the night. People with lanterns appeared on the high bank, beyond the reeds, on the other side of the canal to see what was going on. Those sounds were like music. My prayer for help had been answered. The knife was snatched away. Yards of material trailed between me and the two men. Then unbelievably, like waking from a bad dream, they melted furtively into the reeds.

"Come on," urged Jane helping me to my feet. Without waiting for our invisible neighbours to arrive, we leapt into the car, which for once started immediately. Using full revs and regardless of the bumps and holes in the towpath, we drove back wildly to the main road and sped along it, away from the frontier, for almost a quarter of an hour before finally stopping.

Jane told me that one of the men had vanished, while another had overpowered her. She struggled to keep his arms in the air while remembering her mother's good advice; knee him in the groin.

"Try doing that when the man is wearing a skirt," she commented wryly. Angrily he had flung her to the ground. Even though she had landed on a rock, she jumped back up. It was then that we had heard the voices and the men had disappeared hurriedly and as silently as they had come.

Jane had quickly recovered her senses and dashed back to the car to help me. She switched on the headlights and checked that nothing had been taken. We were lucky. We were shaken, but safe and unhurt.

Shattered and trembling, we parked the car close to a farm building, hoping the presence of those that lived there would afford some protection. We climbed back into our roof tent, still surprisingly intact on top of the Mini. My teeth chattered uncontrollably. Suffering from shock, unable to sleep, alert to every sound, we both waited anxiously for the dawn.

The sun was high when we inevitably passed through customs the following morning. Jane stayed to guard the car while I went inside to have our passports stamped. Three or four men were standing idly in the room. They were tall and thin. Instinctively I knew that the one sitting smugly behind his desk was my attacker; his thumb was wrapped in a white bandage.

While waiting, I walked over to the window to see if Jane was all right, when a voice behind me said: "You know it is dangerous for two young girls to camp alone."

I smiled inwardly. "I know," I replied, "but we are quite capable of looking after ourselves." Meanwhile outside, a man walked past Jane and the Mini, carefully shielding his face as if to avoid recognition.

CHAPTER SEVEN

INDIA

After one and half hours of complicated red tape, inherited from the British occupation, we were finally freed from the tedium of bureaucracy and drove into Amritsar.

Unlike in Pakistan, the shops were abundantly stocked with exotic fruit and vegetables. The market was teeming with cycles, rickshaws, turbaned Sikhs and unveiled women in saris and Punjabi dress – silk trousers, a tunic and a delicate scarf worn over the hair. Skinny cows roamed the streets chewing old comics and scavenging for food. This was India; a land of 400 million inhabitants, 14 main languages, innumerable dialects, colour and mystery.

In the middle of all this confusion, we met a bearded vet and his wife. They had arrived the previous evening in their Land Rover. Their journey overland had been comparatively unadventurous, except for six punctures. But then, their tough vehicle was more suited for the rigours of the unpaved roads of Turkey and Persia. In fact we realized our little Mini had done extraordinarily well.

We acquired their guide; a solidly-built, handsome Punjabi, his long black beard neatly rolled and kept in place by a fine net, his hair knotted and concealed beneath a turban. Long hair is a sign of strength and a requirement of the Sikh religion. He spoke excellent English and after formally introducing himself, somehow managed to squeeze onto the front seat with Jane and direct us through a maze of winding streets to the Golden Temple. It stands in the middle of a small lake and is accessed by a long causeway.

Amritsar (which means 'ambrosial nectar) is the original name of an ancient lake which is continually fed by an underground spring. Since time immemorial, when the land was covered in forest, this has been a place of pilgrimage and meditation; even the Buddha is known to have spent time here in contemplation. The founder of the Sikh religion, Guru Nanak, lived and meditated here and over the subsequent centuries, it became the sacred shrine of his followers. Many temples were built and destroyed. The Hari Mandir, or Temple of God, is 400 years old, and as it stands today combines Hindu and Moslem artistic styles. It was dazzling; richly ornamented with marble walls decorated with floral designs and inlaid with semi-precious stones, brought from all over the world. The domes were clad in gold foil and reflected in the peaceful water surrounding it. Here throughout the day and night pilgrims immersed themselves; a symbolic cleansing of the soul.

A broad walk and office buildings for the Temple staff surrounded the basin. A nearby kitchen run by a team of mainly volunteers fed up to 500 pilgrims each day, including the local poor to discourage begging. All the food was donated. An enormous cauldron of rice stood on the hob and chapattis were piled high ready for the hungry, who sat in rows on the floor, scooping the rice out of bowls with the chapattis. Pilgrims could stay at a lodging house provided, where they ate, slept and mingled with the poor.

Our guide carefully supervised us, ensuring that we stored our shoes in the niches provided and washed our feet out of respect for this holy site. Together we walked across the causeway and entered the temple through heavy wooden doors, exquisitely carved with birds and animals on one side and lined with silver on the other. They were 600 years old and had been imported from Afghanistan. Devout Sikhs bent down to touch the worn step with their hands and then foreheads before entering.

Inside, a three-piece orchestra played inspiring music while a priest read from the Sacred Book; the word of God as set down by his ten prophets. The Book was displayed on a raised platform covered in red velvet and strewn with garlands of marigolds and coins given by the pilgrims. In return they received sweetmeats, flower petals or a garland, symbols of Grace or Blessings. Jane and I were very touched to be given a garland each, which then remained entwined on Honey's roof rack for days. On an upper floor the walls were of cut glass and three more readers intoned the words of the Book.

"The readers and musicians are changed every two hours and replaced from a pool of 12 orchestras and 100 readers," explained our guide as we mingled in a sea of brown faces. "The Sikh religion was founded 500 years ago and there are about 5 million adherents living mainly in the Punjab. It is a monotheist religion. Our Book was written in psalms and hymns telling of God and nature. Unlike in the Christian Bible, history was not included."

Northern India was strikingly green. The rivers were full of flowing water, spanned by fine-looking new bridges. Tall shade trees inhabited by darting chipmunks and screaming green parrots lined the roads, reminding me of the oaks that have stood for centuries in English parklands. Bicycles zigzagged in and out, heedless of the hooting traffic. Creaking carts, loaded with hay, pulled by long suffering white cows with top heavy horns, laboured under the watchful eyes of small boys on their way back to the village. Every inch of the countryside was alive with a mass of humanity. The men wore red, green and orange turbans. Some wore sarongs with their shirt tails hanging out; others wore shorts and shirt tails, slacks and shirt tails, pyjamas and shirt tails. Very few wore trousers with belts. The women in India were not hidden away, so we were no longer a curiosity.

Progress towards Delhi, on the rolling surface of the Grand Trunk Road, was extremely slow and bumpy, though a great improvement on the roads in Persia. Speeds in excess of 50 mph were apt to give me a stitch. It was narrow and not nearly as grand as its name implies. Army lorries with careless young drivers kept holding us up. Overtaking was difficult and dangerous. Fortunately I had managed to repair the horn, an extremely necessary accessory, but it sounded rather feeble, more like that of a scooter.

We arrived in old Delhi early the following afternoon. The narrow streets were jammed with bicycles, rickshaws, ponies and traps, cars and scooters all jostling for space, pushing and hooting trying to make headway. Cows wandered aimlessly, adding to the obstruction.

New Delhi was an amazing contrast, with impressive modern buildings. Wide tree-lined avenues, parks, arcades and markets fanned out from a central square. The residential area, known as the cantonment, was strikingly spacious with beautiful homes set in gardens filled with flowers and trees. The new Parliament buildings were semi-circular, the lower half built of red sandstone and the upper half supported by pillars of white stone. Similarly the nearby Secretariat and National Museum were also built around a semi-circular courtyard overlooking a magnificent park of green lawns, waterways and fountains. The Embassies vied with one another for distinction and originality of design.

A long row of attached bungalows had been built for the new middle class, facing onto a grassy square and divided by a narrow path in the form of a cross. Here the women relaxed on charpoys (low beds with a woven base), carefully combing each other's hair looking for nits, while their children frolicked around them.

Disappointingly, we received little post at either of the main post offices. Neither of the families we had hoped to stay with proved to be hospitable. Well, we did look rather disreputable. So we opted for the YWCA. An official campsite didn't exist. At first, the receptionist was reluctant to offer us a room. She claimed it was full to capacity with delegates from the World Council of Churches, holding its third convention in Delhi that week. These are held every seven years. Eventually she relented.

Twelve rupees per night for three nights was, we thought, rather expensive, but we needed somewhere to stay and a good rest was now essential.

"Come on, let's treat ourselves" said Jane. "Besides it will be safer".

We were worn out after driving long, ten-hour days through the desert on dusty bumpy roads. We hadn't had a break since leaving Teheran. Here we would be able to be ourselves, do our washing, (Never have I seen such black water after soaking my clothes) make new friends, have a real bed to sleep in and not have to do any cooking. We would even be able to lock the door and not worry about whether we would be disturbed during the night. What a treat.

We met some wonderful people. Among them was an English woman, who had driven overland on her way to Australia in a VW camping car with her three sons aged 10, 14 and 16. I really admired her pluck. She had collided with a straying buffalo near Agra, in India, and was forced to pay damages even though the animal was unscathed. She had been hanging about for three weeks trying to sort the insurance out.

An Indian Christian missionary to lepers in the hill-country fired many questions at us. She was fascinated by our adventures. She even offered to dress us in saris, which we wore to dinner on the last evening. Jane's was a saffron colour trimmed with black matching her dark hair. Mine was a pale pink silk, and with my hair, normally plaited, piled high on my head nobody recognized me. We felt very special and pretty for a change.

It was so much warmer, so wearing light cotton frocks, we set out to explore the city. We joined the throng of pilgrims to the new Hindu Temple, built of red sandstone with soaring domes and marble floors; people came bare-footed, trailing noisy children, stopping to mumble prayers at the numerous shrines, throwing coins and flowers at the feet of the gods or goddesses. The surrounding terraced gardens with trees, flowers and lakes offered a haven from the heat of the sun. Profound Hindu texts adorned the walls. An Indian family stopped to put what we were seeing into perspective. The young man explained earnestly: "There may seem to be many strange gods and goddesses, but all these statues actually represent the essence of the one true God and Creator".

In complete contrast the atmosphere, in the small Buddhist temple nearby, was quite different; a place of reverence and calm. A large statue of the Buddha, surrounded by lighted candles and burning incense, was the focal point. Men and women sat or knelt on the tiled floor in meditation and prayer. Here too the walls were decorated with texts from their scriptures, both in Hindi and English.

We spent the following morning trying to get the Mini serviced, driving around in ever more frustrating circles. Near the Red Fort, which we had failed to locate the previous day, horse cabs were drawn up waiting for a fare, the drivers idly chatting under the trees. In front of some squatter homes, a man sat cross-legged being massaged with oils and another was being shaved: A kaleidoscope of impressions.

Back in Connaught Square, we finally found a garage. The plugs were filthy as I had expected and the petrol overflow, for some unknown reason, led into the boot, hence the petrol smell we had recently been plagued with. We had the car cleaned throughout with compressed air to remove the thick layer of sand. Five boys had been assigned to do the work and succeeded in getting in each other's way, having fun and repeatedly stopping to chat.

Honey was freshly packed and looked and felt unusually clean. We took leave of our friends at the hostel, hopefully called one last time at the post office for mail, and set out for Agra. It was the last night of the full moon and we were determined to see the famous Taj Mahal by moonlight; we were in a hurry. But, progress was exasperatingly slow. Either there was dirt in the petrol or the points in the petrol pump had been incorrectly adjusted. The engine kept spluttering and we would grind to a halt. I began to fret that we wouldn't make it, however we arrived with enough time to go on a tour of the Agra Red Fort.

It was surrounded by an empty moat and strong outer wall. An higher inner wall enclosed gardens, fountains, courtyards and buildings constructed in marble and stone and decorated with the usual patterns of semi-precious stones and painted ceilings. It was spacious enough to accommodate comfortably a whole city of people during a long siege.

From the temple courtyard, across the lazy Jumna River, we caught a first glimpse of the Taj Mahal shrouded by a curtain of mist. Leaving Honey parked in the shade of some leafy trees, we walked under a dark archway into a garden. Before us lay two long narrow stretches of water, lined with Cyprus trees and reflecting the glistening white domes and minarets of the Mausoleum. The Taj Mahal was infinitely more splendid than I had imagined.

Barefoot, we descended into the vault to see the actual tomb of the Empress Mahal, for whom the Taj had been built by her doting husband the Shah Jahan. The tomb of the Empress was in the centre and that of the Shah, somewhat larger, lay beside her: he had intended to build a replica of the Taj, in black marble, for himself on the opposite bank of the River Jumna, but died soon after completing the foundations. The original precious stones, set in the marble, have long since been pillaged and the Koh-I-Noor diamond is now among the crown jewels of Queen Elizabeth.

On the main floor, two identical tombs had been placed side by side and enclosed with a marble screen of interwoven design and lit by a webbed light from above. The numerous small rooms surrounding them were used, during the Muslim reign, by women in purdah. Floral motives, carved in the marble, adorned the walls.

Later that evening, as a faint orange glow faded from the sky and the full moon slowly rose, to soften and cast shadows, the white marble domes and the inlaid jewels sparkled in the last rays of light; the dark alcoves enhancing their brilliance. Indeed a crown fit for an immortal queen. It was cool and pleasant to sit by the water, to drink in the quiet beauty of the moment and savour the strong scent of fresh dew and flowers; to reflect how lucky we had been to witness the Acropolis in Greece and the Taj Mahal in Agra on the nights of the full moon.

Someone at the YWCA had suggested we ask at the Holliman Institute for permission to camp in their compound, in order to be free of worries at night and to escape the crowds of gaping onlookers that immediately congregate to stand and stare wherever you stop in India. Maybe we would have been less upset if at the time we had known that in India it is a sign of respect. The Agra mission had a spacious garden with trees. Undisturbed we ate an omelette with fried bananas sitting on the steps of the mission house. We slept, comforted by the periodic rounds of the night watchman thumping the ground with his stick to warn of his coming.

As it was Sunday, we decided to attend matins before leaving. Unfortunately the priest was away, probably in Delhi for the World Council of Churches. His replacement, a lay reader, managed to mislay the readings and get the hymns in a muddle. Attendance in the large airy church was much better than for early morning service in England.

On the way to Cawnpore we drove towards a crossroads. The policeman on duty signalled for us to drive past. He can't have been concentrating or was so mesmerized by such a small foreign vehicle that he failed to see the cyclist approaching behind him. We met with a screech of brakes at the policeman's feet. The poor cyclist went flying and the impact of his bike broke one of the Mini's headlights. After a lengthy time-wasting enquiry at the local police station, we were given 30 rupees towards a replacement, but there seemed to be some controversy among the inevitable throng of spectators. At this point a senior officer arrived, and after identifying himself, declared that we should have been compensated immediately.

Somewhere we managed to take a wrong turning and 34 kilometres later we found ourselves in the village of Etewah. We had to back track past the endless string of bullock carts, herds of cattle, pony traps and cyclists. Honey's peeping horn was completely ignored. However we did see some wonderful birds: a peahen sitting on a branch and a tree housing a colony of storks. The air was full of them flying to and fro with large strings of greenery dangling from their brightly coloured beaks. In the shallow ponds left by the recent monsoon rains, enormous birds with beanstalk legs stood idly waiting for a fishy catch.

The petrol gauge was showing almost empty. None of the villages we had passed through had boasted a petrol station and eventually as darkness fell, we spluttered to a standstill. Not knowing what else to do, we flagged a fast-flying lorry, driven by a couple of Sikhs, to ask for help. They couldn't speak English, nor were they able to supply any petrol as their vehicle ran on diesel. Gallantly they hung around feeling responsible for our safety as we had no men to protect us. Villagers start to gather and repeatedly suggested that the Sikhs should give us a tow. We declined. Just imagine being attached to a fully-loaded lorry driven by a speed-loving Sikh!

Jane became increasingly frightened because of the growing crowd of men. She felt vulnerable, but there is safety in numbers, especially on the perimeter of such a busy main thoroughfare as the Delhi–Calcutta trunk road. At last a government malaria official came to our rescue with a couple of gallons of petrol, carried for such emergencies. The Sikhs quietly slipped away, knowing that we could safely continue on our way. We were grateful for their support.

Cawnpore was another enormous town and we got hopelessly lost looking for the Methodist High School, recommended to us by Miss Schaefer of the Holliman Institute.

A car drew up alongside and the driver offered to lead the way. We pursued his car down one road after another until on the outskirts of the city we arrived at our destination. We sadly refused his offer to take us out to dinner. We couldn't really ask for hospitality and promptly go out again.

Miss Hutchins, an elderly American missionary, her gentle face framed by greying hair, had already retired but was filling in for a year. She offered us the guest room, gave us a bucketful of hot water each to wash with, a glass of delicious warm soup and a slice of apple pie. Thoroughly spoilt and unable to keep our eyes open for long, we thankfully fell asleep enjoying the sheer luxury of clean white sheets. Miss Hutchins even provided the ultimate treat for two nomads: breakfast in bed – bacon and eggs, toast and oranges.

The mission school was built of red sandstone, covered in creepers that almost concealed the archways leading into the courtyard; it was set in an attractive garden of shady trees, flowers and grassy lawns, with swings for the children. The six-hundred students, male and female arrived by taxi, car, pedicab or bicycle, all carrying enormous quantities of books and chattering excitedly. Morning assembly was held in the courtyard. Then the students filed neatly and silently into class.

We thanked Miss Hutchins for her wonderful hospitality and struggled for over an hour to find the way out of town. The wide road soon tapered to a single narrow track, which meant travelling with two wheels in the ditch whenever we passed an oncoming lorry. Even so we made good time and covered 90 miles during the morning. That afternoon we had to change one of the tyres because of a slow puncture. This delay meant that we arrived in Benares after dark, but we easily found the Cantonment area where we took advantage of another Christian mission, the home of the Rev. and Mrs Thompson. The Vicar was at home. He agreed that we could camp under a tree in the garden and offered the use of their bathroom.

After a terrible night plagued by mosquitoes, we opted to spend a quiet morning resting and writing letters. We didn't even want to go and see the pilgrim's ritual morning bathing in the sacred River Ganges.

The Thompsons invited us to lunch to meet Mary, their daughter, who had travelled overland on the Indiaman coach and had seen the Mini somewhere along the way. They had three children and worried about their education so far from home. They found the work of evangelization in the Holy City of Benares to be a losing battle. The life of a missionary was often disheartening and definitely not easy.

We drank coffee in the garden and then drove to Sarnath, where the Buddha is reputed to have gained enlightenment under a Bow or Bodhi Tree. The tree now standing on the site of this momentous event was taken from a cutting off a tree in Ceylon, which had been grown from a cutting taken from the original Bodhi tree in Sarnath. The shrine was set in a spacious garden, fragrant with frangipani flowers, with lawns and red pathways and an adjacent deer park. A small modern temple with murals by a Japanese artist housed a Golden Buddha. A gigantic stone-faced monument, known as a Stuppa and originally covered in gold foil, enshrined a sacred relic of the Buddha. The excavations of monasteries and temples from a bygone age, with bases of thick pillars and stone carvings, were testimony to the rich history of the site. Beads and books were on sale for the pilgrims and tourists.

The museum housed an enormous round wheel, originally used as an umbrella to protect one of the stuppas from the intemperance of the weather. A complicated relief caught my eye. Carved out of stone, it depicted the slaying of the evil demon. God held a bowl in one hand, so that no drop of blood should fall to the ground, thus avoiding the creation of new demons; another hand held the trident that slew the demon, and many other hands depicted the omnipotence of God. With the decline of Buddhist art, the detailed facial expression lost its importance to be replaced with emphasis on the curvaceous figure.

Back in Benares, on the banks of the River Ganges, we shopped for fruit and found the place we should return to at sunrise to witness the hour of prayer. Opposite the food stalls, hopeful beggars proffered their bowls; a leper sat on the steps leading down to the water's edge, his mutilated hands half hidden in the folds of a brown sack wrap; a woman resting on a pile of rubble was eating something stringy and green; a man, his face pitted by smallpox, nursed a child, while at his side a woman offered sequins for sale; a lone Buddhist monk sat lotus style, in deep meditation, at the foot of a flower-draped shrine. Pedicabs pushed past women, in richly embroidered saris of Benares silk, jostling with others in dirty muslin cloth; a goat surreptitiously stole food from a stall. A small boy already showing signs of leprosy huddled in a corner. In the blazing sun, women followed scavenging cows and goats, collecting the droppings to be dried on the walls of their homes or used as fuel for cooking. This was the India I had always imagined, the colour, the rich and the poor, the squalor, utter confusion and timelessness, the pungent smells of incense and spices mingled with cow dung.

Realizing how stressed we had been by mosquitoes the previous night, the Thompsons offered us their spare room and even woke us the following morning at 6 am with a cup of tea, in time to view morning prayer on the River Ganges. How truly Christian and caring the missionaries were. It was so comforting.

The sun hung low over the horizon, dimly visible through the morning haze. The sequin vendors were already in the square; small boys were having their heads shaven, leaving only a few strands hanging like a miniature tail. We walked down past the line of ragged and sore infested beggars, now sitting cross legged on the steps leading to the water's edge and still patiently proffering their bowls.

A cool breeze ruffled the water. For a grandstand view, we settled comfortably onto the cushions of a shapely boat rowed by a young Indian, his slim brown body clad in a sarong. Along the river bank, men in minimums and women fully clothed, wet saris clinging to their shapely forms, were performing the ritual bathing using copper pots to douse themselves. Muttering prayers, they stood knee deep in the Ganges throwing water towards the rising sun, then away to the right, finally submerging themselves repeatedly. Afterwards they washed their clothes, pounding them with a stone and thrashing them on the water. The cloth still looked grubby as it lay on the steps drying in the hot sun. The women changed into fresh clean saris with great skill. Some men were performing gymnastics, push-ups and knee-bends, while others sat cross-legged, facing the sun, meditating.

Temples abounded along the shore, many only tiny shrines representing an aspect of the spirit of God. In front of one temple complex the funeral pyres burnt around the clock. We watched as a body, wrapped in shrouds and tied to a stretcher, was pulled out of the sacred Ganges and placed on a prepared pile of wood, which was then set alight, while from inside the temples came the sound of clashing symbols.

Tourists from the Clark Hotel sat perched on straight-backed chairs with their cameras poised to capture the scene, as they glided by on a double decker boat, propelled along by two oarsmen.

Back in the square, a Holy man dressed in a saffron robe approached and offered to lead us to the Golden Temple. We told him we did not want a guide, but he insisted and explained that it was his duty to help strangers. It was however a blessing we accepted, as without him we could easily have lost our way and seen very little of what the city had to offer. He led us along dark, narrow alleyways, shielding us with outspread hands from the horns of the sacred bulls and cows which we were forbidden to touch. Pilgrims pushed past, carrying in one hand a copper bowl of Ganges water and in the other flowers to sprinkle over the image of their favourite aspect of God. We slowly climbed the steep steps to see the pyramid shaped dome of the three hundred year old Golden Temple. We were not allowed inside any of the Temples; we could only peer through peep holes and see the floors wet with holy water and stained with mud and cowpats. People swarmed in and out leaving flowers, water and sweetmeats. With them came the cows helping themselves to the flowers. In the dark corners sat more beggars and many lepers.

Apparently when the Mongols invaded the region, they had destroyed the original temple and built a mosque on the site, which was still guarded to prevent its desecration. A stone bull, taken from that temple, stood beside the Well of Knowledge, where people came to drink the water and gain easy knowledge. In an adjacent shrine, a phallus, wet with Ganges water and adorned with flowers, was venerated by those desperate for children. It was, unexpectedly, a haven of peace and quiet after the turmoil of the Hindu part of the city.

Against overwhelming odds, a vain attempt was being made to sweep the street. It seemed strange to us that people could live in all this filth and worship a god of such extraordinary forms. Even the monkey was worshipped as a servant of Rama. I felt quite sick as tears welled up with pity that people should have to live this way. The culture shock was extreme, especially as at that time graphic television documentaries did not exist.

After a short lunch snack of bread, tomatoes and baby bananas, we left Benares and headed towards the busy town of Dehri-on-Sone. Here we spent a frustrating half an hour at a railway crossing waiting for the barrier to open. The road beyond deteriorated. We asked for directions but nobody understood. Finally the road petered out into a track, and too late we realized that we should have been on the train ferrying vehicles over the river. This meant another twenty-minute delay to cross back again. While I was making enquiries in an engineering office, Jane drove through only to find we were now once again on the wrong side of the track.

Emptying all our pockets, we still did not have enough rupees to cover the fare. A sympathetic official took pity on us and came to the rescue. He accepted 23 rupees and a few niapesas instead of the standard charge of 25 rupees. I had to reverse up a steep ramp and onto the train. A bus was to follow, but the Mini's wheels were too small to cross the access ramp over onto the next truck and I had to drive down again to let the bus on first. By this time Jane and I were thoroughly overtired and short-tempered and I had a headache, so we both swallowed a couple of codeine to relax.

The train should have left at 4.30 pm, but was shunted onto a siding where it remained for two hours. Time passed quickly though as the passengers travelling on the bus kept us entertained. A metallurgical student fired questions and when we started firing them back we all had great fun. They were so generous, giving us baby bananas, fried rice and guavas to try. When I tipped my empty purse upside down, the peanut vendor weighed out a couple of annas' worth and gave them to me with a broad smile. In the meantime, Jane managed to exchange a couple of our remaining pound notes with one of the other drivers. So now we had a few coins in case of necessity. The tiredness and feeling of desperation slowly dissipated.

The train creaked as the wheels started turning and we left the station. Riding on the first coach, sitting on the roof rack, surrounded by men standing or squatting, we felt the thrill of riding along the railway line as it rushed towards us and was swallowed up beneath. In the dark we could only dimly see the water below, the looming river bank and sandy shore beyond.

An hour later we stopped under a large leafy tree for the night. Few people bothered us, not even the peasants working in a nearby field. One man wrapped in yards of white material did stop and stare too long. An exasperated Jane snapped "Do you have to stare?" to which he replied in perfect English, "No, I'm just going." Jane was dumbfounded. Normally men just stared blankly.

The countryside became more undulating, cultivation sparser and green pastures more abundant. Fewer villages on the meandering road meant fewer pedestrians, carts and animals to negotiate. During the one-hundred-mile stretch that morning, we counted seventeen broken-down lorries that had collided with trees, had a technical fault or just given up the ghost. The drivers sat in the shade beside their wrecks playing cards, brewing cups of tea and waiting for the insurance man to inspect the damage.

Jane was feeling rotten again. I went to fetch water from a nearby farm; a woman in a sarong, bare from the waist up exposing her shrivelled breasts, pointed the well out to me. A dog and a calf lay side by side in the courtyard, while chickens pecked in the dust. During the heat of the day we stayed beneath the trees reading, resting and strolling around observing the people at work. Beside the cart-worn track, women were doing their washing in a shallow pool. I paddled in the muddy warm water of a small stream, so caressing to my dirty, dusty feet. A young boy on a cycle followed me, contriving to keep himself out of sight.

Camping wild in India was not easy. We hadn't intended to travel much further. It was still two hours before dark and we were now more wary than ever of stopping where anyone could see us. The first time we attempted to pull off the road, we spied a couple of armed guards and decided to move on. The region was highly populated. Between the frequent towns, lorries travelling at a reckless pace regularly forced us into the ditch. No wonder accidents littered the roadside.

The second attempt was thwarted by a couple of lorry drivers who came to investigate what a car was doing hidden between the trees. At last, we found a place between two ponds, beyond the beam of passing traffic. Here we felt safe, despite being disturbed by mosquitoes, shrill train whistles and pounding lorries.

Heading on towards Calcutta, we came across a large sign that read: TRIBENI TISSUES.

"Look! That's the home of Daphne Renwicks," exclaimed Jane excitedly. She had been a pupil at Mon Fertile in Switzerland, where Jane and I had met. Thrilled, we turned up the side road. It deteriorated rapidly. Treacherous stones littered the track and despite my efforts to avoid the puddles left by the monsoon rains, mud splashed up all over the windscreen. In the surrounding paddy fields, bare-legged peasants were bent double harvesting an abundant crop of rice.

Almost unexpectedly, peeping out above the green foliage, we saw the shining white walls of a modern factory. The reception and offices were housed in a nearby bungalow. Along another narrow lane, we could see the housing estate where the workers lived with their extended families, including wives, children, uncles and aunts.

Daphne's home was a fine villa facing the River Hooghly. She was still in Switzerland, but her parents, Mr and Mrs Renwick, gave us a wonderful welcome and after a cup of hot, sweet milky tea, showed us to the firm's guest house. Here we had use of a spacious bedroom with ensuite bathroom, a sitting room, veranda and private garden all to ourselves, complete with cook and manservant.

Daphne's mother took us to visit Mrs Green, a school teacher who lived nearby and though retired still taught some of the younger children in the compound. She invited us into her home and told us a little about Indian culture.

"Large feasts are essential to accompany important events such as marriage, birth or death" she said. "In the days before a census was taken, this ensured there would be plenty of living witnesses in case of a family dispute or difficulty over land distribution."

She also explained how the company looked after its employees. It ran a Co-op Shop selling essential items, as well as a Credit Society to protect them from the iniquitous money lenders, who demanded repayment in full and never in weekly instalments. This meant that it was almost impossible for the poor to extricate themselves from debt.

We learnt that numerous factory complexes had been established over a wide area on cleared jungle land. Each had its own garden housing estate with three grades of houses for the workers, junior and senior staff. Club facilities were also provided.

Later we made a tour of the housing estate, which consisted of rows of two-room bungalows, each with a washroom, toilet, veranda and tiny garden. They were unfurnished and the occupants lived on the floor, as many as seven sharing the small dwelling. One of the buildings was used to house religious images fashioned from mud and decorated with bright colours.

"These are not considered to be idols. Hindus pray that the Universal Spirit, in its differing manifestations, will inhabit the image for the duration of the festival. Afterwards it is consigned to the river to disintegrate," Mrs Renwick explained.

In the cool of the evening we played an energetic game of tennis with various male members of the Social Club. Fortunately for us the standard was not high. This was followed by the luxury of a quick bath and change for a formal dinner at nine; an opportunity to wear a dress and look pretty.

Breakfast was also served in style in our small dining room by our manservant and at ten o'clock Mrs Renwick arrived to ask for the car key, so that the chauffer could give Honey a wash. He had such fun, together with their mechanic, playing with and examining our little Mini. They had never seen anything like it.

It was Mr Renwick who escorted us around the mill explaining, without becoming too technically involved, the process of making cigarette paper:

"Old ropes, sacking, hemp and chalk are all finely chopped and mixed together. This is then thoroughly cleaned, cooked and reduced until almost liquefied, before being rolled out through countless rollers to become paper. The full process takes roughly two and half days." It was fascinating watching the mixture become paper.

Mr Renwick continued, "Sometimes the national grid fails to provide sufficient power to keep the mill going, so we have two generators on stand-by. It's important, as we export to most countries around the world."

That afternoon four Indian ladies, dressed in sarees, challenged us to a game of badminton. I thought the long flowing material might slow them down, but no, they were much too good for us. I'd forgotten what an excellent game it was. Jane and I were definitely out of practice. The men also challenged us to another game of tennis but by then, my arm felt ready to drop off.

To round the day off and liven things up for us, the Renwicks invited a couple of young men over for dinner, one a bachelor, the other a grass widower whose European wife was away in the UK. Their hospitality and kindness was an oasis of calm in the ongoing challenges we had to face.

The grand trunk road to Calcutta was chock-a-block with lorries, cars, carts and people. It took a full two hours of patient driving to cover the short distance to the stunning Howrah Bridge, commissioned in February 1943 and built by the British firm Cleveland Bridge & Engineering Co. It united Howrah on the west bank of the River Hooghly, another name for the River Ganges, with Calcutta. It was only the 4th cantilever bridge ever built and considered one of the wonders of the world. The central span between the two 280-foot high towers was an amazing 1,500 feet. The aluminium paint of the super structure sparkled in the dying rays of the sun. Beyond, the sky was a blaze of scarlet.

First stop was the post office, which we found easily, having seen many photographs of it previously. It was open, but no amount of pleading would persuade those in charge to give us our letters. After all, it was Sunday, a non-working day. It did however give us an opportunity to see inside a postal sorting room; parcels and letters were stacked high on shelves and spilling out of sacks. It's a wonder more post wasn't lost in transit.

While studying in London two years previously, I had met an Indian. His name was Jagu, a tall thin man with a hooked nose and black penetrating eyes. He had insisted we stay with him when in India. We had failed to locate his home address in the phone book, which provided only an office number, so we took the Renwicks' advice and went to St Paul's Cathedral, hoping to meet the Canon, who would be sure to help us.

The cathedral was beautifully decorated with flowers and the evening service was comforting after the hardships of the afternoon's journey. The Canon had moved on to another parish and insurance rules forbade the camping of foreigners on church property. Jane, in her inimitable way, approached someone in the congregation to ask if they had a large garden where we could camp for the night. After a short conversation they kind-heartedly invited us to use their spare room. At first our new friends, the Larkins, were naturally unsure of what they had let themselves in for, but soon melted and asked us to share their supper, even inviting some of their friends in for a chat. As we didn't fancy sharing the single bed that night, I slept on our lilo and used a sleeping bag. We were most grateful to have somewhere safe to stay.

Next morning we collected a pile of letters from the GPO. Jagu had not left a note, so we headed for this office. While Jane waited in the car, I was led by an office boy up some dark narrow stairs, through cowboy style swing doors and into a large airy room.

Jagu was impatiently dictating some work to a clerk. On seeing me, he thrust aside his papers, dismissed everybody and greeted me effusively with a warm handshake.

"You have come!" he exclaimed "I never expected it. I am delighted."

After showing me around and introducing me to his uncle, a man strangely devoid of charm, conversation or personality, we collected Jane and he took us to look at the Victoria Museum. It was finished in 1921 as a tribute to the successes of the British Empire; an imposing symmetrical building, built of white makrana marble, a fusion of British and Mughal architecture and surrounded by 64 acres of well-kept gardens.

Jagu then escorted us to the Automobile Association to gather information for our southbound trip. He had forewarned them of our visit, so they were well prepared and full of good advice and suggestions. To the annoyance of all present, Jagu kept interrupting the conversation in Hindi, imposing his importance in a nervous and exasperating way.

It was at this point that we became interested in going to Darjeeling in the foothills of the Himalaya. We decided on the spot to include it in our itinerary.

After lunch in one of Calcutta's exclusive clubs, Jagu ushered us back to the hotel where he insisted we spend the night, on the pretext that his mother would not welcome us into her home. The room was located in a tall, eerily empty building, at the end of a long, echoing corridor. Jane was anxious. I felt a bit put out and couldn't understand why Jagu had shunned the idea of inviting us home, even for a meal. For some strange reason he didn't want us to meet his mother. Were we looking too disreputable after three months' travelling, or perhaps foreigners were not welcome at that time in an old Indian family?

A pang of homesickness for Europe swept over me later that evening, as we watched the film *Roman Holiday*, the familiar sounds, sights and buildings now almost part of a previous life.

We had an appointment at the Austin garage at 8.30 am. Jagu arrived in time to accompany us to the workshop, where the manager promised to get the service done as quickly as possible. The damaged headlamp was replaced with a new one and after tightening the driving shaft and putting grease in the gear box, the mechanic found a bolt missing from the shock absorber. This too had to be repaired.

Meanwhile we sat in the manager's office drinking tea. He was a man in his early forties, slightly greying at the temples; well-built for an Indian, dressed in European clothes and wearing glasses. At first he tried to dissuade us from driving to Darjeeling because the roads were atrocious further north, but then he relented, declaring, "You have enough spirit. You will get through".

The conversation turned to the Indian language. "English used to be the only common language," he told us. "India has 14 main languages and many dialects. After Independence, Hindi became the official national language and is now taught at all grades in all schools. Many educated people objected to this new ruling, especially the Madrasees in Southern India, because English is essential for further education. Hindi is not rich enough for technical subjects."

He also expressed disappointment to hear we would be leaving so soon. "I would have liked to introduce you to the women of my family and perhaps even invite you to stay with us" he said.

Who knows? It was tempting. Perhaps we would take up his offer on our return south.

During the long wait in the garage, Jane had been out gathering information and vividly recounting our adventures. As a result we had to pass by the Automobile Club again to show off the Mini. This was the first time such a small car had travelled so far and they wanted to see it.

Later, Jagu drove us out to the Botanical Gardens to see a Banyan tree of incredible girth. It covered almost an acre of land. The original trunk had long since been removed due to old age, but it had plenty of manmade supports and was sustained by the roots. Banyan tree roots grow down from the branches and take root in the ground. These thicken to form new trunks. It was such a peaceful place; a vast expanse of grassland with shady areas provided by mature trees and a good place to picnic and escape the bustle and noise of daily life in Calcutta.

What a contrast it was returning through the back streets. The conglomeration of large and small buildings, owned by traders, vied for space. The rich and the poor mingled together. Barefooted runners pulled rickshaws weaving between the lorries, buses and trams that crammed the narrow streets. Hurrying pedestrians and men bent over with the strain of pulling overloaded carts added to the chaos. The smells of cow dung, humanity and incense hung heavily in the warm air.

It was quite a relief to take a break and step inside the formal gardens, adorned with mosaic flower beds, that surrounded the Jain Temple. Jagu remained outside. His excuse was that he did not feel like taking his shoes off.

A delightful young Jain took us around, explaining many things. "Jainism is an ancient religion that was widely adopted in the Indian subcontinent. It teaches the way to liberation, from the wheel of karma and bliss, by living a life renunciation and harmlessness. We refrain from hurting even the smallest creatures. Jains do not believe in gods and goddesses," he added, as we continued to walk around the exquisitely-decorated temple, admiring the colourful mosaics and cut glass set in plaster that created myriad reflections. Grandiose chandeliers hung low and stylized paintings illustrated their beliefs. Our guide pointed out one in particular and commented on it.

"The moral is that 'without God, we are nothing and can do nothing'" he said. This statement seemed completely contradictory to us, as we had just been told that the Jains did not believe in gods and goddesses!

On the way back to the hotel, we bought flowers in the market for the hospitable Larkins. Unfortunately they were out, so we left them with the maid.

I would gladly have slept in the following morning, but a hot cup of tea arrived promptly at 8 am, followed by Jagu at 10. I left Jane to finish packing while I went with Jagu to find a back street shop to have my antiquated typewriter repaired. It had belonged to my grandfather and was now clogged with dust. While waiting, we toured the market to stock up on fruit and groceries for the journey ahead. A small boy tagged along behind carrying a basket laden with our purchases. As we passed between the stalls the vendors called out, 'Memsab, this way! Memsab, look here!'

It was time to move on. Jagu had really made us welcome and even drove in front of us to the outskirts of Calcutta, so that we would not lose our way.

The first obstacle we encountered was one of the many waterways that crisscross Bengal. Nearby, as part of the new roadwork, a bridge was under construction. The only way across was by ferry; two flat rafts bound together and secured by bamboo poles, already stacked with loaded carts, bullocks and cattle, leaving just enough room for Honey. It swayed precariously and I worried we would all end up in the water. Several men punted us across for the small charge of 1½ rupees, the equivalent of a few pennies. Once on the other side, we had trouble locating the road again. It proved to be a bumpy, dusty dirt track with occasional fast smooth sections. The manager at the garage had been right. This was going to be tough. It was already dark when we boarded the next ferry and we almost lost Honey overboard as the wheels jammed in the ramp joints. Miraculously we made it to the other side.

Grumpy and unable to find the mission church we were looking for, we drove around in circles until in desperation, we just pulled off the road, polished off the cake Jagu had given us and retired to bed.

Dhulian was a small settlement on the River Ganges. We arrived around 10 o'clock in the morning, in good time for the steamer that would take us to the other side. Beside the river, lorries were being unloaded manually item by item. The goods were then transferred onto the heads of half-naked coolies, who deftly negotiated the narrow planks attached to the stern of the waiting barges, drawn up to the muddy shore. Like pins to a magnet, an excited crowd gathered around the Mini.

It was then that we discovered we had come to the wrong place. We eventually found the booking office. An elderly man wrapped in an eiderdown was sitting on his charpoy, a bed consisting of a frame strung with light rope common in rural villages. He neatly recorded our names in his grubby book and accepted payment for a passage across the river. The official departure time was 1 o'clock, but because of an unsatisfactory ramp on the other side, the actual time was uncertain.

We parked nearby on the river bank where we could read, write and wait. The inevitable spectators soon gathered, dressed in colourful sarongs and saris, shirts or rags. Many of the children were clad only in their birthday suits. They stood and gaped, fascinated by my typewriter clattering away. When asked to leave, one man who spoke English piped up, "We have never seen beauty before". They were dark skinned. Though tanned, we were white and white in their eyes was beautiful. Pale-skinned brides were prized in India.

Whenever the crowd grew too dense and edged too close, a Sikh lorry driver, who had noticed our predicament, came over and dispersed them.

I decided to go for a walk, and as I wandered around with a trail of skipping, grubby grinning little boys in tow, women and girls crammed their doorways to see this strange European pass by.

Dhulian was a typical Indian village. The houses were built of baked mud, or a frame made from cane and stuffed with jute. A woman was busy strengthening the mud walls of her home; on the ground beside her lay a pile of grass complete with roots and two different kinds of damp earth. These she kneaded together with leaves and stalks, then she plastered the resulting sticky mess into the cracks in the wall. She had a toothless smile and chatted away, even though it was obvious I couldn't understand.

Sacred cows wandered at random or lay chewing the cud beside a stagnant village pond. In one hut, open onto the street, a painfully thin old man with a high forehead and horn-rimmed glasses knelt before a hand loom, weaving an attractive pattern into a coarse cloth. Just beyond the village, on the high banks of the Ganges, some men were kneeling on the ground making quilts by flattening cotton onto a gaily coloured piece of cloth.

Once the cotton was evenly spread, they rolled the material into a tube and skilfully unravelled it with the cotton neatly inside. With long batons they beat the cotton into the corners, making sure it was smooth, and then they rolled it up again.

Back at the river I watched fascinated as the women arrived with their large brass water pots and washing boards. One woman stood in the brown water beating the cloth on her board in an attempt to remove the grime. Next she neatly pleated the material and flung it in a wide circle over her head, repeatedly bringing it down with a resounding thud on the board. Then, she swirled it around in the water and threw it onto a pile of supposedly clean washing. Finally she spread it out to dry in the sun, wherever she could find space on the bank. Amazingly, people's clothes always looked spotlessly clean.

Once finished, the woman waded out until waist deep in the brown water to complete her toilet. Still fully clothed, she submerged and somehow managed to undress and rinse her sari, while her nakedness remained concealed beneath the muddy water. Back on shore, the woman, still wearing the clinging wet sari, made her way back to the shack that was her home. Balanced on one hip was a full pot of water, the neck held neatly in the crook of her arm; on her head was a basket of clean clothes and reluctantly trailing along behind, a small barefoot child.

At last the steam ferry arrived. It was a large rusty landing craft with four powerful engines, a lower and upper deck. The helmsman sat in solitary state inside the wheelhouse. We had no difficulty in loading the Mini on board as the landing gear was in good order.

Keeping close to the shore, the ferry made its way upstream, past black-hulled boats with tall bamboo masts waiting to be loaded with cargo; others were tacking into wind or just drifting on the tide. We passed convoys of barges, hauled along by four or five men bent forward to take the strain of the taut ropes. Their mate meanwhile sat comfortably in the stern, on bamboo matting, casually holding the rudder. Smaller craft used for fishing lay tethered to poles on the bank, protected from the strong sun by tarpaulins. Usually manned by two fishermen, one to scull and another to row, they glided to and fro in the lea of the land with a net hanging over the side to catch the fish.

Ten miles upstream we joined the main flow of the Ganges and crossed over to the other side. It took almost an hour to come alongside in the shallow water. We disembarked on to deep soft sand and many strong willing men were needed to push and pull the Mini up a steep hill and on across rough land towards terra firma.

A railway line wound its way over the sand. As we drove across it, the petrol feed pipe was ripped off the underside of the Mini. Again it was a Sikh who came to our rescue. He helped me to jack up the car and crawled underneath to join the broken ends. It was long after dark before we could move on, but the temporary repair only lasted until we reached the road, where another lorry driver mended the joint again, this time with rags and soap. He trailed us all the way into Malda, the next small town, to make sure we would arrive safely. The road was as bumpy as the wash left by a fast launch on the river. You just had to drive slowly and concentrate.

We took refuge for the night in the garage rest house. The beds were hard as tables and I'm sure they overcharged us. That was upsetting, especially as the conveniences were awful. A new feed pipe was fitted in the garage before leaving and we were soon on our way. But what a day lay ahead!

A few miles beyond Malda we came to another river and

another ferry, but with sandbags to fill the gaps in the ramp, boarding was without complications.

The next hurdle was a level crossing that was under repair. The hole between the lines was so deep that the car's small wheels couldn't possibly negotiate their way across. As usual a crowd gathered to stand and stare. Nobody offered to help. I began to feel exasperated and ended up organising some of the men working on the site to fill the gap with a large lump of wood and then drove across without any difficulty.

An hour later, we arrived at the Mahanadi Dry Weather Bridge. To reach it we had to cross a vast stretch of sand. Fortunately it was the dry season. During the monsoon rains, many of the roads become impassable as enormous tracts of land are flooded. Honey was just not wide enough to fit into the hard packed tracks left by the lorries and we soon got stuck. Luckily, there were plenty of men hanging around who came to the rescue, insisting that I reverse. This resulted in the sump guard filling with sand, bogging the car more firmly. Using sign language, I asked all of them to push, even those who had only come to give advice. Soon we were speeding away towards the bridge, waving goodbye and taking care not to lose momentum.

Driving in the direction of Siliguri, we caught a first glimpse of the Himalayan foothills that we had come so far out of our way to see, framing the horizon like a dim, distant wall. The scenery was changing. All around, bushes in neat rows like a detached privet hedge covered the ground, shaded by tall furry leaved trees. This was tea country.

It was then that suddenly and for no apparent reason we ran out of petrol. The gauge was not showing empty. We climbed out, opened up the bonnet and gazed at the engine dumbfounded. At that moment, a nun driving some children home from school stopped and leaned out of the window,

"Can I help you?" she asked pleasantly. She then went out of her way to fetch us a gallon from a nearby village.

"Normally I don't leave school as early as this" she said. "Surely it must be God's intervention that has given me this opportunity to help." She smiled happily as she waved goodbye and wished us godspeed. 'What another wonderful coincidence!' I thought.

We drove on through the Mahanadi Game Sanctuary, which lies some thirty kilometres north of Siliguri and covers some 159 square kilometres of the densely-forested foothills. It was first opened in 1955 to protect endangered animals and birds, including the Indian bison and Royal Bengal tiger; not that we were lucky enough to spot any.

Over a 50-mile stretch, the road climbed from the plains up to Ghum at 7,400 ft/2,254 m. Narrow and steep, it wound its way up through dense jungle and tiny villages perched precariously on the hillside. We drove over the ninety-two level crossings that crisscrossed the narrow gauge railway. The aptly-named toy steam train, belching smoke, climbed slowly, riding on two-foot-wide rails. It was stuffed with freight and passengers. A shrill blast on the siren noisily warned of its approach.

Through gaps in the tall trees we caught glimpses of a glowing sunset over the plain below. It was already dark when we reached the top of the pass. Above and below lights twinkled like stars. The road started to descend and I worried that I might have taken a wrong turning. Just before we rounded a final bend, Jane jumped out to check the map under the glare of the headlights. I needn't have fretted. There, on a promontory just below us, shone the lights of Darjeeling.

It was bitterly cold up in the mountains and I was feeling quite stiff and light-headed after the long steep climb, so we opted for the Bethany Convent, recommended to us by someone at the Oberoi Hotel. Here we were given a room each and a hot cup of tea before retiring. We set the alarm for 4.30 am.

I was awake early listening to the first birdsong. A cock crowed and somewhere a nun stirred. I woke Jane and we quickly dressed and crept outside. It was still dark. To my dismay the car wouldn't start and the battery was almost flat. The convent, surrounded by a well-tended garden was located at the bottom of a steep hill. There was nowhere for a push-start. Even with both of us pushing, we couldn't possibly have moved Honey. Reluctantly, we abandoned her and set off to cover the six miles on foot to see the sunrise at Tiger Hill. We had walked about a mile in the direction of Ghoum when a Land Rover drew up alongside and an American girl leaned out and drawled, "You gals want a lift?" Wow, that was lucky, as it was quite a climb. She told us she was on a luxury tour and had saved for it for eight years.

Tiger Hill is at 8,500ft/2590m and reached by a narrow winding track. The track gradually disintegrated and became so precipitous that even in four-wheel drive and first gear, the Land Rover laboured around the spiral bends. At times we thought it wouldn't make it.

From the lookout at the summit, towering, range upon range, high mountains dimly edged the horizon; the mighty panorama of the Himalayas. It was breathtaking. We were truly on top of the world. These mountains certainly dwarfed the Alps. With the approach of dawn, the massive snow-capped Kanchenjunga emerged slowly from the clear starlit night. A great red sun rose beyond the plains far below, casting rays of crimson onto the uppermost peaks. As it crept higher, other peaks were pinpointed by the rays from this fiery ball; among them, over a hundred miles away, were Lhotse and Everest, the highest point on earth. The light grew brighter. The vivid glow faded and the snow became silvery white, suspending the peaks in icy glory. Away to the right, a guide pointed out the Tibetan frontier and famous V-shaped pass and to the left, Nepal.

On the way back to Darjeeling we visited a 17th century Buddhist monastery, the oldest in the region. The outer walls were richly decorated with paintings. Dragon heads were moulded onto the corners of the curved, tiled roof. At the entrance a pair of dog-dragons stood guard. Encircling the temple were large brass prayer wheels, which the monks, draped in long saffron robes, kept in perpetual motion as they chanted and slowly shuffled their way around.

The hallway was surrounded by murals depicting strange figures, their clothes entwined with beads and shimmering with gold leaf. An enormous golden Buddha in an attitude of peace dominated the temple. A chair had been placed beside the altar, ready for the Dalai Lama. The photograph that hung behind it was of a young man with a mischievous twinkle in his eye. We learnt that the office of the Dalai Lama was not hereditary. The incumbent decides the date on which his successor will be born, so that when he dies the Good Men, who are also monks, can get together and go out to find the child they will then educate to take his place.

Behind the Buddha, figures of demons and dragons were fashioned in minute detail; even the roof of the dragon's mouth was corrugated and he had delicate curly feelers. Incense burnt constantly and bowls of holy water stood ready to be taken home by the devout. Candle power was used to keep the prayer wheels ceaselessly turning. The walls were lined with shelves containing scriptures written on parchment 2500 years ago, each one meticulously preserved in cloth wrapping.

After a delicious breakfast back at the convent, the nuns and a priest helped to push the car back up the steep garden path onto the road. Darjeeling was fascinating. It had the highest and smallest race course for horses in the world; a Tibetan school for refugees, where we watched the children playing a wild game of football; a bazaar teeming with squat little people with round flat faces and almond eyes; Nepalese tradesmen; and Tibetans selling whatever they had managed to salvage from their lost homeland. A large man with a peaked hat set jauntily on his head sat on some steps surrounded by swords, homespun cloth and other trinkets, and at his side, in comical contrast, sat a younger man with muddy unkempt hair, reaching well below his shoulders, wound into ringlets that stuck out in all directions.

It was after examining all the trophies in the museum of the Mountaineering Institute that we were approached by the registrar, a Sikh, who asked if he could help us in any way. He added, "There is a film in progress showing last year's attempt on the summit of Everest", but it was just finishing as we arrived. Glad to rest awhile, we sat through a documentary on Canadian mountain wildlife.

The Institute was run by the famous Sherpa, Tensing, who just a few years before had taken part in the first successful ascent of Everest. Unfortunately he wasn't there, but instead we met five young Indians training to climb the mountain the following summer: Mahon, who had led several expeditions in the Himalayas, Krishna, Bearded Jogindar, who had a bad knee, Surrendra, whose wife was studying art in Paris, and Hari, a Sikh and keen photographer. He boasted that he was married and had several 'ready-made' sons. We didn't think he looked old enough.

They invited us to celebrate Krishna's birthday later that evening, and Hari, Mahon and Jogindar came to pick us up. Jane accompanied Jogi, as he was known, on the scooter and the other two squeezed into the Mini. The extra weight made the climb to the Institute difficult, especially as the plugs were oiled up, until I realized that to zigzag up was the answer. The evening was a huge success. We discussed our trip and their mountains over whiskey and rum, curry and papaya. Then we drove up to the deserted Gymkhana Club, a large hall surrounded by an elegant upper balustrade, and to the accompaniment of records, we took turns to dance with our hosts until our feet ached.

We took leave of the nuns and spent the next day with our new friends. They managed to persuade us to stay on until the following morning, offering us Mahon's room for the night. It was good to have company, to sit around and drink coffee, take photographs and relax. Later we walked around the knoll to enjoy the view and get warm. I found it freezing up in the mountains; such a contrast to the summer temperatures down on the plain. We had been so lucky to have seen Kanchenjunga on the first morning in Darjeeling, because she remained shrouded in clouds throughout the rest of our stay.

Later that evening after another, this time shorter, dancing session at the Gymkhana Club, Hari expressed his surprise to find me fitter than I looked, as we all walked back uphill to the Institute under the star-studded sky. I had prudently left the car parked at the Institute all day, as the police were after me for driving down a one way street in the wrong direction.

The mountaineers gave us a tremendous send-off with kisses all round and repeated invitations to spend Christmas in Bombay, which we couldn't promise to accept; it was a long way back across India to the west coast and back again to Madras in the south-east. However, it was very tempting. Maybe... we'd think about it. Amid raucous laughter, they all helped to push-start the Mini. The battery was flat yet again.

It only took a couple of hours to reach the plain and warmth, where the going was not easy and progress was slow. It was high time to have the car serviced, but suitable service stations were non-existent. The plugs needed cleaning, but I was unable to unscrew them all and new ones were not available in the small garage where we stopped to ask for help. The brakes were playing up; they were pulling sharply to the right and at one stage nearly caused us to collide with an oncoming Jeep. It was the rule of the road that downhill traffic must give way to upward-coming traffic.

That evening, we almost reached the Manickchat Ghat on the river Ganges, but it was too late for the ferry, so we pulled off the road to prepare supper. A man with a torch appeared, walked away and returned with a policeman. To be on the safe side we immediately decided to drive on to a more secluded place, where only the noisy cackles of a jackal disturbed the peace of the night. Fortunately this part of India was sparsely populated, which made camping easier.

We arrived back at the Manickchat Ghat an hour before the ferry was due to sail. We drove on board a large hull, topped with bamboo and iron matting, to await attachment to the Missouri River type ferry, which plied the Ganges with pedestrians. It took roughly an hour to cross over to Ramalganj on the other side.

We then threaded our way through the crowded bazaar and along dusty streets until we emerged into the rolling hills of the countryside, along a dirt road full of treacherous potholes and on into the desert. A spring strut broke, forcing us to crawl along, the wheel almost grazing the wing above. With some of the load moved forward onto the front seat and Jane perched on the roof rack to relieve the strain on the rear right wheel, we struggled on. Jane just took it in her stride, waving gaily to the few people we passed.

Progress was painfully slow for over 100 miles. Part of the road was under reconstruction. It wound through uninhabited, sparsely-treed, undulating country, around boulders and across dried-up streams. It was hot, dusty and lonely and the going was tough and tiring. We seemed to be driving through the middle of nowhere and met only a couple of lorries and three heavily-loaded bullock carts.

As if we were not having enough trouble already, the petrol pump packed up. Jane fortunately discovered a nearby stream, so we soaked the pump in a bucket of water to clean out the dust. Meanwhile, we took the opportunity to freshen-up with a much-needed wash, to make a cup of coffee and down a couple of aspirins. Well-boiled water is supposed to be quite safe to drink. By this time we both had splitting headaches caused by frustration and dehydration.

The petrol gauge was showing almost empty when we finally limped into the next village. A Sikh driver knew exactly where to find fuel and also recommended the best garage in Dumka, a nearby town, for repairing the broken spring strut. But our litany of woes was not yet over. A few more miles and the rear tyre went flat. An audience of small boys gathered to watch us change the wheel. We had this down to a fine art and it didn't take long. Not only had they never seen such a small car, but I'm sure they had never seen a couple of girls changing a tyre either.

Yet again, on the outskirts of Dumka, Honey coughed, spluttered and stopped dead. We hadn't run out of petrol and the fuel pump was still ticking, so I lifted the bonnet to find that a plug lead had come off. But even when repaired the car wouldn't start. Then suddenly, for no apparent reason, the engine burst into life. She definitely needed servicing. She was using far too much petrol and causing a great deal of trouble.

The mechanics at the garage recommended by the Sikh seemed capable and promised to get started immediately. Someone hailed a rickshaw. Trustingly we left Honey behind, quickly gathered a few necessities and headed for the Lutheran mission on the outskirts of the town. It was run by a Norwegian couple with accommodation for 60 people and was used for conferences. When they heard our plight they welcomed us, gave us each a bed for the night and immediately showed us to the bathroom. We must have looked a sight.

After the sheer bliss of a hot water wash, we joined the missionaries, their guests and children for dinner. We sat down and before tucking into the most delicious meal of different curries, we all sang grace. I thought that was much nicer than chanting, 'For what we are about to receive...' as we had done in boarding school.

Next morning the garage mechanics made a new head for the spring strut and fixed it in place. Apparently dirt in the air cooler was causing the over consumption of petrol. Honey was given a free wash, including the engine, a thorough service, a top up with 10 litres of petrol and 3 pints of oil; all for the small sum of £2. She had been well tuned, sounded much better and pulled well for the first time in ages. I was confident that she would run better from now on.

While waiting, the garage proprietor explained all about the Indian marriage customs. Parents with sons or daughters of marriageable age go to a broker, who knows all the different families of similar status in the region. He confidentially finds out all about the prospective family and especially about their financial position. The parents are then introduced to the future bride or groom, approve the choice and arrange for the dowry, usually in the form of a down-payment. The future couple meet to consent. According to status, one member or the whole family, including all the relations from every family in the town, are invited to a feast, lasting three days. The bride then goes to her husband's home for the wedding night, returning to her own home for a month. She goes back to her husband again, this time for a little longer. This coming and going continues until the bride no longer feels homesick.

It seems the people were so steeped in tradition and convention that little change could take place. The mostly illiterate villagers were bound by taboos and could not understand anything they couldn't see. No wonder the missionaries made little headway in teaching hygiene.

The dirt everywhere was beginning to pall, especially in the towns, and what I found picturesque had become an area to walk through quickly, my nose tightly closed to the smells.

After only fifteen miles on the road, we had to return to Dumka again. The rear shock absorber had been too loosely fitted and I was unable to tighten it. The mechanics were apologetic and soon we were on our way.

We did manage to cover sixty miles that day to Deogar, where we sought out two delightful Anglican English missionaries running a school on English lines for middle-class Indian girls. They were doing a heroic job with practically no finance and loving it, supported by the diocese and modest fees. We found most Europeans were hankering to go home, but not these two. They proudly showed us around their school where the resident girls slept in overcrowded dormitories, did their own cleaning, cooking and drawing of water from the well. They even ate their meals sitting on the floor, native style.

The older woman was such a gentle lady, her grey hair held neatly in place by a fine net, her specs perched on the end of her nose. Her companion, younger and full of fun, was absolutely dedicated and really happy with her mission in life. After first sending us upstairs to wash the dust off, we shared a frugal meal in their sparsely-furnished parlour, together with the Indian matron, who arrived with a little box of sweets. They all seemed so delighted with the unexpected company. Jane felt so guilty afterwards as she had too generously helped herself to the lemon juice which they had obviously saved as a special dinner drink.

What a treat! We had a call at 6.30 am with tea, toast and sweetmeats on a tray. The hospitality and kindness of the missionaries in India was wonderful, especially as we were both beginning to miss the comforts of home.

Repeatedly throughout the course of the following day the distributor was troublesome. We made little progress inspite of my repeatedly cleaning the points. A lorry hurtled past, dust flying, swaying across the road in a drunken manner. The yellow turbaned head of the driver was leaning out of the window facing backwards to see what two girls were doing under the bonnet of a diminutive car. The lorry stopped; the occupants climbed out and walked back to help. Neither spoke English but despite their disreputable clothing, they were charming and ready to lend a hand. One of them had dashing black eyes and a twirly moustache. Between us we managed to get the engine started.

Our litany of woes was still not over. Sixty miles further on, in a village, the Mini suddenly came to a halt and refused to budge. There we were stuck in the middle of the road, surrounded by an ever-increasing crowd of curious onlookers. This time it was the local doctor who came to our rescue and found a mechanic who managed to get the car going, but I was sceptical. The doctor spoke fluent English. He invited us to his home. The mechanic came along too, so that he could clean the distributor properly, undisturbed by the crowds. He also made sure the timing was correct as the engine was running too fast. Meanwhile we sat on the terrace drinking tea and eating fried rice.

By the time Honey was ready, it was so late that we gladly accepted the doctor's invitation to park and camp on the veranda, and to take our cooking things into the courtyard in order to prepare supper. He was sure we would be happier eating our own food.

The family were refugees from East Pakistan, displaced by partition, and had left hurriedly with nothing, so despite being educated people their living conditions were basic. They ate in relays; first the men, then the women, squatting on the floor eating off shared brass plates, using chapattis or fingers to scoop up the food. As Europeans, we were honoured with a small table and chair each.

The focal point of the house was the courtyard, around which the rooms were built. A garden of potted plants adorned the flat roof. The cooking arrangements were almost as primitive as ours. The wife squatted before a bucket of hot ash, which she fed with wood or cow dung in the corner of an otherwise bare room. Washing took place at the pump in the courtyard where a bucket was provided. This was the only source of running water available and after use was swilled across the yard.

Grandfather, 74 years old, was a great character. He had thick silver white hair and flowing beard, was thin as a stick, still sprightly and surprisingly well versed in European history. In a friendly way he disagreed with my politics and my belief that private enterprise was essential. It transpired that he was a communist and had been imprisoned twice. His eldest granddaughter was to be married in three months' time and he told us she was delighted with her parents' choice of husband. Her youngest sister loved to dance and performed gracefully especially for us. She had never had a lesson.

The family slept under mosquito nets. It was early to bed and early to rise.

The first morning train-ferry across the River Son was full. Even though we arrived in good time, we had to wait until 11.30 am for the next loading. Also waiting for the train were some Indians from East Africa whose womenfolk were proving tiresome. They didn't want to do this and that and found India dirty. Two of the men spent quite some time talking about the different conditions in India and their home country.

Once across the river, we battled for an hour with heavy traffic and unable to find anywhere to buy bread, we stopped briefly for a meagre lunch of tinned spaghetti. From then on to Mirzapur things improved. The wide unfrequented road ran across a vast plain, until it climbed into hilly country. It was semi-arid with deep crevasses left by the monsoon rains. A causeway ran across a dried-up river bed, which for a short time each year would be impassable. Towards evening the main hold-ups were caused by herdsmen and their cattle returning to their villages from the grazing grounds.

It was dark and late when we wearily arrived in the small town of Rewa. We headed straight for the hospital to ask permission to camp in the compound. It seemed the best option. The nurses were wonderful. They invited us to supper and even found us a room for the night. It was a Government-run establishment, and normally they would not be allowed to have guests, but the House Mother let us use the vacant room of two nurses who were away for an interview. We learnt something about hospital conditions in India and the near impossibility of teaching sanitation to illiterate people, who believe only what they can see.

Both Jane and I woke up next morning feeling as if we had hangovers. To make things worse, the car had a sprung an oil leak. The sump draining nut had worked loose. It seemed that the little things that could go wrong were never-ending. Luckily a man delivering a car to the Mother Superior of the hospital saw me struggling, towed the Mini over to his garage pit and tightened up the nuts for me. Our guardian angels were still keeping an eye on us.

Short of rupees, we then went to the bank, which was in a litter-strewn back street; it was a dingy building, heavily guarded by army personnel standing slovenly in the doorway. Inside was equally squalid and disorderly. The safe stood in one corner, the door wide open, while soldiers unpacked large boxes of bank notes.

We expected the proceedings for changing traveller's cheques to be prolonged, so we settled down with a couple of magazines. From the Manager's office came the unexpected sound of an English North Country accent. Eventually a man emerged and introduced himself as Harold. Amazingly he hailed from Sandbach in the north of England and often played the organ in Gawsworth Church, in the very village I grew up in. Harold was exceedingly talkative and we couldn't get a word in edgeways. He worked for UNICEF and was delighted to meet a couple of compatriots; he invited us to have lunch with him. The delicious meal of Samba venison, the first meat we had eaten in a long time, lifted our flagging spirits; we were exhausted from the long hours of driving and coping with so many set-backs.

Silver City ferry to Le Touquet (Sept 5th 1961)

Camping in France

Typical dirt road in Greece

Meteora

Mt Olympus

On the way to Istanbul

A mosque in Istanbul

Honey after her accident

The Black Sea coast

A Turkish woman and her son

Turkish men

Jeanne, Jane, Carem, Hans and Honey

A typical Iranian road through the desert

Jeanne and Jane with Iranian students

Jane and Honey on pass into Baluchistan

Baluchistan camels

Honey with Sikh flower blessings

Ferry north of Calcutta

Jeanne and Jane with Dr and his family

Western Ghats

Dhobi

Women road-workers

View from Redcliffs in Ceylon

Buddhist monks in Ceylon

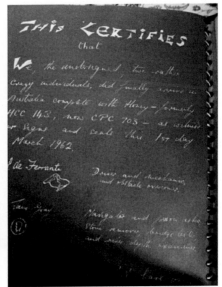

Fisherman on the
Ceylonese south coast

Jane's certificate on arrival in Australia

Boy and Jenny Budgerigar, Australia

Surfer's Paradise

Boarding the *Fairsea*

Tasman Glacier

Honey at Milford Sound

Jane

Pacific coast, NZ

Cathedral in Acapulco

Siesta in Acapulco park

Proud fisherman in Acapulco

Arrival in Miami

An orange grove in Florida

Main street, New Orleans

A long straight road through Texas

Refuelling the Mini in Mexico

Mexico City

Campers' wash day, Mexican desert

Young men spinning

Teotihuacán

The Painted Desert

Mules in the Grand Canyon

Colorado River

Zion Park

St Francisco tramway

Honey beside a truck

Redwoods,
California

Jeanne and Jane

Jasper Park Canada

Prairie farm, Canada

Changing the Guard, Ottawa

Jane and Mr Wu in New York

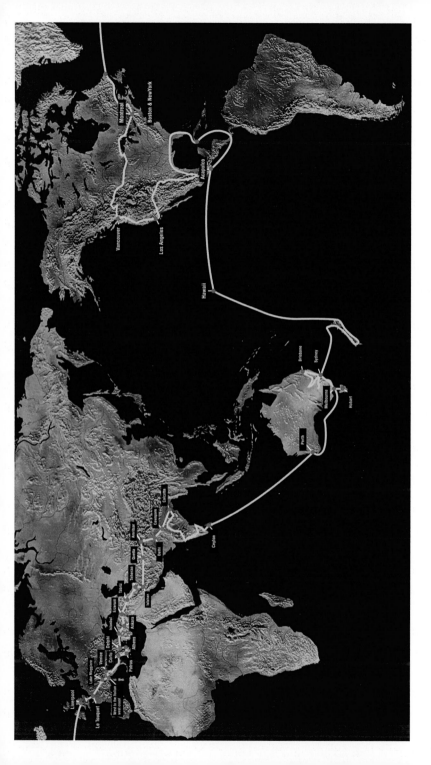

Later in the afternoon, Harold took us to have tea at the home of an Indian doctor, whose bungalow was set in a real English garden. The walls of the sitting room were painted green, decorated with Egyptian tapestries and on display were religious icons of the Hindu faith. His charming wife and daughter served home-baked coffee and papaya from the garden. We sat in a circle on high-backed chairs, looking out onto a typical inner courtyard which was spotlessly clean and tidy.

Back at Harold's bungalow, we met the ADC of the local Maharajah, a loud-voiced man, already drunk and still drinking heavily, who imposed his muddled views, gesticulating wildly and constantly addressing Jane, "Am I right, sister?" Harold, meanwhile just calmly agreed to his every whim.

Suddenly the lights failed. The ADC was furious with the servants when they brought oil lamps instead of gas.

"In my house," he declared as he waived his hands around vigorously, "the servants come running to do my bidding. Everyone obeys Tay Saab." To quieten him Harold assured him this was correct.

The ensuing two hours were hilarious. The ADC insisted on reading the lines of our hands. Some character details were correct, but most of what he said was quite incomprehensible. He put ink dots on Jane's hand to prove she had a mole there. He even showed us the soles of his feet with a deep line running through the middle, an indication of high birth. But by 10.30 pm I could have screamed. We were starving and longing for bed. At last supper arrived, but we had to wait for the ADC to finish talking before we could sit at table and eat.

Soon after, we excused ourselves and retired to bed in the next room, which the servants had prepared for us. Silently I locked the door and the intercommunicating door, which I hadn't noticed before and which now to my surprise was open. It took time to fall asleep as the two men were still drinking and playing a rowdy game of cards. My suspicions proved correct. When, for no apparent reason, I awoke in the middle of the night, Jane whispered: "Someone has been trying the doors!"

Sleep eluded me, so I sat and wrote letters until one of the servants brought the morning tea, followed by four buckets of hot water for a two-inch bath. Loud voices and clatter heralded the appearance of Tay Saab with his almost silent bodyguard. Tagging along behind was the elderly, now retired ADC, a quiet mild man who had fallen asleep in his chair during the evening's raucous party. He wore the most startling diamond earrings.

It was raining cats and dogs. Lightning streaked across the sky and thunder rolled; a truly heavy tropical downpour. Harold arrived with the car to take us to breakfast on the other side of the garden.

Mysteriously, the Mini's radio had been left on. The battery, which was pretty weak anyway, was flat. It was impossible to start the car. A dead fuse had to be replaced and the battery had to be taken to the garage to be charged. One of the cells was found to be defective and we were told to return at 4 pm. Tay Saab tried to command immediate delivery of a new one, but it was Sunday and just not possible. I was happy about that as I was most embarrassed and worried about being compromised.

Everyone was at Tay Saab's beck and call. Harold continuously played up to him while his daughter, who we met at breakfast, tried to smooth things over. Suddenly we found ourselves compelled to stay another day and yesterday's pressing invitation to stay until Monday suddenly became an almost insistent "You are dying to leave and must get away."

'*Let that be a lesson to lecherous old men who invite unsuspecting young girls to enjoy their hospitality'* I wrote in my diary. I wondered if Tay Saab would have liked his beautiful 21-year-old daughter to experience this when travelling in foreign lands.

The day passed peacefully reading and writing letters. This was the first time since leaving Ankara that we had a few hours with absolutely nothing to do and nowhere to go. The enforced rest did us both a lot of good and we felt so much better.

Late in the afternoon we all returned to the Indian doctor's house. He showed us around his garden, which was full of flowers and vegetables, and impressed me with his knowledge of all the botanical names. Many other doctors arrived to meet us, but this time the womenfolk were nowhere to be seen. A table on the veranda was laden with sweetmeats, jellybeans, curried peas, tiny meat cakes spiced with chillies, banana chips, guavas, papaya and a sweet cheese cake; a veritable feast! The guests helped themselves as often as they liked, finishing off with tea and yogurt. Before leaving they stacked their plates beneath the sink in the corner or under the table. All the while, Harold remained in close attendance to our host.

Back at the bungalow the men played cards and drank whiskey until the early hours of the morning. We made the most of another long, undisturbed and comfortable night's sleep with door firmly locked.

Now that the battery was fully charged, the car started immediately. At 8 am, Harold appeared just in time to wish us a hearty goodbye. Refreshed, we covered a record three hundred miles in the day. Initially the narrow highway was covered in a layer of skiddy mud, due to the heavy rain; a bus had ripped a tyre while overtaking and ended up in a ditch, leaving a trail of debris. Deep ruts lined the verges where lorries had half driven off the tarmac to avoid collision with oncoming traffic. Soon, however, the surface dried up and further south, no evidence of the storm remained.

We travelled on through dense forest over many *ghats* (an Indian word denoting a difficult passage through the mountains). At one point, the trees reached away to the distant hills on the horizon, broken only by a shimmering mirage of blue water. Intermittent long straight stretches of road broke the monotony of continuously winding up and down hill. Camels and cattle grazed in the clearings and long-tailed monkeys sat in the road, scampering to safety at the sound of the horn. How we laughed to see one glade occupied by a school of monkeys sitting around imitating a human family having a picnic in the next.

In daylight and at the end of a long satisfying day we reached Nagpur, a large industrial town, cleaner than most with wide roads. Men were stationed on the white lines down the centre during the rush hour to ensure that pedestrians, cyclists, bullock carts, buses and other vehicles kept to the correct side. Someone directed us to the Church of India, just beyond a cathedral, a union church and a couple of temples; religious tolerance very much in evidence.

The Bishop and his wife greeted us warmly. "No way can you camp in the compound" he said, "but you are most welcome to use our recently vacated spare room." Once again we felt very spoilt. Hot water, a washing line and supper in the bedroom were provided. Downstairs we could hear a dinner party in full swing.

At breakfast the following morning, the family celebrated their 19-year-old son's birthday. The Bishop read the lesson for the day and said prayers, before we all joined in singing Happy Birthday. While we spent the morning ironing and shopping, the Bishop's two sons washed the Mini for us and before leaving, his wife made sure we ate a wholesome lunch by providing an enormous meal on a tray in the bedroom, even though it was only 11.30 am.

For a change we had an uneventful day on comparatively good roads again through forests alternating with semi-desert. As people were sparse, we risked camping in a field of maize. The moon was nearly full and we could easily see to cook without showing a light. We even slept under the stars for the first time, without the canvas cover because it was so warm. Unfortunately I slept badly, disturbed by tinkling bells and convoys of bullock carts, creaking and squeaking their way past throughout the night, carrying cotton to market.

Now that we were so much further south, sunrise was much later. Lying on top of the car we watched a glowing red ball creep up over the horizon, suddenly flooding the sky with light. A dog barked. A cock crowed and sounds of people stirring in a nearby village prompted us to dress quickly before anyone discovered us.

Somehow we missed the way and only realized it thirteen miles further on, after a long steep climb to a plateau. As we retraced our steps, the front wheel started to make ominous noises.

"Oh no," moaned Jane. "It sounds as if another spring strut has broken!"

She was right. It was the front right shock absorber, the damage caused by consistently travelling with one wheel on the sunken verge whenever we passed an on-coming vehicle. With Jane once again perched on the roof rack, this time on the rear end, to take weight off the front of the car, we crawled at snail's pace along the interminable sixty miles to Jalgaon. These constant setbacks were beginning to take their toll and how we longed for a break from travelling.

The garage mechanic skilfully made a new spring strut on

the lathe and after a trial run, we asked for the bill, which came to the outrageous sum of 35 rupees.

"Last time we only paid 26 rupees for a service, a new bearing, oil change and 10 litres of petrol" I protested. "We'll only pay 15 rupees for this job". He accepted without protest. It just goes to show he was trying it on.

While waiting, the Reverend Caps engaged us in conversation. He told us he was a missionary and invited us to dinner with his friend, a doctor, who in turn asked us to an informal discussion at the Rotary Club later that evening. With them was a Christian pastor, an Indian, who later returned as promised to show us the way to the Caps family home. They had a pleasant bungalow beside the government hospital and had already prepared their guest room and a bucket of hot water. This was a great surprise, as we had not expected it. Over dinner, the reverend and his wife talked to us about the Hindu religion and the slow progress of Christianity among a people bound by tradition and family ties.

Later that evening the Reverend Caps accompanied us to the Rotary Club, which met in the home of the doctor we had met earlier. We all sat around in a circle and the doctors fired numerous questions at us. They seemed to have incredible ideas about the English.

"How do you manage without liquor?" someone asked.

"Do you smoke?"

"How many children do you want?"

"What is the purpose of your journey? Surely only rich people could ever hope to make such a journey."

"Two girls travelling alone, Isn't that rather dangerous?"

Coffee was served, while one of the doctors explained enthusiastically, "We are involved in carrying out a sterilization program. The population growth in India is such that it is impossible to control and only the educated understand the need for family planning. This means that we are reducing the good brains and increasing the common run. We offer the men 20 rupees to undergo the operation and have already performed over eight hundred interventions."

We had a conducted tour of their home; the kitchen had two gas rings and brass pots for eating from. They were kept spotlessly clean using ashes and lemon juice. Several children shared a bedroom with the parents, all cramped together and protected by mosquito nets. The communal bathroom was in the courtyard.

It rained during the night and continued throughout the following day, sometimes in torrents, forcing us to stop and wait for the storm to pass. The distributor kept playing up, the petrol pump overheated and once we had a loose plug. It was stop-start behind struggling lorries and buses belching black smoke, up and across the Western Ghats. We saw that erosion had sliced the tops off the mountains, giving them the appearance of tables.

When at last we reached Bombay it was stifling hot and humid after the cool, fresh breezes in the Western Ghats. We arrived just before lunch, along a narrow road jammed with traffic crawling nose to tail, engines overheating and stalling frequently. The first stop was the post office, to collect a whole stack of Christmas mail. It was the 22nd of December, my birthday, and we were a long way from home.

There were no messages so we decided to locate Surrendra, one of the mountaineers we had met in Darjeeling. We knew he worked somewhere in the port, and that was where we found him. He welcomed us warmly and installed us in his 5th floor flat overlooking the harbour before disappearing for most of the next two days. He was a Sikh, though he didn't wear a turban, and was filling in for his Christian colleagues during the holidays. It really didn't matter as we were so exhausted; all we wanted to do was to take it easy. Poor man, he had only received our letter the day before announcing our arrival and wasn't really prepared.

The next morning was spent in trying fruitlessly to get the car serviced and repaired. Then while scrutinizing the map to find the way back to the flat, a businessman approached and realizing our distress, told us to follow him to a suitable garage. He thoughtfully helped with the organization of the servicing and I suspect he even paid to have the distributor fixed. When he went to pick up the bill for us, he told me they had done it for nothing. Such kindness, when we were feeling low, was quite overwhelming.

No way was Jane going to forego celebrating Christmas properly. Surrendra, in one of his free moments, accompanied us to a nearby market to buy a turkey and potatoes. To Jane's great delight, she even found a Christmas pudding in a shop frequented by the English expatriates. In sweltering heat in that tiny kitchen, she set to and cooked the turkey, with all the trimmings that go with it; little sausages, prunes wrapped in bacon, and stuffing.

Meanwhile I went out for a walk, with my thoughts far away in England and digesting some exciting and totally unexpected news; my parents had written announcing their imminent arrival in Ceylon. What a wonderful Christmas present. Nothing could have pleased me more.

The dinner was festive and delicious. Surrendra joined us, together with a delightful French lady called Marianne, which made it a great party. She was his mother-in-law, the daughter of a Sikh father and a French mother. She was cooking for him and his little girl, Anuradha. His wife, Sita, was away in Paris on a two-year scholarship to study art. Anu, as she was usually called, was a pretty child with curly blond hair, two and a half years old who spent most of her time with her *ayah*.

Later Surrendra drove us to church, where we sang carols in English. This helped to make it feel more like Christmas. There was no air-conditioning, but I was frozen. Wearing only a light cotton dress and sitting in the direct draft of whirring fans, I gathered my shawl tightly around me to try and keep warm.

Back outside, in the heat and humidity of the Indian night, festive lights and painted balloons hung over the streets. Christmas was a holiday everyone enjoyed.

Whenever he could take time off from work or in the evenings, Surrendra would take us out for a drive and show us around. Bombay was a fascinating place. Cricket was played in the evenings on the Oval, an elongated square surrounded by palm trees and tall picturesque buildings. The Marine drive was one of my favourite with its twinkling necklace of lights; families out for a stroll, the brown water lapping against the quayside and a cool breeze blowing in from the sea.

Malabar Hill was home to the affluent, who lived in attractive bungalows surrounded by well-tended grounds with views across the city. At Beach Candy there was an open-air swimming pool frequented by the Europeans and their children, accompanied by their *ayahs*, who came to bask in the sun and eat ice-creams on the immaculately kept lawns.

A peninsula of reclaimed land, the bustling port and smoking chimneys in the west highlighted the contrast between rich and poor. The homeless slept on the unkempt streets because they had nowhere to go and had failed to find work in the city. Many had come from the rural areas dreaming of a better life. Their hardy babies, huddled in cotton wraps, cried themselves to sleep.

Bombay was a prohibition area, but foreigners, if they wished to drink, could have their passports stamped, permitting them to be labelled as 'alcoholics'. This Jane did. So with a good supply of whiskey and beer, we brought in the New Year on board a Pilgrim ship anchored out in the harbour. I didn't particularly enjoy it as drinking was not my thing. It was cold and we had to make polite conversation with a rather obnoxious, overpowering colonel. We then moved on to another party, invited by a friend of a friend, where the women wore richly-embroidered saris and jewels in their hair – a very glamorous affair. The guests just sat around exchanging small-talk. I would have much preferred to dance the night away. Though an interesting experience, I found it all rather dull.

The Mini was our worst headache, for no matter how many garages we took her to she persisted in stalling at the traffic lights. Eventually, after fitting a new gasket, new brakes, a new petrol pump and giving her a thorough tuning and servicing she ran as new, except for the suspension, which was hardly surprising. We even took her to Thana, a 'hill climb' on the outskirts of Bombay, to successfully try her out.

One of my most vivid memories was the arrival of the *dhobi*. He came with the laundry wrapped in a sheet and balanced on his head; a tall, slim Indian with a droopy moustache, large doleful eyes and a smile playing around his lips, as he watched us observing him. His hair was longish, curling at the ends. He wore a long piece of white cloth wound around his loin and attached between the legs, to look like baggy breeches. Barefoot, he glided across the room and sank cross legged on to the floor. Only then did he remove the laundry from his head and place it neatly beside him. He untied the knot slowly and meticulously counted out the clean clothes. He then retreated to one side to wait for the dirty linen to be placed ready for him to count out, wrap up and take away.

The *dhobi* was suddenly shy and embarrassed when Surrendra asked him to let us take a photograph. He stood stiffly to attention on the small balcony, not wanting to smile for the camera.

We had only intended to spend a few days in Bombay, but we ended up staying three weeks. Whenever departure was mentioned, we were told not to be so mean. Surrendra was obviously enjoying the company. It was wonderful to relax and not worry about breakdowns, campsites, food, water and all the other little things that go to make up the overland traveller's day. We made many friends and were brilliantly entertained.

I suppose it was my fault we tarried so long. It hit me all of a sudden out of the blue; I had fallen in love with Surrendra. Jane was not at all pleased – or was she a little bit jealous? He was not the sort of man I would have noticed in the street; older, fairly thick set and married. But somehow he grew on me, his shock of curly black hair and his winning smile, and we shared many common interests. Perhaps it was the novelty of having so much attention and being so far from home. For days I floated on a cloud.

Time slipped rapidly by. It was much hotter than in northern India, though the evenings were cooled by the sea breezes. We went sailing, cooked cakes, learnt to make true Indian curries, listened to the Muslims and Hindus making music and dancing in the evening to the sound of a beating drums. We spent several afternoons at the Beach Candy pool, swimming. The sea water looked dirty and uninviting. Surrendra was often free and took us out sightseeing or to visit friends.

Before leaving, we met up with the dashing Lt. Kohli, a naval officer, one of the Mountaineers we had met in Darjeeling. He invited us all to Circarama, together with his brother, wife and child, whose dark appealing eyes were heavily made up with kohl. Jane was delighted to meet him again, especially as she had been disappointed to find Jagu was away on a three-week course. We learnt that he had been a member of the Indian expedition to Everest in 1960 and had reached the South Col. He subsequently scaled Annapurna 111 and as leader of the expedition, was one of those who reached the summit.

It was time to say goodbye and move on. My parents and youngest brother Mark were already on board the P&O liner *Arcadia* and heading south towards Ceylon, no doubt curious to know how well we had survived the adventure so far. It was still dark when we packed the car and formally shook hands all round.

That first day was difficult. I had left a part of me behind, and we drove away in silence. The rush hour had not yet started and though we lost our way once, we were soon out of town and on the road for Poona, past Thana and the mountaineering school, overlooking some lakes dotted with small fishing boats, just visible in the encroaching dawn.

Honey climbed stoically and at one stage she found the gradient of the ghat so steep that after trailing a lorry for some time, she struggled to keep going. We ate sandwiches for breakfast on the go and later stopped for an early lunch under some shady trees by the side of the road. I couldn't rest or keep my mind on the book I was trying to read, so I set off uphill barefoot for a walk. Going up was fine, but coming down was painful, as I had stupidly burnt the soles of my feet on the hot stones. From that vantage point I could see the road stretching away to more hills on the horizon.

Sitting alone, I let my thoughts wander over the events of the past three weeks and wondered sadly that one could feel so much for someone in so short a space of time, at the understanding between us, and the unexpected pain of parting.

The afternoon didn't drag as the morning had done. We chatted about many things and easily covered a record 300 miles, to stop for the night just beyond Belgaon, which was hidden in the middle of nowhere, sheltered behind some bushes.

The countryside was kinder as we headed south, more scientifically cultivated and well irrigated by small lagoons. The towns were cleaner and spaciously laid out, though lacking comprehensible signposts. Bewildered by the Sanskrit, I asked the way to Bangalore and was mistakenly directed to the 'Bungalow', the local rest house, situated several miles in the wrong direction. The people were darker skinned with less defined features and lived in neat little houses, rather than in crowded hovels as along the Ganges. In the shops we found large red juicy tomatoes and unripe tangerines, but little else.

At lunchtime the usual audience gathered to watch us eat. I lost patience when a man approached too close for comfort, jumped up and yelled angrily "git!" He was as surprised as I was by the sudden outburst and he ran away. The crowd sitting under a neighbouring tree roared with laughter.

At the frequent railway crossings, we somehow nearly always managed to pull up behind or just in front of a waiting bus. Several men would jump out and taking advantage of the enforced stop, squat to relieve themselves on the grass verge in full view of everybody, jumping back on board at the sound of a loud whistle from the approaching train.

We reached the garden city of Bangalore without further incident and as usual, headed for the first Christian Church we could find. It belonged to the Methodists. The caretaker directed us on to the home of the Gospel Missionaries, Mr and Mrs Smith. They welcomed us as if we had been friends from back home and offered us a room, a bath and some bacon and eggs for supper. He was a tall nervous man and his wife was a typically welcoming American. They were both such caring people, eager to hear about our adventures so far. In one way we felt bad about taking advantage of Christian hospitality, but on the other hand we brought a breath of fresh air to a routine life.

In the morning, after having our photograph taken, we stood around the car asking God's blessings for a safe onward journey. Smiles all round and we climbed into the car, eager to be on our way. The Smiths stood at the front door to wave goodbye... but Honey disgraced us by refusing to start; so embarrassing after such a send-off. She had to be pushed a good hundred yards down the street before the engine sprang to life. What a pantomime that was, especially after the prayers!

The road wound on through hilly country, towards the east coast and the sea 3,000 ft below. Huge boulders lay scattered haphazardly and moth-eaten palm trees towered into the deep blue sky, giving no shade to the parched, sandy earth. The villages were clean, the whitewashed mud huts topped with thatched roofs. The people here were even darker. The women worked bent double over young shoots that sprouted in the flooded paddy fields; the intense green was such a contrast. Near the *tanks*, reservoirs of water collected during the monsoon season, buffaloes wallowed contentedly in the mud, absent-mindedly swishing the flies with their skimpy tails.

Madras, where we arrived in the early afternoon, was

surprisingly beautiful and spaciously laid-out. It was hard to believe that it was home to over two million people. A long promenade, known as Marine Drive, ran parallel to the sea. I loved the attractive public gardens, lined with architecturally interesting high-rise buildings. Large private bungalows were set back from the street. Poverty seemed less evident.

A whole heap of letters awaited us at the General Post Office. Great news - my parents were already in Ceylon! Sightseeing suddenly lost all attraction and we rushed around madly enquiring about ferries at P&O and the AA.

We spent the night at the Deaf School, which was run by a pair of old spinsters. They were sisters, the elder rather bitter with a forced smile and the younger full of life and laughter. Next day, we returned to the AA to have our only remaining spare tyre repaired. We had had a puncture the previous day on the way into Madras. Such small tubeless tyres were irreplaceable in India at that time. The only solution was to use an oversize inner tube and hope that it would carry us a few hundred miles more.

The office manager was a disagreeable, middle-aged man with puffy features and little desire to assist. However our complaints of the previous evening seemed to have helped and this time he sent us to see the boss, who was of course unavailable. So it was back to where we had started. Eventually, through dogged persistence, we managed to find out something about the ferry and its new place of departure, from Mandapam further south.

I sent a telegram to the AA office in Madura requesting a reservation and another to my mother to let her know our whereabouts and possible date of arrival in Ceylon. It was midday when we finally set off south in the direction of Mahabalipuram. In our haste, we took a wrong turning and were soon hopelessly lost in the back streets. Jane leaned out of the window and asked some young boys on a scooter which way to go.

"Follow us and we'll take you there" they said. Riding ahead, they accompanied us back to the correct junction. Then out of the blue, a cyclist, oblivious to the world around him, cut straight in front of the scooter and sent the boys flying into the ditch. Dusty and bruised they picked themselves up, perhaps a little shaken, but nobody was hurt.

The road meandered along the coast through small palm-thatched hamlets, teeming with colourfully-dressed people and congested with the usual bullock carts, then on across flat, green and palm-treed terrain. All of a sudden, I heard a strange sound. Slowing down to listen, I asked Jane, "Can you hear that noise?"

"It's the rear tyre going flat", she replied as she leant out to look back. One of the tubeless tyres had developed a large air bubble and was almost flat, so we took it off and replaced it with the one we had had repaired.

Mahabalipuram has been a holy place since time immemorial. Five rathas or temples, carved out of solid rock over 2,000 years ago with richly-decorated sculptures dedicated to the glory of Lord Shiva, remained undamaged by time. To my surprise the site had already become over touristified. Guides and small boys ran around pestering Indians and the few foreign tourists alike, vying for custom.

"Follow me, I show you temples!"

"This way, better temple!"

"I am official guide, come with me, I show you all!"

The Shore Temple stood at the water's edge, guarded by a sacred stone bull. Carrying our flip-flops and a lighted lantern, we ventured into the dim interior. Half hidden behind a broken column of black stone, it was just possible to make out the muted form of Lord Shiva lying abandoned among fallen stones.

Hungry, we sat on the breakwater to enjoy the most delicious juicy pineapple I had ever tasted; it had been cut lengthways in four and peeled. Two black-eyed little imps pleadingly hovered around until, in the end, we gave them some and told them to skedaddle. They ran off giggling delightedly, as we waded into the soft sea water to wash the sticky mess from our fingers. In a way, it was comforting to notice that a group of rowdy Indians, picnicking nearby and serenaded by their transistor radio, were as surrounded by inquisitive villagers as we were.

Soon and not unexpectedly, the outsize inner tube developed a puncture; not having another spare tyre, we pumped up the blistered tyre, the one that had been making a noise earlier in the day, and used that. As Honey crawled into Chingleput, the boil grew with every turn of the wheel, until quite suddenly it miraculously disappeared, making it difficult to explain to the mechanic what the trouble had been. An enormous patch of recycled tyre was fitted inside the offending one, while we sat people watching, perched on the raised platform of the village shop which also mended cycles and sold cigarettes.

Villapuram was a much bigger town that we had imagined and it took us quite a while to find St James Church, which was run by Canon Manichan and his elderly wife. They allowed us to sleep on the veranda of their tiny house and use the washroom, which had a tub in the corner and two tins to swill the water. He was a tall man with white hair and a droopy moustache, who stooped and spoke with a croaking voice. To keep out the cold night air he wore a length of white towelling like a turban wrapped around his head.

The night was hot, humid and thick with mosquitoes that bit us unmercifully. Jane thought, judging by the animal groaning sounds from the old lady as she lay on her bed nearby, that she must be very ill. Her nursing skills came to the rescue; codeine to help cure a cold and splitting headache.

The Canon explained next day that the sounds of drums and merrymaking that had woken us at dawn were the Tamils honouring one of their goddesses with early morning dances and music. It didn't matter as we needed to be in Madura in time to go to the AA to check that the ferry booking was in order.

We treated ourselves to lunch at the India-Ceylon Hotel, in a special section reserved for 'LADIES AND FAMILIES'. Hot spicy curry was served on palm leaves rinsed in a plastic bowl of water and eaten with the fingers. Much to my disgust, Jane was too fastidious to do this and insisted on using a spoon. After all, a small basin in the corner was provided for customers to wash their hands before and after eating.

Madura boasted a very fine temple with four *Gopuram* (monumental ornate towers). The richly-carved superstructure was being renovated and painted in gaudy colours. Within the high walls were many shrines to the diverse aspects of the Divinity, and a *Mandapam* (pavilion of a thousand pillars), all different. A giant statue of God supported the roof. The temple market was similar to the one described in the New Testament where Jesus scattered the stalls in anger. Garlands of bright orange flowers were among the many devotional objects on sale for the Hindu pilgrims. Men slept on the temple steps sheltering from the heat of day. Sari-clad women walked gracefully along the narrow dusty streets, bejewelled, rings in their noses and ear-lobes elongated by the heavy earrings. There was so much to see, but we had a ferry to catch.

A few miles beyond Madura, the blistered tyre grew another bubble, this time in the tread. We reduced speed until it too stopped making a noise and returned to normal. Somehow it carried us the remaining 70 miles to the village of Mandapam, where rounding a corner and to our great surprise, we saw the sea stretched away to the distant horizon; dark-hulled boats lay high on the sands. This was the end of the road. We had made it; all the way from the UK to Southern India, in a Mini. We climbed out of the car, hugged each other in delight and ran to dip our toes in the sea.

The booking clerk directed us to the quarantine camp. Judging by the number of abandoned barrack type buildings, it must have housed an army at one time. The next ferry did not leave until two days later, on the Monday, so we rented a bungalow at one rupee per night. It consisted of a tiny garden, a veranda, two bedrooms, an open-air wash room with the usual tap and deep trough, and a kitchen with the possibility of making a wood fire. Two wooden beds, two chairs and a table were provided, but no mattress or bedding. That didn't matter as we had our own equipment and it was much more comfortable than camping. Our neighbours were François, a Swiss citizen, and Dorothy, an Irish girl, both stranded for a week because their cholera vaccinations had expired.

Food was unavailable in the nearby village, so after much merriment watching a hungry François chase a scraggy hen fruitlessly hither and thither, we settled on a large dish of shared spaghetti for supper. François was quite a character. Fascinated by Indian culture, he had studied philosophy at Lausanne University. Disillusioned by the reality of life in the sub-continent, he was now returning home to study medicine instead.

In the cool of dawn, we set off for a long walk along the beach. Miles of golden sands lined the coast, but we soon learned that it was better to admire them from afar. After about half an hour, we couldn't take the stench anymore; the mixture of rotting fish and human excrement was just too much. Toilets didn't exist in the villagers' homes. Men and women alike squatted down under the palm trees, unfazed by others in their vicinity, quietly gazing out to sea while going about their business.

A fresh breeze rippled through the palm fronds which hung low over the village that lined the shore and extending someway inland. A young Indian boy, his long dhoti turned up and tucked in at the waist, was watering his coconut palms with two buckets made entirely from palm leaves and incredibly waterproof. Chickens scampered around pecking in the rusty brown earth. Little children with runny noses, played happily with sticks and stones, their eyes decorated with pesky flies, stared open-mouthed at the two strangers in their midst. Women smiled. Life was hard but unhurried and peaceful.

All vehicles had to be loaded a day early. A train service linked Mandapam with the ferry at end of a long spit of desolate land. The station procedure seemed interminable. Before the Mini could be loaded onto the train numerous forms had to be filled in, in triplicate. While battling with the reams of paperwork, we talked to Louis and his wife Mirena, who had arrived earlier that afternoon on a motorbike, as well as a couple of Singhalese business men who had arrived by car.

We had plenty of time to laugh and exchange views as we waited until Honey was loaded, together with the motorbike. We helped Louis anchor it safely with a length of tow rope given to me in Bombay by Surrendra. After yet more form-filling and checking that the vehicles were going to be safe, we all walked back along the railway track to the camp a mile away. François and Dorothy were waiting for us to go and have supper at the local hotel.

Rice with a thin, hot fish curry ladled out of a giant size cooking pot was served on a palm leaf. This had been splashed with water from a plastic basin by the waiter to ensure it was clean. We ate at trestle tables, sitting on long benches in a vast and crowded barn. The walls were woven palm leaves, allowing the cooling evening breeze to penetrate. Horror of horrors; rats scuttled visibly around the rafters. Cutlery was not provided, so Jane was finally forced to eat with her fingers. The forks she had asked for didn't materialize until after we had finished eating.

Dorothy woke us early the following morning and it wasn't long before the doctor arrived and summoned us to his office. A family of nine small children already sat patiently in a tidy line on the long bench outside his waiting room, neatly dressed, wearing new shoes and accompanied by an elderly bearded gentleman, clad in a dhoti and fez. Stretching out beneath the monsoon shelter was a long queue of men, their chests bare, squatting or standing idly, waiting for the cholera needle.

Vaccination certificates had to be approved prior to sailing. Jane was very smug. Hers was still valid. I had had to add two ones to the Roman five on mine, but fortunately the doctor either didn't notice or couldn't have proved it otherwise. That was a relief. The last thing I wanted was to be stranded on the camp for another week.

We collected our certificates and in a nearby office, our embarkation cards. The lengthy formalities completed, we embarked on the train in cheap class with our newfound friends, to sit squashed together on narrow, hard benches.

"If you come at night" someone told us, "it is best to grab the luggage rack and sleep up there, as you are less likely to be disturbed." I would have been frightened of falling off.

The train steamed slowly out across the narrow sandy

peninsula which was sparsely inhabited by a few fisher folk; a waste land yielding only a poor crop of coconuts and scrub for the animals. It was hot and humid on the train and at the frequent stations everyone jumped out for a breather, to buy lemonade or nibbles.

A causeway, built by the Germans at the turn of the century, linked the peninsula to an island and the port. Through erosion, 150 government buildings had been washed away during the previous five years. It was a lonely life for the officials who worked here and who came only for short periods, leaving their families at home.

Our papers were checked and rechecked. Goodheartedly, we teased the clerks about the incessant queuing and form-filling. By three o'clock Jane and I were starving. She finally managed to buy a few biscuits to fill the void; the only food available. Nobody had warned us.

At long last, a few minutes before sailing, already an hour delayed, the cars were whisked on deck in a dilapidated net, dangling on the end of a rusty looking crane. This time we travelled upper class. No-one queried our right to be there, even though we only had tourist class tickets. The smooth sea crossing passed quickly in conversation with François, Dorothy and the Sinhalese, having supper and filling in more forms, this time for the Sinhalese authorities. Soon we would be in Ceylon.

It was amazing to think that we had arrived in India on the 30th of November and it was now the 15th of January, 1962. We had been travelling since the 5th of September, so this part of the journey had taken just over four months to complete. We no longer knew the exact distance covered as the milometer had ceased to work somewhere in Persia. We had seen and learnt so much. It had been tough on the Mini, but she had made it. Now a new country to explore lay ahead of us and best of all, my parents and brother Mark were somewhere on the Island to meet us.

CHAPTER EIGHT

CEYLON

The ferry docked in Talaimanar that same evening, at 11 pm. Disembarkation and customs formalities were surprisingly quick and efficient and within an hour we had left the pier. François and Dorothy boarded the train for Colombo. The rest of us headed for the local rest house. Almost immediately the motorbike ran dry. We tried to help, but with little success. Somehow they managed to ride some of the way into town. The rest house was full, so we all ended up camping in the grounds under a large, ancient tree.

Excited, we slept little and were under way early, heading due south for Colombo, via the hill country and Kandy and on along increasingly improving paved roads, praying the tyres would last. Everywhere was so green after the aridity of southern India; the villages were cleaner and the towns more substantial. Petrol was cheaper, though food seemed to be more expensive. But before long one of the tubeless tyres went flat and had to be replaced with the spare, which wasn't much stronger but good enough for the remaining miles.

At the General Post Office in Colombo, we collected a pile of letters, including a message from my parents, who were touring the country. Their room at the Mt Lavinia Hotel, some seven miles south of Colombo, was available for our use, so we headed there. It was the favourite haunt of tourists and day trippers from the cruise ships who came to sunbathe and sip cocktails by the pool.

The Mt Lavinia was in need of a thorough spring clean and a fresh coat of paint. It was a relic from the luxurious old days, overrun by innumerable barefoot porters, room boys, waiters and helpers. We took possession of the family's bedroom and settled down to enjoy an evening of great comfort. Here we could lock the door and relax. What a contrast from camping and roughing it. This was high living!

Dinner was served in the dining room with white tablecloths, polished cutlery and large white napkins. Fans whirred overhead. Waiters took our orders. We were dressed in cool cotton frocks, doing our best to look the part. Mum rang and we made arrangements to meet up-country at Polonnaruwa the following evening. It was so good to hear her voice. Excitement rippled through me.

The next morning the sound of waves crashing on the rocks below pulled me out of a deep sleep. Noisy jackdaws perched on the window sill were sharpening their beaks on the bars, awaiting the arrival of early morning tea and pineapple slices, greedily expecting the hard juicy core.

Before leaving, we battled to get help at the local garage. In their opinion the flat tyre was irreparable, but I kept insisting that all we needed was an inner tube. Eventually a kind-hearted Sinhalese came to the rescue and gave us his spare retread, because, he said, it was slightly faulty. It may have been, but the tube was new and in perfect condition.

It was another cloudy, hot and humid day. Even though the Mini was running well, the starter motor had decided to go dead on us that morning. This meant that the car needed a gentle push to get going. We decided not to waste precious time trying to get it fixed and set out for Polonnaruwa.

The road north wound through straggling suburbs bounded by neat little bungalows, past coconut and rubber plantations, then paddy fields and on up into the hills at Kandy. This time, we took a break to walk around the botanical gardens, which were famous for orchids and rich herbaceous borders. A lazy river meandered beneath the trees and clusters of bamboos and bright yellow and green songbirds fluttered from branch to branch. It was refreshingly cool up in the hills. No wonder the English loved to escape the heat of the coast and take their holidays here.

We were no longer the source of curiosity that we had been in India, which was a great relief. The people were happy and smiling. The men were dressed in sarongs, while the women wore saris draped differently to those in India, or long skirts and blouses with puffed sleeves revealing a bare midriff. Young girls had pretty dresses with full skirts to their knees.

Back in the car, we drove on through the jungle. Tall palm trees, laden with coconuts, leaned across the road, almost shutting out the sky. Monkeys leapt from frond to frond, swinging recklessly while hanging on with one skinny arm. Plodding elephants carried stacks of palm leaves in the curl of their trunks; others helped load heavy tree trunks onto lorries. Modern tractors, rather than bullocks, were being used for cultivation in the fields. Amazingly, even Minis were a popular form of transport.

Without any warning, a cyclist wobbled and suddenly shot

straight across the road in front of me. I swerved sharply onto a providential siding, thus avoiding a serious accident, but the cyclist collided with the offside front wing, breaking the useless radio aerial and scratching the paint. To my dismay he landed in a heap with a grazed shoulder, somewhat dazed but unhurt. He picked himself up and we motored on.

My parents and brother were already at the rest house in Polonnaruwa. It overlooked a mosquito ridden tank (the Ceylonese name for a reservoir). It was great to see the family, happy and tanned after the long sea voyage. They had been given the Queen's Suite and as no extra rooms were available, it was turned into a dormitory for the night.

The rest house was high class by our standards, with mattresses on the beds and real bathrooms. However Mark and I slept badly. Not only was it uncomfortably hot and humid, but we were plagued by mosquitoes because of a shortage of protective nets. Jane, as the guest, had been the lucky one.

Just before dinner the police arrived to summon me to the police station for careless driving. The superintendent wanted to test the Mini's brakes. He was a large man, smelling strongly of alcohol, and had great difficulty squeezing himself into the car. We set off across the yard in first gear.

"Stop", he yelled before I had gathered enough speed to change gear. I jammed on the brakes. I had failed my driving test the first time by applying too soft a touch. The new linings, fitted only 1,000 miles previously, worked like a dream.

"I'm... I'm so sorry to have troubled you", he stammered apologetically, as he struggled to extricate himself, "but it was a necessary formality."

A long day of sightseeing lay ahead of us. Polonnaruwa had been the medieval capital of a great civilization that had flourished briefly in the 11th century and subsequently relinquished its riches to the ravages of the jungle. While Jane was buried in a book, Mark and I were duly dispatched to find an official guide at the Archaeological Museum.

As we all walked among the ruins, we learnt that the dynamic King Parakramabahu had erected buildings, drained swamps and planted vast areas of crops, created wildlife sanctuaries and restored existing monuments. He was also responsible for the 2400-hectare tank (reservoir) providing irrigation, so large that it was called the Sea of Pakrama. Within a rectangle of now crumbling city ramparts, he had built a richly-decorated palace that once stood seven storeys high. Some of the impressively thick walls and an amazing drainage system remained. The steps at the entrance were supported by stone dwarfs; a cobra's raised head was a sign of protection and a coconut flower a symbol of welcome. The many other buildings, temples, dagobas, standing and reclining Buddhas were a lasting testimony to the greatness of this thriving Buddhist city. The Audience Hall was embellished with lion portals and a well preserved moonstone doorstep. It was also decorated with carved elephants representing strength, with ducks signifying wealth and horses power; attributes needed to be discarded in order to pay homage to Buddha. The King had even thoughtfully provided a temple to the god of fertility for his Hindu wives, who came from Southern India.

After getting the Mini's starter motor and yet another flat tyre repaired, we cooled off in the invigorating water of the tank. A fisherman glided silently by in his craft, roughly hewn from the trunk of a tree. The setting sun cast a gentle orange glow. Imperceptibly, the outlines faded, the cricket-concert started up and the mosquito war began. It was time to make a quick retreat.

My parents had imported a Mini for their own use during their month-long stay in Ceylon. To avoid the worst heat of the day, we set off at 6 am on the lengthy journey to the east coast. The narrow paved roads were full of potholes and frequent rivers had to be forded.

The three-room Kalkadah Rest house was delightfully homely, only a few paces from the sea and utterly remote. The food was excellent; delicious curries served with tantalizing dishes of shredded coconut, mango chutney, chopped tomato and other goodies to appease the palate. It was so much tastier than the simple meals, made with rice or spaghetti, we cooked on our small gas cooker. This was paradise; the perfect place for a honeymoon.

A carpet of miniature pale blue flowers connected the rest house to the beach. Coconut palms lined the horseshoe shaped bay, sheltering hidden villages of palm-thatched cottages. My father, a stickler for exercise, his bare torso burnt chestnut in sun and wearing a tiny kerchief round his neck to ward off sunstroke, marched us a good three miles along the beach. Flat-bottomed boats lay pulled up on the sloping sands and under the leaning palms, away from the waves crashing lazily on the shore; long slender oars were placed ready for use. Women and their mischievous children filled the villages with colour and life.

To reach Ininyagala, our next destination, we drove on through heavy monsoon rain, slaloming round the potholes, the windscreen wipers working overtime. Here the rest house, in total contrast, was large and built originally to house the Americans who came to Ceylon to construct a dam and hydro scheme. The scenery and surrounding mountains cast deep reflections into the reservoir they had created, enhancing the sheer beauty of the area.

In the course of conversation later that day, I was asked what I had thought of the area. Not realizing that the gentleman asking the question was Indian, I replied, "Oh, I loved it, the variety, the colour and culture. It was so interesting, but extremely overcrowded." That was definitely the wrong reply to give to this gentleman, who immediately launched into a lengthy lecture on trying to do for others as Christianity teaches; that was what the Indian nation was doing in promoting birth control, not only so that families would be smaller and easier to support, but to secure better living conditions and less crowding in the poorer areas. Jane was in her element and was soon deep in earnest conversation with him.

Next day we arrived in Tissa to find the rest house had recently been burnt down. Bang went our visit to the game reserve. Jane and I had so been looking forward to it.

"Well" said my father, who never bothered to book anything in advance, "we'll motor on to Hambantota Rest house." It was an hour's drive further along the busy coastal road but it too was fully booked.

This was another disappointment as the rest house was at one end of Hambantota bay, high on a cliff with a fantastic view. After making enquiries, a local touring agency came to the rescue and sent us to one of their bungalows, even though they were expecting a group to arrive for a week's stay. My father had somehow managed to persuade them to let him have a room for the night. We three youngsters slept on camp beds out on the veranda. The group never turned up, so we stayed two nights.

Once installed, we trooped down through the village for the regulatory, and welcome, evening swim. The beach below the rest house turned out to be a disaster, as the drains ran out into the sea at that point. It was unsanitary and the cleaner open sea, a short walk away, was unsafe for swimming. We did however enjoy jumping over the rolling waves that came crashing in. Our secluded bungalow, half way along the beach in the opposite direction with its almost private swimming and accessible walks, was by far the better bet.

A tall slim, greying Englishmen in his early sixties was also staying in the bungalow. We soon discovered that he had been to school with my Uncle Vincent, my father's older brother. Bronzed and fit, he looked not a day older than forty. He had lived most of his life in Ceylon and now found England far too cold. He was a mine of information for my father, as well as being knowledgeable about the birds and animals in the district.

The attractive Ceylonese man running the bungalow couldn't have been more than thirty years old, though he was already growing a paunch, a sign of prosperity in that part of the world. He joined us on the beach early in the morning, probably the first time he had ever been out swimming before breakfast in his life. We soon discovered that he was actually quite enterprising. He had completed a nine-day walk from Colombo to Anuradhapura - a distance of approximately 130 miles. This impressed us. He was also preoccupied with the perplexity of religion; in a country so full of diverse beliefs – Buddhism, all forms of Christianity, Islam and Hinduism, each one claiming to be the one true path. Jane, always good at questioning people's views on life, embarked on another lively yet inconclusive discussion.

Mum wanted to return to Yala to visit the nature reserve, reputed for its abundant birdlife, elephants, leopards, wild water buffalo, crocodiles and turtles and many other species. She decided to drive us there, but was not very brave when it came to negotiating the deteriorating road. As we ventured deeper into the jungle, it steadily became a rutted, sandy track. It didn't bother us as we were used to adventure and out of the way places. But she just refused to go any further, frightened of being lost and stuck in the dark. Disappointed, we turned back.

Before leaving Hambantota the following morning, we had one final, hazardous swim. The waves came rolling in, higher and stronger than previously, crashing on the beach with a thunderous roar. I found it exhilarating to try and ride the waves, but an undertow made it difficult to claw my way back to safety. In a moment of fear, one caught me unawares, dashed me to the sand in a foaming turmoil, rolling me over, throwing me hither and thither, and filling my eyes with grit, tiny stones attacking my skin, until it dumped me unceremoniously on the beach. It was ghastly. Shaken, I crawled out of harm's way and refused to go in again.

Heading south once more on the busy twisty coastal road, we had frequent glimpses of palm-lined sandy beaches and beautiful bays. Fishing boats were pulled up under the trees and small dwellings with palm-thatched roofs lay hidden in the lee of the land. The villages teemed with barefoot pedestrians; lithe, straight-backed women balanced bundles on their heads and impish boys and pigtailed girls carried stacks of books as they trudged along the verge to school. The men coaxed reluctant donkeys pulling creaking carts laden with goods for market. Overcrowded buses and ancient cars vied for space. All day dark grey thundery clouds, tinged with deep purple, scudded across the sky, casting ominous shadows on the angry green sea, threatening rain which didn't come.

The bustling market town of Welligama was protected from the open sea by a large bay, fringed by golden sands and distinctive red cliffs falling into the distant ocean. Flamboyant tropical bushes draped themselves around a private bungalow, the centrepiece of an exotic island, separated from the shore by a narrow strip of shallow water. We waded across, carrying our sandals, and wandered shamelessly around as if we owned the place. From behind the house a servant appeared, his betel nut stained mouth making him look sinister and more like a pirate. "You are trespassing" he snarled, "Please go." But on coming face to face with my smiling father, who looked incredibly Ceylonese, his dark skin and black hair only faintly tinged with grey and his European family in tow, he changed his mind and proceeded to introduce us to his master; an Irishman who at first barely opened his mouth to speak, had a limp handshake and low hanging stomach, but my father won him over.

"Come," he smiled, "Let me show you around the garden."

My father was thrilled. This was just the place he had always dreamed of owning.

"I would like to buy the island," he suddenly announced. "Would you like to sell it?"

Mum was horrified. Unfazed, the Irishman replied that he had already sold it, quite recently. But he said pointing to the far end of the bay, "Can you see the house on the red cliffs over there?" It was barely visible nestling among the palm trees above the cliffs. "Now that house is for sale."

As an afterthought as if to put him off, he added, "It has a metal tank full of snakes round the back".

Well that didn't worry my father and we went to buy some bananas for lunch before driving the four miles back to the village of Mirissa to find 'Redcliffs'. The Master was out, so we snooped around admiring the view from the promontory while the suspicious servant followed at a discreet distance. Steep steps led down to a private cove completely hidden from the house above. The little beach was just wide enough for a family to sunbathe and the water was clean and inviting. Hot and hungry after the climb back up in the heat of the day, we sat under the trees gratefully enjoying a cooling breeze and eating bananas, observed by a couple of peaceful, cud-chewing cows and the self-effacing servant.

At three in the afternoon we gave up and set off down the steep and rutted gravel drive to the main road, where we met, coming up towards us, the large car of the ex-finance minister of Ceylon. He graciously invited us to tea and explained he had been negotiating to buy the house for over a year, but the eccentric owner consistently said he had had a better offer.

Redcliffs was a long low bungalow with an overhanging roof providing ample shade. The airy sitting room was pleasantly furnished with wicker chairs and a round dinner table. The two large bedrooms, with simple en-suite bathrooms, were reached via a long passage. The kitchen was at the back, a bare room with a primitive brazier for cooking and buckets for the washing-up. As was the custom, the servants sat on the floor.

We sat on the veranda overlooking Welligama Bay, drank strong sweet tea with milk and tasted *juggeries* wrapped in a plantain leaf, a local delicacy that tasted like Demerara sugar. My father was enthusiastic.

"Could we possibly arrange to rent the house for the remaining two weeks of our holiday?" he asked.

Well, the ex-finance minister wasn't sure whether it would be possible. But he would be glad to recommend us and better still, provided the address and phone number of the owner.

Later that evening, we sat on the terrace at the Welligama Rest House, looking out over the sea and watching the sun go down, a great glowing ball of fire that sank slowly, casting a flickering red carpet over the water. A dark sturdy tree silhouetted against the sea and sky caught my attention.

"Look at those large black flowers hanging off that tree!" I commented to Jane who, lost in thought, was quietly sipping a Coca Cola and enjoying the cool of the evening.

"Hmm" she replied, unimpressed.

I was absently wondering what sort of tree it was when the flowers began to unfold, to stretch, to croak and then one by one, they flew gracefully off into the fading sunset and gathering gloom. They were bats.

Within a couple of days everything had somehow been miraculously arranged and we returned to spend an idyllic fortnight at Redcliffs, swimming from the adjacent beaches, basking in the sun undisturbed by curious onlookers, eating delicious hot curries prepared by the cook and served by a slim, elderly but always smiling servant, gliding silently across the lawn on his bare feet with his little tray held high. Best of all, we didn't have to worry about cooking, finding a secure place for the night or battling with the Mini's constant woes. Neither did we feel under-dressed waltzing around the garden in skimpy shorts.

We made many forays out to explore and to walk. Sometimes we accompanied Mum and the cook to do the shopping down in the village or to buy fish in Welligama at the open air market. Though food was plentiful, it was different, and my mother had no idea what to buy. The invasive flies bothered her, along with the dark faces and the lack of products she was familiar with. Britain had not yet become a multi-cultural society and she was completely out of her element.

Welligama was famous for its exquisite lace, made by the local ladies toiling with fine silks for many hours to produce gossamer-fine tablecloths, doilies and lace-edged handkerchiefs. Mum loved these and spent many happy moments choosing from the piles displayed in the dimly-lit shop down by the beach. They would make good presents and were so easy to pack.

Once, Jane and I heard drumming in the surrounding jungle and decided to investigate. After changing into skirts, we ran down to the palm-fringed golden sands of the village beach via some small steps hewn out of the rock. First we came across the cemetery. A patch of soil had recently been turned and covered in fresh flowers. A funeral had taken place earlier in the day. A woman called us over to her garden to meet some of her friends and chatted away in Tamil. We couldn't understand a word.

Further along the beach we turned inland towards the sound of the drums. We crept through the undergrowth, through a plantation of young palm trees and from a safe distance watched a fantastic ancestral dance, similar to that of the African tribesmen. As the men and boys warmed up, they became increasingly wild, gyrating vigorously. The dance culminated with a low bow in the centre of a tightly-closed circle.

Gingerly, we picked our way across a muddy stream to get a closer view. One of the dancers saw us and with a broad grin and large gestures invited us into the garden. He broke a few pieces of string that tied the palm fronds together to create a fence and ushered us in. Everyone in the village knew we were staying at Redcliffs. A couple of chairs were produced and strategically placed so that we could sit and watch the dancing in comfort. They performed their whole repertoire especially for us with great energy, their lithe bodies twisting, turning and seemingly flying through the air. They carried long batons in both hands, which they beat together and against those of their partners to the compelling rhythm of the drums, continuously stamping their feet and moving around in a circle. The drums were made from a hollowed-out palm trunk, across which a skin had been stretched and sewn on with leather thread. Amidst much laughter and cheering, two of the women showed us the way out to the main road, and so back to Redcliffs.

A cool, revitalizing breeze heralded the approach of evening as the sun slowly sank below the horizon. We gathered to sit on the terrace sipping cocktails and to watch the blackbirds coming home to roost in the swaying palms overhead. Soon the small islands and Welligama with its long golden beach, framed by the low hills in the background, faded into the night which comes so rapidly in the tropics. Twinkling lights filled the black space as the fisherman set out for their catch. Just as suddenly the mosquitoes materialized and we beat a hasty retreat indoors.

All too soon we headed back to Colombo in the Minis. It was time for my parents and brother to head back home on board the P&O liner *Arcadia*. An overwhelming sadness filled me as we waved goodbye to the diminishing figures standing high on the upper deck. We stayed to watch the ship sail away, shrinking in size, until it was swallowed up in the darkness. Once again we were on our own. It had been a wonderful holiday, a time to recover and gather strength for the journey ahead. I was so grateful that my mother and father had come so far to check up on us.

"Come on Jane," I said climbing into the car, blinking back a stray tear, "Let's go back to the hotel."

My parents had left me enough money to pay for a week at the Galleface Hotel. It was as spacious and grand as the Mt Lavinia, but not situated directly on the beach. The usual giant fans whirred overhead to keep the rooms cool. Air-conditioners were a thing of the future. Two waiters wheeling in a table, laden with delicious fruits and breads, brought us breakfast in bed and we dined in style sitting at elegantly-laid tables with white starched cloths and lines of cutlery.

We spent most days on the beach or by the pool at the Mt Lavinia, drinking Coke and eating pineapple with some of the officers from the aeroplane which preceded the American Admiral's yacht. It was nothing like the British royal leisure yacht. Painted a naval grey with gun turrets, it sported the usual paraphernalia of war and looked daunting. When it arrived we were treated to a 'royal' tour by the chief cook. We saw the engine rooms, the crew's quarters, the bridge and the kitchens.

During that week we witnessed two Ceylonese weddings. The first one caused great excitement. The chieftain of an important Kandyan family was to be married. 750 guests were invited, the women clad in brilliantly-coloured silk sarees, many embroidered in gold and worn in the traditional manner of Lanka. Each guest greeted the bride's father by joining hands as in prayer and bowing low; lower still if rank demanded it.

The famous Kandyan dancers arrived, prancing along to the rhythmic clash of cymbals and sound of their elongated drums. These hung horizontally, leaving both hands free to tap out the tempo. They wore traditional long, white voluminous skirts trimmed with red and silver. The young bride followed, clothed all in gold, gliding solemnly along like a queen. The groom wore the national costume; his baggy white breeches looked more like a skirt, with swathes of material gathered up between his legs and wound round his waist. He looked imposing and four times his normal size. A dashing four-cornered hat perched on his head.

The ritual was complicated. First the groom slipped the ring onto his bride's finger and with their hands tied together, she circled him three times. Once they were installed demurely on a large ornate throne, two men stood before them chanting prayers and blessings. This was followed by a troupe of Kandyan girls gracefully swaying, leaping and twirling their hands in a ritual dance. To conclude, the bride ceremonially served her groom with tea, modestly pouring it from the pot into a tiny cup and offering it with two hands. Next she knelt and kissed the feet of her own parents and then his parents. Finally, they signed the register and greeted the guests in turn. All this took place on a raised dais.

Wedding sweets, wrapped in silver paper were passed around and some of us lucky peeping toms who were playing paparazzi were given one too.

We were so lucky to later see a complete performance given by the Kandyan dancers for a Bavarian film crew who were also in residence at the Mt Lavinia.

Someone wanted to buy Honey. He offered me a good price, which was very tempting considering the thrashing she had had coming across the deserts. The only difficulty was taking the money legally out of Ceylon because of their strict currency laws. On the other hand she was an essential part of the team and our home and we would have hated to part with her. So our faithful friend, our precious Mini, stayed with us.

The week flew by and it was time to say goodbye to Ceylon and set sail for Australia, the country I had so long dreamt of visiting.

CHAPTER NINE

AUSTRALIA

We sailed out of Colombo on board P&O's SS *Oriana*. It was a fantastic experience to be out on the Indian Ocean with no land in sight, except for a brief sighting of the palm-fringed Cocas Islands on day two. They are so remote that the supply ship only called there every three months. The ship was air-conditioned to such a degree that a heavy sweater was needed below deck to keep warm. We were no longer used to such cool temperatures and were proud to be the darkest Europeans on board after all those weeks in India and Ceylon - and still our tan deepened.

We had booked the cheapest accommodation available, a four-berth cabin which we had to ourselves, complete with wash basin, cupboard and two drawers each – even a radio. We were amazed to find so many amenities on board: two swimming pools, two large games' decks, ping pong, a cinema, library, pleasant bars, a ballroom, nursery and TV room. Over a thousand tourist passengers were travelling out to Australia on the six-week voyage from the UK, so at first it was rare to see the same faces over again. Most were immigrants paying £10 sterling a head. Meals were eaten in an overcrowded dining room in two sittings, served by almost as many waiters as passengers. I wished Mark could have been on board too. He would have loved to be surrounded by so many girls of his own age.

Jane and I felt a little lost to begin with and seemed to have little in common with our co-passengers, who had been on board for several weeks already – that is until we joined a group of rowdy young English, Australians and New Zealanders, spending the days sunbathing, swimming and playing deck tennis and the nights dancing and drinking. It turned out to be quite a hectic week.

No way were we going to miss the dawn arrival in Perth, so we were up early, excited to be arriving in Australia at last. The coast, a slim line on the horizon in the dim morning light, was the land we had travelled so far to see. As the *Oriana* drew closer, we could pick out more and more details and finally the harbour.

Perth was a gracious provincial town and such a contrast to the countries we had recently visited. The residential area consisted of pleasant red brick houses, large gardens and wide tree-lined avenues. The shopping centre was modern and extraordinarily clean, as portrayed in American films. Long sandy beaches stretched out along the coast in either direction from the port as far as the eye could see. What a pity we had so little time to explore. The ship set sail again in the early evening.

By comparison, Melbourne was a disappointment. It was just an ordinary seaside town, similar to those found back home in the English Midlands, except that it was cleaner. What struck us most were the elegant women dressed in smart clothes, court shoes and Ascot hats; the latest Australian couture, one or two seasons behind Europe.

I was so excited when, on the 1st of March 1962, we finally arrived in cosmopolitan Sydney. We marveled at the amazing natural harbour full of little boats, yachts and ferries. Tall buildings sprouted in the city centre and Sydney Harbour Bridge dominated the skyline. Here we were at last.

Once the Mini had been safely offloaded and the formalities completed, we set off to find Jane's cousin, Michael. He lived in one of the overcrowded suburbs, where the houses were so squashed together one almost fell over the neighbour's garden hose when trying to reach the front doorstep. People lived predominantly in houses, and whether large or small, all had gardens and all were different. Very few flats had been constructed – they were apparently only allowed in designated areas. Sydney was a pleasant city to live in with myriad views across the harbour, choc-a-bloc with colourful sailing dinghies at the weekend. An excellent network of roads was well organized to suit the commuter at different times of day.

Envisaging a long stay, I had asked my mother to arrange with Jane's cousin, a nursing sister on the SS *Canberra*, to send out my large blue suitcase, which was already packed ready in my room at home, as well as my skis, sticks and boots. Short of money, we immediately started job hunting, hoping to find work outside Sydney so that we could see more of the country. But it wasn't that easy.

To fill the gap, we went to an agency that specialized in placing temporary staff for short or long periods and the following morning we both started work; Jane in the city in one of those tall smart blocks and myself in a factory in the Eastern industrial suburbs. It turned out to be quite pleasant. The factory and office building were fronted by a lawn the size of a football field, planted with young trees. The offices were modern, with a canteen for the administrative staff. I earned £15 per week, plus holidays and my fare paid from the city centre. Though Jane was a qualified nurse, she had worked as a secretary in Switzerland at Mon Fertile. My qualifications consisted of six European languages and a secretarial training, with eighteen months' teaching experience.

That first morning we used the public transport; a ferry from Mosman where we lived to Circular Quay on the city side of the harbour, just below the bridge, followed by a taxi ride as directed by the agency. Returning home in the evening was more complicated; first a bus, then a train and finally the ferry. Though we both enjoyed the ferry, we found it cheaper in the long run to use the car and pay the one shilling toll on the bridge. It had celebrated 30 years on the 19th of March 1962 and had apparently cost over £10 million to build, with an £8 million debt still outstanding.

I was thrilled to be in Sydney. People in the street were smiling and happy and even though I only had a mundane secretarial job, I enjoyed my new life. I was tired of being a nomad and wanted to settle down, at least for the next six months. Jane on the other hand had numerous relatives in New Zealand and wanted to move on as soon as possible. We decided to compromise and stay in Sydney during the three-week period we had been contracted for, then tour the various places in Australia on our 'to visit' list. I would have to make up my mind whether I wanted to return to Sydney to live and work or go elsewhere in Australia. Jane would travel to New Zealand, just as soon as she had saved up enough cash and rather than tag along visiting her relations which I felt loath to do, I would join her later in the year.

One Sunday, Jane's cousins accompanied us to Katoomba in the Blue Mountains; it was similar to Delphi in Greece, the same red rock formation and wooded valleys, but without the olive trees. It was overcast, so the mountains were not as spectacular as they were reputed to be. I was also horrified to find that the sixty-mile road to Katoomba was a long line of straggling suburbs and at no time did we emerge into the countryside. This was not the Australia of wide open spaces I had imagined. In the evening, an endless stream of cars snaked its way back to Sydney. The traffic was as bad as in England. At least it moved faster.

I finally managed to persuade Jane to settle for a permanent job until we had earned sufficient to pay for the passage on to New Zealand, spending the weekends seeing as much of the surrounding countryside as possible and doing a grand tour before leaving Australia.

The room we rented in a building directly under Sydney Bridge was ideal. It had parking for the Mini and convenient access to the ferry and the city. But our social life was limited to a naval party where everyone got drunk, an evening at the theatre to see 'Oliver' and walks on Manly Beach with the cousins. Television wasn't worth watching except when they showed movies on Saturday evenings. Settling in was difficult.

On the way to work I had yet another flat tyre. Nobody stopped to help. The Australian attitude was: 'You wanted emancipation, you got it mate!' After all the help and consideration we had experienced in India, this came as a total shock.

The thrill of office life in a big city soon started to wane. I felt hemmed in. I was not energetically occupied at work and felt bored spending the day typing figures. My back ached and I complained of eye strain. Substantial unemployment made it difficult to find further temporary work, so in answer to an advertisement in the local paper, we wrote off for a job in a school to work as Sister and Housemistress. If we didn't get a positive reply, we planned to drive south to the Snowy Mountains project, where we had heard there was plenty of money to be made.

Barbara, a drama art student and a sweet girl from my office, invited us to join her folks on a drive north to Gosford and Avoca Beach, and on along the Hawkesbury River to Wiseman's Creek which we crossed by ferry and back to Sydney. The sun was shining and the river was alive with water-skiing enthusiasts weaving in and out. It was a wonderfully relaxed family day-out with lots of laughter; just what was needed to cheer us up, in spite of the dog going berserk, and the fact that the picnic area, alongside a pretty river, turned out to be a swamp with swarms of annoying little flies that nipped. The attractive countryside was covered in scrub, or bush as it is called in Australia. Sadly new houses were springing up all around.

The days slipped by and I earned enough to pay for a complete set of new tyres. We made daily visits to the main post office, but I received no news from home and was beginning to feel quite upset. After work and 'tea' as the Australians refer to their evening meal, Jane and I explored the district on foot; the urban areas, King's Cross and Sydney's amazingly multi-lingual Soho. Exploring on foot was the cheapest form of recreation; otherwise we went to the cinema. We thought of joining the All Nations Club so as to meet some more exciting people, but not only would that have eaten into our meagre savings, a lot of red tape was involved. Life was not easy for two girls alone in foreign country, even if the language was your mother tongue. It was difficult to meet other girls our own age except in the office.

Depression set in, probably because neither of us had made

any friends and the cousins, though extremely kind and thoughtful, were rather dreary and their house uncomfortable.

Determined to do something more interesting, I went for an interview as house-help to look after a child in splints. It would have been better than sitting in an office all day, but the woman was only prepared to pay me £7 per week, instead of the £10 or £11 + keep as advertised, so I turned it down. Afterwards Jane and I drove over to see the famous Bondi Beach. What a let-down. It was so short and surrounded by barrack type houses. No doubt that didn't bother the surfing addicts riding the long high breakers rolling in.

Jane had been out of work all week as the agency had nothing else for her, and she was feeling frustrated and bored. Once the three weeks were up with the company I worked for, I too had a day to wander around town with her, hoping that someone would report sick. For me, at least, this was a paid holiday.

We called in on the Grazier firm again to enquire into station vacancies, that is domestic work on one of the big agricultural properties, and we struck lucky with job offers; both on stations, or so we thought, and by coincidence working for the same family. Jane's Mrs C was the sister-in-law of my Mrs C. Jane was to stay with the family in Sydney for roughly five weeks, by the sea, while mother produced her second child. Her salary as mother's help was £8 per week. Then they would go south to Wagga. Apparently the postal plane called three times a week. Where I was going was more remote, and it only called once a week.

I was delighted, because not only would I be earning £10 per week, I would be going to the 'back of Bourke'. This Australian phrase meant anywhere off the beaten track. Literally, I was going nearly 200 miles due west of that famous town Bourke, at the end of nowhere, to a large sheep station. Several acres per head were needed to feed each animal as the grazing was so sparse. It was 40 miles beyond the settlement of Wahringer, which consisted merely of a pub and a shop. The family employed a governess and a cook. I would do the cleaning. But then that was the only way to see the Outback as a girl. All governess jobs were filled for the year as from January.

I planned to stay for three or four months, as this would give me time to save up enough to continue our journey. Jane seemed quite happy with this idea. We would meet up again and head north to explore Queensland together. Instead of sitting idly in the office with little to do, I wrote home to announce that finally, we had both landed another job.

The Mini had been for repair earlier in the week. The front suspension had collapsed completely and the engine was resting on the sturdy sump guard. It was so lucky it hadn't fallen out in the street, which would have meant a very expensive repair. At least now the car was in good order and ready for the long journey west. It had also given me a chance to enjoy the peace of going to work on the ferry, instead of battling with the traffic over the bridge. It carried six lanes of impatient cars weaving in and out into the city in the morning and six lanes out in the evening. That didn't leave much room for those travelling in the opposite direction.

It is amazing how everything happens at once. The day after we had accepted to work for the families C, a letter arrived in the post in response to our enquiry sent to a junior school for girls in the small town of Mittagong. Jane wanted to write immediately and tell them that it was too late as we had already accepted another post, but I felt it was too good an opportunity to miss, especially as the duties would be right up my street. I would act as matron looking after the girls' dormitories and do some of the shopping and any secretarial work required. Jane, with her nursing qualifications, would be responsible for the girl's health. The remuneration was far better than it would have been in an English boarding school. I was offered £625 + keep per annum and Jane £700 + keep with one month free in August and two at Christmas during Australia's summer break. The long holidays would be ideal for travelling. We planned to stay at least until Christmas or until Easter the following year, as this would more than adequately replenish our dwindling resources and enable us to travel home via the USA.

Jane, as always, wanted to do things correctly. First we went to see her new employer to explain about this alternative offer, as the sisters had already engaged us. If they were not prepared to release us, we would forget about it. They took this turn of events philosophically, as so often people go to the outback and leave after only three weeks because they can't cope with the lonely life.

That same afternoon, after ringing, we drove down to Mittagong for an interview. The Headmistress, who was in another meeting at the time, came out especially to meet us. She warmed to our enthusiasm and showed us around the school. It had only been running for nine years and housed fifty pupils. The buildings were modern and Spartan. We would each have our own small room at opposite ends of the corridor furnished with a bed, wardrobe, desk, bedside table, a lamp and rug, even a heater for the cooler winter nights; a little home from home after all those months of camping.

"Now you can go away and think about it and let me know if you are interested," said the Headmistress.

Jane turned to me and asked "What do you think?"

"Fine," I replied as I turned to towards the Headmistress, "We'd like to accept".

"OK. The new term starts at the beginning of May in six weeks' time".

We had already packed our things and vacated the flat under the bridge, so Jane caught the train back to Sydney to start work with her Mrs C while I drove as far as Orange. The coastal country was covered in gum trees and thinly inhabited. I camped undisturbed in a quiet spot for the night. I had decided to sleep on the back seat, with the doors locked. It felt more secure than sleeping on top of the car and was less effort than putting on the canvas cover and blowing up the Lilo. It wasn't as cramped as I had expected, but it was cold and to my surprise I wasn't a bit nervous out there all alone.

From Orange to Dubbo, I drove through a remote and compelling landscape of rolling hills. Farmsteads nestled in the almost treeless valleys. Further east, the land became flatter and the vegetation meagre. At Nygam, I hit the dirt road and the dust. I took a break in a shady spot to rest awhile and listened to the amazing songbirds, the only sound breaking the silence.

Bourke was a quiet market town, some five hundred miles due east from Sydney. Two hundred miles remained. Australia in the early 1960s had a population of only three million people. This was the land of wide open spaces I had dreamed of. In and around Sydney it had seemed hard to believe. This was quite different, and so exciting.

That morning, I noticed a change of tune in the engine and discovered, on investigation, that a spring in the distributor had broken. After a quick repair at a nearby garage, I called in at Dalgetys, the grazier firm, to check for directions. They asked me to give a young man a lift as he was also going to work on the same station. At least, he would be company on the lonely journey ahead, especially as the next 118 miles were along a deeply corrugated road. Occasionally it deteriorated into shallow sand-drifts where Honey wallowed and the wheels spun, but somehow we managed pull through. Only emus and kangaroos populated the rusty-red sandy plain which stretched as far as the eye could see. A few bedraggled eucalyptus trees broke the monotony.

Were we glad to reach Wanaaring, a settlement of a few buildings and a store which also sold gasoline from a solitary pump! After a top up and making enquiries, we continued along the final 65 miles of narrow track. This sometimes petered out into a stony waste or was lost under deep sand. We passed a couple of isolated homesteads and finally, dusty and weary, we arrived at Budgerigar.

Mrs C met us at the kitchen door and eyed us up and down suspiciously. What were two dusty strangers doing out here?

"What do you want?" She asked grumpily. Apparently she had not expected us until later in the day, hence the poor reception. She invited me in and sent the young man off to the men's quarters.

"You will share a room with the cook" Mrs C told me as we walked across the garden to a new wooden cottage. "There are two bedrooms and a common room which doubles up as a school room." Like the main house it was encircled by a wide verandah. She left me to settle in and I was pleased to see we had a bathroom with a bath and shower and better still, plenty of hot water.

Sharing a bedroom with the cook didn't last long. She smoked in bed, so I opened the windows wide on the windy side to dispel the smoke, which didn't please her. Soon I chose to sleep out on the verandah instead. After all, I was used to the great outdoors.

Dawn, the Governess, was only 21 years old and an ex-trapeze artist who turned out to be good company, so we enjoyed many long walks together; though it did seem ironic that although I had the better education, I was employed as a maid.

I soon learned that my boss was suffering from a duodenal ulcer, so I suggested a fat-free diet. I knew this because my father had the same problem and had followed a very stringent diet. I wasn't sure whether it was my imagination, but she began to look less sour and more cheerful. Even so, she had a foul temper if she chose not to like you.

I was expected to be up at 6.30 every morning, though sometimes I managed to stretch it by another 10 minutes. I had to do all the cleaning and dusting, washing of floors and windows, also set the table for breakfast, morning and afternoon tea, lunch at midday and high-tea at 6pm. It was just as well the nuns had taught us all the household skills when I was at school in Spain. At home, we had enjoyed the privilege of having both a cook and a maid during my formative years. It seemed strange to be living in the kitchen in a reversed role. I felt very definitely out-of-place, but was happy enough. I enjoyed the exercise, which was slimming, and it was a relief that my eyes no longer felt tired, as they did when working in an office. I came to realize that remote properties were great if you owned them, but limiting as an employee. However it was just the opportunity I needed to experience the real Australia with its hardships and challenges.

One of the advantages of doing the chores was that I was not mentally tired in the evenings, nor distracted by cinemas or TV, so I could settle down with my typewriter and write for a couple of hours, sending the articles in instalments home to my mother. Sadly nothing ever came of them.

I loved the wildlife; the galahs (white parrots) that came to drink at the fountain, the wild budgerigars flitting around in the bedraggled eucalyptus trees, as well as numerous songbirds; the kangaroos and emus that inhabited the endlessly flat and seemingly inhospitable plains, competing with the sheep and cattle for what little grass there was.

The weather was perfect, neither too hot nor too cold. But when it rained, the track became impassable and Budgerigar was isolated for days. A small plane flew in on Wednesdays with perishable foodstuffs as well as to deliver and collect the mail. If, however, the runway was too wet, it couldn't land. A truck came at the weekend, also bringing mail and other larger items. These were our only contacts with the outside world, apart from the radio, the great lifeline of the Outback, used for communication with the neighbours and for home schooling, supervised by the governess.

Since leaving Ceylon, I had had no letters from home and when my mother finally wrote in April, it was in a censorious tone. She did not approve of my job as a maid, even though it was temporary.

'What do you think we educated you for?' She asked. 'Certainly not to work as a maid! After your year's holiday, it is time to find a suitable job. I quite understand you are anxious to have something definite to do. It seems rather silly to stay long in Australia, where there is so much unemployment, when there are so many places where people are crying out for girls with your education and qualifications.'

Worse still, she did not seem to understand the achievement of driving a Mini part way around the world. For us it had definitely not been a holiday. It had been a stiff challenge and we had made it. I hoped she would be happier when she received the news about me working in the school.

My employers were obviously well off, owning a fleet of stations in conjunction with two brothers. But frankly I wondered where their ancestors hailed from, judging from their 'grand' manners and the condition of the area surrounding the homestead – dust-covered tins, boxes, broken vehicles and engine parts littered the back yard and the state of the men's quarters was quite revolting. I was glad of our pleasant cottage set apart, where we could retreat after work.

One morning, I spent some time down in the shearing shed watching the speedy progress. Four men stood in line, each one bent over an animal. Conveyor-belt style, sweat oozing copiously out of their pores, they sheared an average of 180 sheep per day with electric shears. Two helpers gathered up the wool and spread it on a table to have the soft stomach fur separated from the rough fleece by another two men. It was subsequently graded and thrown into cubicles, one for each grade. Someone else was employed to bale it into compact sacks. They were paid so much per head sheared and the proceeds divided up at the end of the day. The men were careless in their haste and the animals suffered many cuts.

Meanwhile, the Boss played chess with the shearing team's manager, stopping intermittently to help with the branding and dipping. The terrified animals had to pass through a tunnel fitted with jets set at every angle to ensure that they were thoroughly disinfected against ticks and other parasites.

That first weekend, Dawn and I drove the 65 miles into Wanaaring. Along the short main street we passed the pub, post office-cum-bank and the police station. We found the Country Women's Association, where Dawn enrolled as a member of the 'Younger Set'. They were putting on a dance in the local hall, so we volunteered to help decorate and prepare it for a first class dinner/dance. We blew up the numerous balloons with the Mini's foot pump. That saved a lot of effort. As it was the Association's first attempt, they went all out to make it a success, especially as people came from up to 80 miles away. It was amazing how many turned up and I wondered where they had all come from. After all, we were out in the sticks and our nearest neighbours in Budgerigar were all of 20 miles away.

It wasn't long before one of the shearers attached himself to me, declaring that he wanted a wife, telling me how miserable he was and how I could make him a happy man. Somehow I managed to shake him off and spent an amusing evening with Keith, a kangaroo shooter. He was a bearded Englishman, tall, slim and creative. He loved woodcarving. He promised to take me out on an all-night shoot. That sounded interesting and I envisaged bringing home a 'roo', as they are called in Aussieland. The dancing lasted until four in the morning. We ate supper at midnight, with extra snacks at two-hourly intervals.

Apparently, the Country Women older-set were staid and unfriendly and didn't greet or welcome newcomers. But it seemed a good organization for bringing communities, living in such isolated conditions, together and the younger-set had really given us a good reception.

Dawn and I stopped a couple of miles out of town and slept until dawn in the car. We had to be back at Budgerigar in time for Sunday school at 9.30 am. Dawn looked after the two children, Boy and Jennie, and was responsible for their education with the help of the radio teaching program.

Later in the week, Keith arrived to give a message to one of the station workers and then went to look for me at the cottage. At the time, I was laying the table for lunch and the first I knew of his visit was Mrs C. screaming at the top of her voice, "I won't have young men entertained in the cottage." Keith was promptly dispatched. Poor man, he was only standing on the steps chatting to Dawn.

"There goes my hunting expedition down the drain" I moaned inwardly, exasperated. The atmosphere around the house grew heavier. It was Good Friday, a holiday and the men were having time off. Why shouldn't we too have a bit of fun? We asked the gardener's boy if we could borrow the horse. We had dropped hints galore that we wanted to ride, to no effect. This time he let us ride round the paddock for an hour, while two of the men hung around to make sure we came to no harm. It was brilliant to be in the saddle again. Riding had taken up so much time in my teenage years.

Again that high-pitched scream pierced the air, "You haven't asked for permission to ride that horse. Who allowed you do it?" Mrs C was angry. We knew she would never have given permission and quickly retreated back to the safety of the cottage.

Later that day, she dismissed me for inappropriate conduct, using the incident as a pretext. Dawn was to leave also. The cook was given the option to give in her notice or go home for a month's holiday, which the poor old dear could ill afford. It would have cost her at least £60 because of the vast distances. Next morning three of the men, dissatisfied with the stingy 'tucker' allowance, also gave their notice in. It seemed that there was to be a grand exodus from Budgerigar.

Fortunately I had seen Keith that morning and he had promised to take me 'roo' shooting on Saturday night. He arrived bumping along in his banged-out Land Rover. It was fitted with a spotlight, which he flashed all around in a wide circle. This way he picked up the glinting green eyes of the sheep and foxes, and the distinctive red eyes of the kangaroos in the dark. It took me a while to get used to spotting them. I was allowed to shoot a small buck with his .22, much lighter to handle than the rifles we used back home in Scotland for culling the deer. First I had to get used to seeing through the telescopic lens. I shot it cleanly, but a little low. Fortunately it didn't hole the skin, which he pegged out for me the following afternoon.

Bill, his friend, who worked from an ancient Ford, a beautiful though scruffily-kept veteran car, joined us later. By the light of the full moon, we lit a small fire and boiled the 'billy' (strong tea in a battered pan) and roasted fresh roo meat in the ashes. It tasted scrumptious, even if it was a bit tough. Everything looked alike in the bush country, so to return to the station, we followed the scintillating stars shining forth like beacons without the competition of artificial lights.

Keith's job was to cull the kangaroos, as they propagate fast and eat too much of the sparse vegetation. The men didn't go for a full-scale slaughter that evening so that I wouldn't be disgusted. No wonder Mrs C. thought Keith was disreputable; not only was he tall and extremely thin with a jaunty curled-up moustache, he wore blood-bespattered drainpipe jeans and high-heeled riding boots (the fashion in the outback) and sauntered around in a laid-back manner. It didn't help that he was English. As a parting present he gave me an unpolished opal that he had picked up on his travels.

According to gossip, when the Cs took their holiday, the staff was sacked to save money, so no disgrace. The shearing was over and the place could quietly tick over for a couple of months with minimal supervision. The family was going to Sydney. Grandmother was ill and I heard that Jane would have to stay in Sydney and miss out on the station experience. I was not sorry to leave the chores and the dishes behind, but regretted parting with the 'bush', the wide open spaces and the birds. I had also enjoyed the warm temperatures and knew that it was already getting quite cold in Sydney. Winter was not far away.

It was nearly the end of April when Dawn and I left Budgerigar and headed off down a little used rough track to the roo shooters' camp to collect the skins that had been cured and pegged out to dry in the sun. What a mess! Engine parts and bits of two old Ford cars littered a wide area surrounding the site. The men were using the parts to reconstruct one good one. Keith offered us cups of tea, made from such cloudy water that it looked more like coffee, and then they escorted us back to the main track. It was just as well as we could have got hopelessly lost. As it was, we stuck in the soft sand and had to be towed out. Bill, full of bravado, tried to shoot an eagle for us, but it outwitted him and with ruffled feathers, it managed to dodge the flying bullets.

We left them standing in the hot outback sun, surrounded by swarms of flies, cheerily waving goodbye, until the dust from the Mini's skidding wheels hid them from sight. That night we camped near a billabong on the outskirts of Bourke, taking a dip in the altogether after dark to cool off.

The next day was spent in Trangie on a ranch owned by the parents of a girl who had been at Mon Fertile in Switzerland. Their welcoming hospitality and kindness changed my shattered opinion of Australians. We rode out across the flat dry land with the shepherds to see how the lambing was progressing and in the evening we were taken to party given by another Mon Fertile girl who lived in the same district. It was good to be back on the family side of life and to feel looked after.

Soon after leaving Trangie a large stone shattered Honey's windscreen, giving us a breezy ride all the way back to the

Sydney, where Dawn and I parted company. I wished her well and went to meet up with Jane. She complained bitterly of overwork and was upset that the Cs had not yet left for the country.

"I'm expected to do everything, the washing, the cooking, the cleaning and look after the child" she moaned. Stoically, she was determined to put up with it for another three weeks when we were due to start work at the school, especially as the exchequer needed replenishing for the next leg of our journey.

It was hardly worthwhile looking for another temporary job for only three weeks and once the windscreen was repaired, I decided to go 400 miles south to Wangaratta, where my cousin Gillian and her husband Toni had recently bought a farm. They were new immigrants to Australia, a land of opportunity for young farmers. The long, solitary and monotonous drive took me south through stark, yet attractive country. Although there was little traffic on the road, the police were unexpectedly active and I was caught speeding. I think they were surprised at how nippy my tiny car was. As I only had an English home address to give them, though I promised to register the car in Victoria, I didn't expect they would catch up with me with the fine.

'Give me the Outback any day,' I thought. 'No restrictions and no police!'

The farm nestled comfortably in an unspoilt valley, only ten miles from Wangaratta, five miles off the main road, along a dirt track and across a range of scrub-covered hills. Gillian and Toni were living in a caravan, together with their two young children. Their attractive brick bungalow, unusual in that part of Australia where homesteads were normally built of wood, still needed a fresh coat of paint and furniture.

The thousand-acre property was surrounded by undulating

fields, gentle hills and vineyards. Numerous orange trees provided shade and fruit in the back garden. Hereford cattle grazed in the pastures together with two tiny ponies. There were, however, no sheep because of the recent outbreak of foot-rot.

After spending the first night sleeping in my car, I was allowed to camp in the large airy sitting room as it had started raining for only the third time since the beginning of January. I found it bitterly cold and damp. It was even too cold to sit in the caravan, so we all spent the evenings indoors on the floor, huddled around a blazing fire. It kept on raining and took some getting used to after months of sunshine and high temperatures.

I loved the life on the farm. It reminded me of growing up at home. Every day we had to spread hay to feed the cattle, as the grass was sparse. The previous owners had left a mischievous Friesian cow behind and much to Toni's annoyance, she would nimbly clear the fence to feed from the lower bales of hay in the barn, causing the upper bales to come tumbling down. One morning, quite surprisingly, a bull calf was born; this wasn't supposed to happen until July.

Gillian and I painted the woodwork on the veranda that enclosed the house, weeded the garden and split a great pile of logs ready for the fire. The children went to a school three miles away, on the other side of the valley. It had only twelve pupils. In the evening they loved to ride their ponies round the paddocks.

When the cattle had to be separated and moved from one field to another. Gillian, mounted on her horse Joco, stylishly zigzagged along behind the steers, keeping them in order every time one tried to break away. I had to make sure the gate was shut promptly so that we didn't lose any. On another occasion, I proudly managed to move the cattle on my own, on horseback. Imagine my amazement when Toni's new cattle arrived accompanied by a drover on a bicycle!

The day Toni was away at the cattle market I spent on the tractor cultivating a vast field with the drill, preparing the ground for the winter wheat. I just managed to finish before dark. Clouds of dust flew in all directions, thickly coating me and everything in the neighbourhood. Gillian took-over for an hour to give me a break, while I collected the kids from school. I earned some pocket money for that day's work. I don't think Gillian was very pleased about that. After all she worked hard every day from dawn to dusk.

Weekend entertainment was an outdoor barbecue, held at different venues; a chance for the local farmers to get together. It was our turn and bitterly cold, so we ended up eating in the empty sitting room. I met a young and reputedly excellent farmer who had been to New Zealand. It made a fantastic difference to Australian men to have been abroad. It widened their horizons and they were much more interesting to talk to. All the children loved these occasions and ran wild.

One Sunday we went to church. Four Church-of-England families lived in the valley. All but one turned up. The vicar was responsible for six churches in the district and had to make a terrific effort to keep his parishioners happy. His singing wasn't brilliant, but at least it livened up the service and encouraged the rest of us to join in.

Midway into the second week my cousins, fed up with caravan life, finally moved into the house, still without furniture, making do with mattresses from the caravan, packing boxes and a picnic table. The kids had been covered in spots and we thought they had chicken pox. Then I too began to feel unwell, sick and groggy and noticed a couple of spots on my neck. The little girl, Janet, and I were sent to the doctor. It turned out that we had contracted ringworm from the cat, a very prevalent disease in the area. It manifests as a circle of small spots and can be itchy. It is extremely contagious and can be picked up by touching someone who is infected. Special powders and lotions were prescribed and we were told to pay special attention to hygiene and wash clothes and sheets every day.

"It should clear up in about four weeks" the doctor announced encouragingly as she showed us to the door.

A letter arrived from Jane, who had now moved to the homestead near Cootamundra and was enjoying the attention of the jackaroos (student farmers). She asked me to meet her at Albury station on the Wednesday as her contract was up. She was delighted to be leaving her job as mum's help. The little girl was very spoilt and consequently Jane had found her difficult to cope with.

It was time to say goodbye to my cousins and move on. Jane and I had planned a couple of days in the Snowy range but the weather was terrible, so we called on another family whose daughter was at Mon Fertile while Jane was there. Her father was the local MP. They were charming people who welcomed us formally and treated us with the same deference my parents showed their potential customers in the business world back home, showing us proudly around their five thousand acre property. I thought the Shorthorn cattle looked somewhat undernourished. No wonder, as the reservoir had dried up during the drought, and I was fascinated by the circular spray dip used for mass dipping, fifty head a time; a round container with jets on two levels that ensured a thorough disinfection.

In the early evening of the following day, we arrived at Gib Gate School. Miss Wilson, the Head, greeted us warmly, as did her beautiful young spaniel who talked just like Sugar, my dog at home. I was delighted to have a pleasant room I could call my own with the added bonus of a little heater, especially with the onset of winter. The school didn't have central heating and it was getting cold. Jane's room was at the other end of a drafty corridor. We were expected to spend the evenings segregated in our rooms and on call. Neither of us was very happy about that.

Life at Gib Gate School was not as rosy as we had expected. It was very different from the finishing school in Switzerland, where our responsibilities had been varied: secretarial, teaching, driving and generally keeping a bunch of teenagers in order. This was a junior school and our main duties consisted of an endless round of getting the children up in the morning and putting them to bed at night, keeping track of their clothes and making sure they had remembered to bath, plus entertaining them at weekends with games and supervising prep. I was beginning to think I preferred doing the chores in the Outback, as there was always something interesting happening during the day. We enjoyed a full day off on Thursdays, but sadly we were too far from the snowy mountains to go skiing. My other free day was from 9am to 5pm on Mondays and Jane's was on Wednesdays.

The school doctor discovered that I had caught impetigo and not ringworm, so he put me on a course of antibiotics, which soon cleared up the problem.

Gib Gate celebrated its birthday on June the 2nd. We spent a hectic week preparing for the event, which was attended by the parents who came to a stand-up buffet, followed by a children's fancy dress party and games, the cutting of the cake and obligatory speeches. We had had to get the children dressed in their best for lunch and then apply make-up and help with their fancy dress. During the meal we rushed around brandishing dishes, ensuring that everyone had their fill of food. It wasn't until after 10 o'clock that night that we finally put out the lights, exhausted and more than glad it was over.

On my day off, I had the Mini registered in New South Wales so that she was now legal, sporting smart bright yellow number plates. Both Jane and I were still very restless, but we tried to make the most of our free time and even drove into Sydney one Thursday to go to see *El Cid* at the cinema. It was difficult to meet other people and we began to tire of so much female company.

Miss West, the founder of Gib Gate and two other schools catering for nearly 400 pupils, was an astounding woman. She was 82 years old and still full of vitality. One Sunday morning, she led the school service and then stood for almost an hour chatting in the staff room before returning home.

School service was always held in the Assembly room and from where I stood I could observe the kookaburra in the tree outside the window. A terrestrial kingfisher, native to Australia, this large white bird with blue-grey wings and beak has evolved to eat snakes, lizards, rodents and insects. The kookaburra has a very distinctive laugh. This one must have enjoyed the singing, as it seemed to join in with gusto.

Jane and I decided that it was time to reform the school. The young hooligans we were responsible for were steadily getting out of hand. They were noisy and rude, answered back and simply ignored anything we said. In desperation we pounced on Miss Wilson and told her we were quite ready to walk out unless something was done about it.

"The children just ignore every member of the staff except you" Jane told Miss Wilson. She was a great believer in 'self-expression', which to my mind was all very well if you didn't have to bear the brunt of it. It took almost an hour to convince her that something had to be done. Apparently the last Sister had left because she wasn't prepared to put up with it any more.

Things improved greatly after a lecture on behaviour. The girls were almost polite!

We started to make plans. I was now quite prepared to go home, as I missed my friends and family. I had achieved my goal and made it to Australia. Jane, however, still wanted to go to New Zealand to visit her extensive relatives. In the end we opted for that, as I couldn't let her down, and we discussed returning to the UK via the Panama Canal and the States. All my idealistic illusions about a perfect country with plenty of room had been dispelled; that only existed in the great desert regions of the interior. The term ended on the 22nd August and we secretly planned to leave then and go peanut harvesting.

One Thursday, we drove to Wollongong to have lunch with Jane's friends, the Backlands. It was much warmer at sea level and the sea breezes revitalized us. The Macquarie Pass was one of the finest I'd seen in Australia. The rocky cliffs, a few miles inland and richly covered in trees, formed a natural barrier to the mountains. The road wound precariously down the side with extensive views across the plain and out to sea.

I had finally bought a new aerial for the radio. With the music blaring we felt relaxed and festive driving along, free from petty restrictions for a day. Mrs Backland was a kindly and understanding woman. She even invited us for a return visit. Her son was away in England and she missed him. She could sense that we too felt cut-off and homesick. That day she was dreadfully upset because her son was due to come home soon and had just announced that he was engaged. She had not met his wife-to-be. What would she be like? We did our best to cheer her up.

Jane had been very low all the week, so I thought some male company at the local dance hall would help. The energetic exercise and lively music certainly improved her mood. It was good fun too. Australians enjoyed barn dancing non-stop for half an hour at a time and constantly changing partners, a good way to meet an extraordinary assortment of people.

On our next day-off we drove to the garden city of Canberra, the purpose-built capital of Australia, with grandiose buildings and wide boulevards lined with a large variety of trees. It had once been the tribal home of the Ngunawal and was chosen as a compromise between the two rival cities, Sydney and Melbourne. The word *kamberra* meant reunion in their language. It was and still is the seat of Parliament and the Supreme Court, enjoying the highest median income in Australia. We had hoped to visit several South American Embassies to gather information for further travel but found none. The consulate representatives resided in the more cosmopolitan city of Sydney where they could have more fun.

Jane received a curt note from Miss Wilson, summoning her to be reprimanded for going out every evening. The council had complained.

"The injustice of it!" exclaimed Jane when she told me. "We have only been late once, on our day-off, otherwise we had never been further than the kitchen for a drink in the evening." Still, Miss Wilson had been very offhand lately. Possibly she didn't like people with initiative and suggestions, or had found others more suitable to replace us.

"Maybe it's just as well we are planning to leave", I replied.

We had one full weekend off a term and took advantage to go to Perisher Valley skiing. It was a small ski station with a couple of tow bars and a short chair lift with moderately easy runs, a strange white paradise set amidst blue leaved eucalyptus trees. It was a deliciously warm and sunny day. The snow was perfect unspoilt powder, in spite of a few icy patches developing towards the end of the day. It was pure joy to be on skis again and free from school duties. The people we met were friendly, though mostly immigrants. All had the same complaint: it was difficult to meet young Australians as they tended to live in cliques. An introduction was a must and most married the first boy or girl they met.

After dinner in a nearby motel, Jane retired early to the car to sleep. We couldn't afford the luxury of a room. I stayed sitting alone for a few minutes before being joined by Jim, who was of Danish extraction and a Queenslander by birth; he was a good dancer and lots of fun. His friend Bruce, who had spent most of his life on stations in the outback, had come to 'civilization' in search of some excitement. The live band had everyone on the dance floor throughout the evening. It was bitterly cold back in the car when I finally curled up, around midnight, fully dressed in my ski clothes.

After another full day's skiing, it was sheer willpower and the radio on full blast that kept me awake on the drive back to Gib Gate. Our conversation turned to the future. We had already found out that to travel through South America presented too many difficulties and we had more or less decided to go to New Zealand on the 19th of September, where we would spend a further six months, before booking a passage on the *Oranje* sailing to New York via the Panama Canal on the 6th of January 1963.

As usual I wrote home every week, making the most of the hour I spent supervising the children's letter writing to do so. My letters were full of moans about the school and our constantly-changing plans for the future, with endless questions about what was happening, to which I rarely received any answers. I knew my parents were frantically busy preparing my brother's twenty-first birthday party, as well as expanding their business, but even so this was disappointing. Despite this I was feeling on top of the world after the short weekend break, but Jane was again down in the dumps, mainly because Miss Wilson became very critical whenever we were away for a day. I was all for floating on the tide and ignoring the warning signs, as only six weeks remained until the end of term. They would be hectic anyway. The children were preparing an 'operetta'. The music teacher was giving me piano lessons and in return I was teaching her to type. At least, I had planned to make the most of it.

On a cold, but bright sunny morning, we took a crocodile of girls out for a walk down the road towards the village of Mittagong. They walked two by two in a reasonably orderly fashion, Jane in front and I brought up the rear. All went well until one of the girls started to misbehave and I told her off, telling her to get back in line. Suddenly this minor incident turned into a major confrontation. The girl reported me to Miss Wilson, who summoned us to her office.

"I cannot allow you to reprimand my girls in such a manner" she announced primly.

"Well" I replied indignantly, "If I have no authority, how can I possibly keep the girls in order, when I'm supposed to be responsible for their behaviour and safety?"

"Nevertheless, I can't have these complaints. You will just have to change your attitude." and then almost as an afterthought, she continued, "Or you may leave if you prefer".

I turned to Jane, who was sitting calmly beside me. "Do you want to leave?" I asked her quietly. Her reply came back like a shot. "Yes. Let's leave."

Miss Wilson gave us a week's notice. We were pleased as punch with the outcome, like kids let out to play. Now we could head north to Bundaberg in Queensland, where Jane had another set of cousins. It had all happened so suddenly I could scarcely believe it. No wonder I'd been on top of the world recently and now I knew why. Jane looked a different person. She had got to the stage where she couldn't wait to leave.

We had a great send-off on the Friday morning. All the girls came out to wave goodbye, showering us with gifts. We can't have been so bad after all. One of the staff, Mrs Fury, who had been supportive all along, asked us to take a cake to her daughter at the Armidale University, situated half way between Sydney and Bundaberg in Queensland, and of course we agreed.

It was wonderful to be back on the road again, to be free to discover new places. After a brief call on the cousins in Sydney, we headed north into the bush country with its naked, stark ring-barked trees and vast paddocks. The long yellow grass, parched by the hot sun, made them look like cornfields. The surroundings were unkempt, punctuated by villages; a few wooden huts had been hurriedly put together, litter scattered in every direction. We easily settled into the nomadic way of life, happy not to have to worry about prying eyes as in India.

The border between New South Wales and Queensland was marked by an open gate. The highway immediately deteriorated as we passed on through orchards and vineyards. Gaudy birds, as brilliant in colour as the fish swimming around the coral fields of Hikkaduwa in Ceylon, darted through the trees.

Brisbane, situated on a river of the same name, reminded me of Manchester. It became the State Capital when Queensland was proclaimed a separate colony from New South Wales in 1859. The humid subtropical climate was so much warmer than down south in Sydney. What struck me most was the way people crossed the road from corner to corner, jaywalking, when the traffic lights turned red for the cars.

Honey now needed a 12,000-mile service. One of the rear shockers had completely gone, but no spares were available, so we would have to make do. The front wheels were fitted with new tyrodents (weights) to eliminate wheel wobble. Not that that was dangerous, but I liked to be on the safe side.

It wasn't long before trouble struck again. Half way between Brisbane and Bundaberg, because of metal fatigue, the exhaust broke away from the frame, severing the wire providing power to the petrol pump and bringing the Mini to an abrupt halt. Eventually we found someone to tow the car to a garage in the next town. We arrived stressed out, long after dark. It was not easy to be towed along such roads at speed as the risk of running into the front vehicle was highly probable. It required intense, unbroken concentration.

Bundaberg was a small town where everyone knew everyone else. The women were invariably elegantly dressed, even to walk down the street. Most of the houses were built on stilts. Originally this had been swampy land. Being high above ground came with the added benefit of cooling breezes.

We suddenly found ourselves in a social whirl. Jane's eighty-year-old aunt had numerous cousins, many times removed, living in Bundaberg, all with grown children away in Brisbane. They invited us for morning tea, lunch, cocktails and tea (the evening meal) and whisked us from house to house so everyone could meet 'the girls'. We attended amateur theatricals, a 'bring and buy' and went to the cinema. What a contrast to life at Gib Gate! Even the local radio station interviewed us on air; a nerve-racking experience. Jane spoke extremely well and I was surprised when she later told me how nervous she had been.

One morning Jane's cousin Bice drove us down to the sea, somewhere north of Bundaberg, to discover a fabulous beach and later up the only hill in the district, known as the Hummock. The panorama of sugar cane fields stretched to the coast in one direction and to a lonely foothill on the Great Dividing Range in another.

The sugar cane harvest lasted for six months, from June through December. The remaining six months of the year, the casual labourers, cane cutters and factory hands were out of work. We visited a sugar cane mill and learnt that the cane was crushed several times to release the juices. The residue was used to fuel the furnaces, which created the steam to vaporize the water content, leaving a solid molasses, some of which was boiled until it crystallized. Finally it was cleansed and shipped in bulk from a new purpose-built port. The rest was stored in underground vats and eventually distilled by the Bundaberg Rum Company. Some of the molasses was mixed with yeast and vaporized, then cooled to form pure spirit and used for industrial methylated spirits. The remainder was boiled and caramelized to add colour to the rum.

Back in Brisbane, we again tried to find work. The Town and Country agency that catered for jobs on stations was not yet open, so we joined the queue of hopefuls leaning lazily against the passage walls.

"Good morning Miss Rossman" the old timers chorused when finally she put in an appearance, only to have their hopes dashed immediately and told to come back later. That included us. Though Jane tried hard to convince her that we were genuinely seeking work it was impossible to break through her passive resistance.

In answer to an advert in the newspaper and a phone call, it transpired that jobs were on offer in Blackall in central Queensland, a mere eight hundred miles away! I dithered and asked Jane if she was prepared for such a long drive. Unsure, I rang off only to find the number thereafter permanently engaged. Jane found the advertiser's address in the phone book and off we drove, several miles to the south of the Brisbane.

A friendly grey-haired woman greeted us on arrival. She sat outside on the veranda eating an apple while combing her long, freshly-washed, flowing locks. It seemed unbelievable that this was an employment agency. However after some discussion, she sent us back to the north of the city for a seemingly successful interview. Jane was offered a job as barmaid and myself as waitress.

Unfortunately, I had mentioned that we planned to call at a nearby garage to have the rear shock absorber changed. This was now imperative. The mechanic had just hoisted the Mini on high to do the repair when the phone rang.

"Is one of you Jane?" he asked. "It is for you."

She took the phone. "Hello. Yes that's me. Oh no! You don't mean it!" Her face dropped a mile. "Well if that's the case, thank you for ringing."

She told Jane that the agency had just heard after we left that the vacancies had been filled from the other end. So that was that. Such a shame as it could have been fun, but then the journey would have been along endless, probably corrugated, dirt roads.

"Let's head south," I said, trying to sound cheerful after this latest setback.

The pearl of the Queensland's gold coast was and is Surfer's Paradise, with its long beach stretching for miles, the sand bleached white, merging with the sea and glistening in the evening sunlight. The Pacific rollers had played havoc with the coastline and a sea wall was under construction to stop the erosion. A few houses stood precariously at the very edge of solid earth, ideal for summer holidays.

"It is just like Yarmouth," exclaimed Jane.

Next day we came across another beach, this one unspoilt and hidden away behind some rolling dunes. We walked for miles and found amazing twirly shells and natural sponges. It was quite beautiful.

Just south of Newcastle, a pleasanter version of the sister town in England, a near- hurricane wind struck, apparently travelling at ninety-one miles per hour just to the north. Rain fell in torrents. Branches, twigs and pebbles whirled through the air and not surprisingly the car ground to a halt. This was in spite of a polythene bag protecting the distributor. Maybe it was just as well, because nothing was visible through the windscreen. Fortunately no trees stood in the vicinity. When the storm abated, almost as suddenly as it had arrived, I wondered if Honey had perhaps suffered from the cold. I resourcefully put a sheet of newspaper inside between the engine and the grill and hey presto, she sprang to back to life.

Immediately on arrival in Sydney the following afternoon, Jane rang the agency we had worked for before and landed a temporary job for the next morning. I was on-call and put on the payroll. Jane's cousins, Cherry and Michael, were unwell, so we found digs with the added novelty of a television. It was down by the waterfront, an easy mile's walk into the centre; an interesting place with a mixed bunch of residents including a couple of social workers involved in the repatriation of five thousand refugees, not eligible for ordinary migration, who had to be returned to various European countries. One man came into the lounge and produced a large wad of notes from his jacket. He had just won a thousand pounds at the races and had decided to move into more expensive accommodation down the road. Another walked out owing a week's rent.

My first day's work was with a firm of stockbrokers. They stood in front the Telex all day long in communication with London, Texas and Melbourne. It was difficult to tell the difference between the brokers and the clients. I was given an electric typewriter, quite a novelty, but I barely wrote any letters. The next day wasn't nearly so much fun. I had to type out an eleven-page 'costing' for somebody's death duties.

It was August and midwinter down under. The weather was pretty awful and it rained almost every day, but we both had work most of the time. I enjoyed my stint with Wills, the cigarette people, as I found the reports I had to type interesting, especially a long extract from Frank Clune's book 'The Saga of Sydney', a history of the cigarette industry in Australia. Wills was an enormous concern, the 5th largest in the southern hemisphere. The description of 'the catering services' showed a staggering loss of fourteen thousand pounds the previous year, so they had a blitz and found a lot of theft and underhand goings-on.

Our social life improved. People we had met on our travels passed in and out of town. The Cross, Sydney's equivalent of London's Soho, was a great attraction, with pretty clothes in the shop windows beautifully displayed. The Canberra Lounge at the Rex Hotel had a band featuring Maoris and Kiwis from New Zealand. The drummer was a fantastic showman, twiddling his drumsticks with a flourish and playing behind his back. The songs were infectious and delivered with terrific enthusiasm and personality.

A young Indian, a friend of the mountaineers we had met in Darjeeling, arrived on our doorstep. He was a chief engineer in the Merchant Navy and brought with him some photos that had been promised. He treated us to a real Indian curry for lunch. That was scrummy.

As the last Friday of the month was a day off, we left Sydney after work and headed south to meet up with two of the Gib Gate staff who we had promised to introduce to skiing. Neither of them had ever been to the snow before. We again camped at Wilson's Valley, sleeping in the car. Our friends booked into the motel. I put the skis under the car for the night, and then forgot about them. A few miles down the road next morning, I realized that I had left them behind, did a quick U-turn and raced back. To my great relief they were still there, lying on the ground where I had put them, completely unharmed.

Saturday was glorious, though the snow on the lower slopes was a bit heavy. Having organized lessons for the beginners, I abandoned Jane and headed up on the chair lift to have fun on the steeper slopes. I found her later, ensconced at the bar with a couple of young men and drinking beer. One was Australian, the other a German-speaking Frenchman. They shared our picnic and in exchange bought us 'tea' at the Wilson Valley motel. That night the wind blew so hard I thought Honey might blow away.

It started snowing early on Sunday so I quickly drove up to the resort car park before we needed chains. They weren't very strong and were covered in grease for protection, so I wasn't too keen to use them. The previous day, an on-duty policeman insisted everyone put on chains. We started to do so. Suddenly I changed my mind, much to Jane's amusement and made a quick departure when he wasn't looking. Well the Mini didn't quite make it and we had to put them on anyway. One promptly broke, taking the paint off the wing as the loose end whirled around; that meant tying them up with string.

It continued snowing all morning and blowing a gale. The visibility was hopeless. Disappointed we gave up at midday and started the long journey back to Sydney. Several accidents had already occurred on the ski slopes and it wasn't worth taking the risk.

Twenty boisterous basketball players between the ages of fourteen and eighteen had invaded the normally quiet Sydney hostel and the peace and quiet of a leisurely Sunday breakfast turned into a hurried affair, so as to make room for the second shift. They stayed for a week.

For a change from evenings with the television, I went to one of the local coffee bars, an innovation of European origin. This one had a lively South American band and I danced until closing time at midnight. On another occasion I was taken to the other end of Sydney by a Greek who had been born in Egypt and spoke five languages, including Arabic. I was very impressed. The floor show was incredible. A young Greek boy in his early twenties, dressed in sexy feminine clothes, with exaggerated breasts and long stylish black hair, did an amazing striptease dance. Before signing off he removed his wig and apologized to the men for the deception. It had taken me some time to realize that he was a fake. This was followed by a lively traditional Maori war dance.

This 'land of opportunity' was full of anomalies. The newspapers carried the story of an immigrant lawyer from Yugoslavia who had recently died in Brisbane. His qualifications weren't recognized in Australia and he had had to work as a tram cleaner - a dream of a better life shattered. Many such stories abounded, though this was perhaps the most controversial. It seemed that the tradesmen earned more than the highly-trained and most brilliant men, which was one cause of rampant inflation. So much wasted talent. But then, he must have felt it was worth leaving the difficult conditions in his home country behind to give his children a better start in life.

The weather did a U-turn and started to warm up, and once again I fretted at being shut in an office all day. With the advent of spring, Sydney harbour came alive. It fascinated me, especially in the evening when the Sydney Harbour Bridge was lit-up and the neon signs of the city reflected red, green and yellow on the water. I thought the new uncompleted Opera House was a monstrosity, its burgeoning beauty hidden within mounds of concrete.

Passenger ships galore were arriving: the *Arcadia,* the *Iberia* and the *Oriana,* as well as cargo ships. Ferries, small craft and the sound of sirens added to the early morning commotion. The call back to nomadic life sharpened. It would soon be time to move on.

Our last week was spent running round in circles before work and during the lunch hour getting the Mini dispatched, arranging insurance, tax clearance and collecting tickets. At the same time, we made a definite onward booking on board the SS *Oranje* leaving New Zealand for Acapulco in Mexico on March 22nd 1963.

Jane went to the Insurance office and exploded with exasperation when no one took any notice of her. To her amused delight, the following morning, the company sent a really nice young New Zealander with the proposal forms out to our abode at 8 am. He then drove us into town and returned the papers that evening after work.

The Mini was delivered to the docks midweek, loaded onto the *Karamu,* a cargo ship, and sent ahead to New Zealand. It had been frustratingly difficult to get into the correct lane on the bridge and then drive in circles around miles of side streets. Just when I thought we'd arrived at the docks, a policeman diverted us back to where we'd started. That evening I dreamt of Honey tossing on the reputably rough Tasman Sea, strapped onto the upper deck of a beautiful pea-green boat. The *Karamu* was indeed pea-green.

Jane and I were booked on the *Fairsea*, due to set sail across the Pacific on the 22nd of September. I began to feel excited about moving on and visiting a new country. Jane on the other hand was more pragmatic, always thinking of food. She could eat to her heart's content and still stay slim. It just wasn't fair.

One morning, Jane went out before work to buy some brown paper and string for packing. Somehow she managed to get the shopkeeper to open up half an hour early. In the course of conversation, he discovered that we were world travellers. Impressed, he gave her the paper, one hundred square feet of it, and plenty of thick strong string, with the compliments of the house. This was in exchange for permission to print this item of news in the company's monthly booklet. She was really pleased with the deal.

During those last five weeks I enjoyed working as an agency girl in the Personnel Administration Department of a large company; an interesting experience and to my surprise they actually thanked me for my help, speed and efficiency. We continued to work until the last minute. Cherry and Michael kindly put us up for the last three nights as we had to vacate our rented room.

CHAPTER TEN

NEW ZEALAND

On the 23rd of September 1962, early spring in the southern hemisphere, we set sail for New Zealand on the SS *Fairsea*.

"That was a great send off" I commented to Jane. From the aft deck, we gazed back at Sydney Bridge receding into the distance. One of the finest natural harbours in the world was humming with activity with small craft speeding along and brightly-coloured sails criss-crossing the water, carried on a light breeze.

Michael and Cherry had come to see us off, bringing a bottle of sherry. The Grindleys, who we had met in the hostel, and George, who had been driving me around those last few days in his Aston Martin, turned up too. So we had quite a party in the main lounge until it was time for non-passengers to leave the ship.

Despite the thrill of setting out on a new leg of our journey, tears welled up in my eyes. Australia had been my dream and the reason for undertaking the long car journey in the first place, and just as we finally seemed to be settling in and having fun, we were moving on again and into the unknown. The *Fairsea* steamed towards the setting sun, past the Sydney Heads framing the entrance to the harbour and out into a light swell; The North Head, a promontory of sandstone covering an area of 3.85 square kilometres, was until the 1980 a quarantine station, where new arrivals had to stay to minimize the spread of communicable diseases, such as smallpox and whooping cough.

The famous Hornby Lighthouse, with its distinctive round lantern gallery and vertical red and white stripes, was located on the South Head. New South Wales's third-oldest lighthouse marked the southern entrance to Port Jackson and Sydney Harbour as well as lighting the South Reef, a ledge of submerged rocks.

Jane had to skip supper that first evening and retire to bed feeling sorry for herself, especially as she had been looking forward to a good feast on board, after the monotonous meals at Kirribili. It was during the following morning, interrupting the quiet tedium of the crossing, that the *Fairsea* abruptly lost speed. We wondered what had happened. Soon the Captain announced over the tannoy: "A drifting ketch flying a distress signal has been sighted on the horizon. We are lowering a dinghy and going to the rescue."

Passengers crowded the decks to watch, chattering animatedly. Two Frenchmen, sailing from Sydney to Nouvelle Caledonia, had met with fifty-knot gales over the course of twenty-four days. They had lost their mainsail, engine, rudder and propeller and been adrift for the past eight days. Fortunately they had stores to last them up to four months, and though they appeared unkempt, they had survived their ordeal unscathed.

It was impossible to hoist the ketch on board the *Fairsea* because there was nothing to attach the cables to. In spite of the now deteriorating weather the Captain decided to tow it. But he had a schedule to keep and once we speeded up, it turned turtle and sank. Apparently the insurance wouldn't pay up if it was found adrift.

The following evening, the New Zealand coastline loomed out of the grey mist, reminding me of the Scottish Highlands. We were due to dock at 5.30 am and even though we partied until the early hours, both Jane and I were up to witness our arrival in Auckland, North Island. New Zealand's largest city looked inviting in the brilliant morning sun. It seemed to be a small, leisurely town, sprawling and suburban in style with mostly one-storey houses built on quarter-acre plots.

Customs formalities were minimal and it took no time at all to collect Honey from bond, where she had been impounded until we turned up with the documentation. But ironically, after dealing with the insurance and licensing paperwork, we had to wait all day for our luggage to come ashore as there was a go-slow. To add to irritation ours was the last off! Jane complained that she was still going up and down. It must have been the previous day's storm. In fact it took her four days to recover.

The good weather didn't last and was replaced by damp, grey skies, just like in my memories of the British Isles. The small intimate fields that covered the rolling, rounded hills were a luxuriant green, filled with abundant flowers and birds; truly quiet and peaceful. The roads were narrow and winding with infrequent traffic. I soon found myself nostalgically missing the wide open spaces and dry sunny climate of Australia, but Jane loved it, so much so that I wouldn't have been surprised if she had decided to settle in New Zealand. These were her dream islands.

The first three days were spent on an eight hundred acre

property owned by the Mains, one of Jane's many New Zealand cousins. They were sheep and cattle farmers who also owned more land in a less fertile area, much of it still covered in scrub that apparently made the sheep or cattle sick. But this could be cured by spreading superphosphate and cobalt, the main deficiency in the land, which was being cleared for their second son to eventually take-over.

Mrs Main took us to Rotorua, famous for its thermal springs. Stinking sulphurous steam seeped out of the earth all over the place. The water was boiling hot and mud baths bubbled like a witches' cauldron, reputedly a great cure for rheumatics. Part of the land was home to a Maori settlement, the original settlers of New Zealand and part was white man's territory.

The Maoris had carved images representing episodes of their history and used them as fencing posts and housing decorations. The long hall was especially ornate and used for occasions such as weddings, funerals and meetings of an important nature. As it was open for a wedding between a white girl and a Maori man later that evening, we were able to admire the inside. The Maoris gathered together from miles around to party boisterously and at night they laid their beds out on the floor, side-by-side, and collectively bunked down for the night. They were large, solid people with a strange gait, cheerful and happy, yet unpredictable after drinking too much beer. Their church had exquisitely-carved pews, altar and pulpit. The walls were covered in reed tapestry, each panel different, representing the diverse tribes. The dead were buried in concrete tombs, placed above ground, to protect them from the fiery volcanic heat below; even so they tended to crack.

The Mains also invited us to their holiday cottage or *bach* on Lake Taupo; it was nothing more than a hut lost in the bush among a jumble of others. I could only imagine how pretty it was, as the supposedly spectacular views were masked by the rain. This did not stop us enjoying the comfort of a thermal bath, six of us sitting outdoors, in the altogether, in a square bath, just large enough to swim six strong strokes of the crawl. Though we were warned that we'd experience drowsiness afterwards, I emerged renewed and full of bounce.

On the way back to the farm we stopped by the Steam Works at Wairakei. Steam belched forth from stumpy chimneys, out of the ground and from cracks in the pipes. It was tapped ecologically for electric power and in my imagination, it looked ripe for an almighty explosion.

The next few days were spent 'relation-hopping', mostly farmers, each with a totally different life style. One night we stayed with Anna's mother (she was the Sister working on board the SS Canberra who had brought my luggage out to Sydney), a lively old lady whose home was an old-fashioned cottage, full of knickknacks arranged higgledy piggledy. Her sprightly husband impressed me. At 82, only two years previously, he had flown to the USA to buy a bull. It was difficult to understand him as he'd lost his two front teeth. Their home was also shared by his 87-year-old brother and Graham, a young lad in his twenties, another relation, who managed the remnants of their farm.

Graham took us to see the amazing Waitomo caves, which were renowned for the spectacle of *Arachnocampa luminosa*, commonly known as glow worms and a species found only in New Zealand. They thrive in humidity. Attached to the high, vaulted ceiling by gossamer threads about four inches long, these tiny gnat larvae radiate an unmistakable pinprick of luminescent light from their tails, with which to attract their prey. Mosquitoes are duped into thinking they can see the sky and become ensnared in the gossamer threads.

The caves were hewn out of the soft rock aeons ago by an underground river. Aboard a small boat, we glided past stalagmites and stalactites, silently gazing upwards in wonder at the thousands of tiny lights above. The guide assured us that any sharp noise would cause them to go out as he hauled us along slowly, noiselessly using the conveniently placed overhead wires to do so.

We had lunch with Graham's family. Their pretty homestead was perched high on a knoll with fabulous views - or so he said, because they couldn't be seen through the interminable curtain of rain.

The next day we stayed with yet another set of relatives, an elderly man and his two sons. Their homestead was miles off the beaten track. After a lengthy tour of their eight hundred acre farm, Jane and I borrowed a couple of horses and rode up to the top of the highest hill. Those horses had a will of their own and obviously knew exactly where they were expected to go. We had no option. First we took a round of the sheep, then a path down on the other side of the hill and in a circle back to the farmstead.

Most farmers top-dressed their land by air and had a convenient private airstrip on rough reasonably flat ground, suitable for small aircraft, with a gentle incline for faster take-off and speedier braking. A diesoline spray was also used to set the scrub on fire for clearing, after which grass seed was spread on the ashes.

By this time, I was keen to head south, as I wanted to find a job and start saving for the next leg of the journey. We had now met most of Jane's cousins and experienced something of life on North Island.

The capital, Wellington, was one hundred miles further south, so we had to make an early start to be there in time to catch the ultra-modern drive-on ferry the *Aroana* for the three and half hour crossing to South Island.

Torrential rain greeted our arrival. Unbeknown to us, the strong gusts drove the *Aroana* into the quayside causing some damage; meanwhile we sat in our cars, patiently waiting to disembark, wondering why it took so long.

The steep hills were blanketed in mist and rain and the paddocks bordering the road, in the narrow valley on the way to Blenheim, were flooded with brackish water. It could have been Scotland. At last the sun came out to reveal the enchantment of the coastal road to Canterbury. On one side, the light green gently-sloping hills and on the other, black sandy beaches framed the turquoise sea. It was unbelievably beautiful. White surf sparkled in the sunlight. In the far distance snow-capped peaks reached as high as 8,600 ft. The numerous rivers we crossed were in spate. Brackish water coursed down under narrow, rickety bridges to spill fan-shaped out into the sea.

After a while we turned inland and climbed along steep, narrow winding roads over the hills to the Canterbury plains. The trees were just breaking into leaf, clad in that youthful spring green that barely lasts a week.

In the gathering dusk we found the Butts' home a few miles outside Christchurch. They welcomed us with open arms. Mr Butt was a jovial, rotund man with twinkling blue eyes, who loved to joke and tease. He and Jane hit it off instantly. His wife had a gentle personality. She was tall and thin, her grey hair always neatly dressed, but she tended to be thoroughly scatter-brained. The house could have done with a good spring clean and the farm definitely needed the help of a younger man. The

130 acres of flat land was originally marsh, but had been well drained and carried 800 sheep and lambs as well as a few cows and a field or two of wheat. Hens, ducks and pheasants wandered freely around the yard – a lot of work for an elderly couple.

A few days later, we started job hunting and went for an interview as 'vote counters' for the up-coming local elections in Christchurch. All the counts had to be checked and counter checked and entered into books. It was well paid but only for one long day, from 8.30 am until 10 pm. Not quite what we were looking for, so the following morning we applied to be housemaids at the Hermitage at Mt Cook, reputed to be the best hotel in New Zealand. One of the vacancies had been taken, but even so we decided to drive up there anyway and hope for the best.

For want of something better to do, we set-off over the hills south to Littleton Inlet, along the picturesque coastal road to Diamond Harbour, to visit the 'spirits'. Jane's old Aunt Inez and her husband lived in a double decker house near the Post Office. They were spiritualists. But I didn't really like the atmosphere. It was spooky and a strange presence could be felt lurking about. Inez greeted us kindly and insisted on showing us round.

Presiding over the tiny entrance hall was an enormous portrait of an illustrious ancestor. A large round table and bookshelves made it practically impossible to get in through the front door. The sitting room was stuffed full of furniture; great easy chairs were stacked one behind the other leaving just enough room for a small coffee table in the centre. A fire burned merrily on the hearth. Photographs and amateur paintings decorated the walls.

A narrow staircase led to the tiny upstairs bedroom, equally brimful; a king-size bed and books galore tumbled off chairs and bedside tables, but it did have a spectacular view over the harbour.

A small cross had been cut out and put in one of the pictures to ward off the ghosts, as apparently one resided in the house when they moved in. *Hmm*, I thought, *I don't believe he has moved out!*

Aunt Inez explained, "One day we called in a spiritualist medium and when she entered the bedroom, she fell to the ground complaining of cancer of the bowel." Apparently the previous owner had died of it. This sparked off the local doctor's interest in spiritualism. No wonder I had sensed something unhappy.

Uncle Harry was a tall gentleman, bent with age, charming manners and with the gift of healing hands. He held them up, slightly apart, and explained that he could feel something like a current passing through them.

"While staying on North Island", he went on "I healed someone of a slipped disc." Meanwhile Aunt Inez, worried that she was neglecting us, kept offering more tea and biscuits.

"Atlantis", continued Uncle Harry, "was destroyed because people became too clever. You know, it is rising again at the rate of six feet per annum."

After lunch the following day we took leave of the Butts and travelled due south towards Winchester, along straight deserted roads, to visit another set of Jane's numerous relations, the Pembertons. We arrived just in time for a scrumptious afternoon tea of delicate sandwiches, home-made cakes and biscuits. Jane duly delivered a picture sent from North Island to Uncle Sep (Septimus). He was an active 90-year-old, lucid as a man 40 years younger. He was so disappointed that we wouldn't accept an invitation to stay overnight, but we were eager to reach Mt

Cook National Park as soon as possible. Besides the house was already bursting at the seams, what with four young children and a man from the Agricultural Ministry, sent to test the cows for TB.

Beyond the plains, attractive rolling hills, deep gorges and mature trees were a delight to the eye. Then came harsh, bare foothills and soon we emerged onto a vast plateau, flanked by the snow covered mountains of the Western Coast. The contrast was unexpectedly breath-taking. A few miles further on and over the brow of another hill lay Lake Tekapo, an expanse of deep turquoise water glinting in the setting sun. The sheer beauty of the scenery left a lasting impression.

Tired and hungry, we managed to buy a begrudged sandwich in the nearby hotel before setting up camp near the lake for the night. "We only serve meals to residents" grunted the grumpy man behind the bar as he reluctantly buttered the bread.

The tiny chapel of the Good Shepherd had been built overlooking the lake and snow-capped mountains. Big picture windows framed the view behind the simple altar topped by a wooden cross. It was the night of a full moon. It lit the interior as if it were daylight, casting wondrous shadows. Outside, the night air was clear and bracing and the quiet sound of water lapping on the shore soon lulled us to sleep.

The last sixty miles of the journey were on reasonable gravel roads. But we had only covered fifteen of them when I happened to glance in the rear view mirror. A large black car was speeding towards us. I pulled over to the side. Dust, pebbles and stones flew in his wake as the driver came haring past, and wham! A large one crashed into the windscreen, leaving it in shreds.

"That was just what we needed," I mumbled angrily under

my breath. Snow threatened, with already a few stray flakes, and in spite of wrapping ourselves in jumpers, coats, blankets and the ground sheet, it was impossible to keep warm and dry. The nearest town was Timaru, one hundred and thirty miles away on the east coast. The only option was to keep going.

The Hermitage hotel was a vast rambling complex of buildings, surrounded by magnificent mountain peaks reaching over 9,842 ft/3,000 m; the tallest was Mt Cook at 12,316 ft /3,754 m and permanently covered in snow.

The interview went well and yes, they would employ us both. Room-staff were needed and in those days these positions were mainly filled by temporary workers wanting to earn enough money to continue travelling. We each had a simple carpeted room in the accommodation wing and bathroom facilities were shared. Our uniforms were brown and white striped overalls and the housekeeper, Mrs Jameson, kept her team in order with a rod of iron. The beds had to be meticulously made; nothing was to be left out of place, not a speck of dust escaped her eagle eye and even the bathroom taps had to be gleaming. The wages seemed very low at £8 per week, but we managed to save it all as board and lodging were included. We really appreciated the tips left on the side table or under the pillow, which we used for unavoidable expenses.

Working hours were from 6.30 am to 2.30 pm, with a further hour in the evening to turn down the beds ready for the night. Afternoons were free to explore. It was great to be together with young people again, and such a mad crowd.

To our surprise, after only one day's work, we had a day off, so we lazed in bed before climbing Wakefield, three miles away across the valley. It was approximately 3,280 ft/1,500 m and quite a challenge especially after weeks of sitting long hours in the car and weren't we glad when someone offered us a lift back across the plain at the end of the afternoon.

The climate was typical of the mountains and varied considerably from hot to cold. It was a wonderful day for sunbathing, disturbed only by the frequent passage of light aircraft used to ferry tourists to the Tasman Glacier. Then out of nowhere a DC3 appeared, sneaking up the valley and up over Mt Cook before circling overhead and coming into land. Weather permitting it provided a daily service from Christchurch.

Sitting in the bar later that evening and unbeknown to me, Jane was eyeing a young man on the other side. Later he followed us downstairs to the lounge and suddenly Jane jumped up and disappeared with him into the dance hall.

At 2 am she woke me out of a deep sleep, bubbling over with excitement.

"I'm engaged" she exclaimed. "His name is Bob."

"Really!"

"Well, I don't actually love him," she giggled. "It is all so ridiculous."

"Did you have to wake me up to tell me this?" I replied grumpily and turned over.

Jane vaguely remembered getting into bed and the following morning she found she must have got up sometime during the night to pee in the waste paper basket. In her letter home she told her parents that she had drunk six gins, a beer and a vodka and orange, followed by another beer.

First thing, we delivered morning tea to the guests. Then we had a half-hour break for breakfast before going back on duty to change towels and sheets, make dozens of beds, clean bathrooms, vacuum the passages, wash rags and iron tea-tray cloths. There was also a short morning tea break and a half hour for lunch. Time flew by.

Mrs Jameson disapproved of my long flowing hair, even though it was tied in a ponytail. That was a bit much, but I had to conform, so I wore it plaited thereafter.

Bob was waiting for Jane when she finished work and she vanished in a flash, complaining bitterly, that I was wasting her precious minutes when I knocked playfully on her door.

Just one week after our arrival, during the morning shift while I was working over at Sefton, one of the outside wings of the hotel, I heard a rumble and roaring as if the water heater were about to blow up. The ground started to lurch and shake, like a ship plunging deep into the troughs of an angry sea. I felt dizzy and stood rooted to the ground, hanging onto the basin I was cleaning to steady myself.

Suddenly it dawned on me that this was an earthquake. Once it stopped and I'd recovered my senses sufficiently, I rushed outside with the receptionist, who had been in her room nearby, to watch in awe the avalanches come thundering down Mt Sefton and Mt Cook and sending great clouds of snow up into the clear blue sky. It took time for the shock, shakiness and stiffness in my legs to wear off.

On our next day off we decided to do the eight-mile hike to the Hooker Hut, across swing-bridges and up the side of the moraine leading to Mt Cook. The second bridge had been damaged by the earthquake and was under repair. The rangers were perched precariously on bits of wood removing the cross bars which held it together. Tom was in charge. He laid a plank across the gap to let us pass.

"You'll be all right mate. That's for sure" he drawled encouragingly.

Looking straight ahead and treading warily, it felt literally like walking the plank. Luckily two thick wires ran conveniently overhead, providing something to hang on to.

A little further on a party of hikers was debating whether or not to cross the avalanche debris. Unfazed, we passed them and climbed a little higher to where it was not so wide. We scrambled across without sinking into the snow any deeper than our knees. Then we had to cross another one and continue on up a steep slope of moving stone and earth to reach the path again. Somehow I got stuck and panicked, unable to put one foot forward or back.

"Take it easy. Don't worry." called Jane soothingly, "I'm coming." She had to crawl across to help me back. I was mortified. I couldn't understand what had hit me.

Soon after this we reached the hut, tired, hungry and happy to have arrived. It nestled on a grassy slope overlooking the moraine, Mt Cook towering above. Built of corrugated iron sheets, it was small and serviceable. When, at long last we succeeded in lighting the paraffin stove provided, it burst into flames. Still we managed to make some weak tea to which we added loads of sugar and the dregs of a whisky bottle we found on a shelf. Re-energized, we all trudged back to the Hermitage just before the rain set in.

During the first two months I spent every available opportunity with Don, a tall Kiwi, going on training runs to try and slim down. I thought he was English because of his clipped accent. He was the outside porter, well read and well-built with powerful limbs, taciturn simply because he had difficulty in expressing himself.

It was tough going. We ran straight up and straight down. My legs ended up like jelly and I was so stiff those first few days, but then I always had plenty of energy and needed the exercise. Max often came too; he was English and an overlander. He had a wonderful sense of humour and was a good storyteller, always cheerful, extremely game and incredibly agile in spite of a pronounced limp caused by polio. He danced well and could climb every bit as fast as Don. We really hit it off, until one day he decided to give up girls altogether. Maybe he thought I was too interested in Don.

We climbed Sebastapol, Wakefield, Müller and Sefton. We swam in the cold water of the blue lakes and went on the Kea Point Nature walk in the Hooker Valley. Jane and I especially enjoyed coming down the scree. It was exhilarating to go leaping down a thousand feet of shingle as if skiing, with short sharp turns. It certainly strengthened the ankles and stomach muscles.

One epic trip to Müller was with Max. It took us two and half hours to reach the hut, which was good going. We huddled together to keep warm, the wind howling all night. Despite the cloudy, misty damp weather the following morning, we set off across the snow for the Annette plateau. That was fine, until we arrived at the edge and looked down at the hazardous descent on the snow-covered cliffs below. Neither of us was adept with a rope. That was not for us. The weather closed in and feeling miserable, shivering with cold wet feet, we retreated back to the hut for a cup of steaming hot tea before making our way back to the Hermitage.

Other staff members included Gene, a Dutchman. He had ambitious ideas and a good brain, but lacked the courage to carry them out, fearing the burden of responsibility, from which he had escaped by joining the army and subsequently migrating to New Zealand.

Kevin served the meals in the staff canteen helped by Earl, a

Canadian who nobody liked because he was excessively familiar. He made a beeline for every skirt in sight and then wondered why all the females shunned him. He was far too smooth for my liking.

The girls were mostly office workers before becoming amateur housemaids and they livened up the Saturday night dances.

One Sunday morning when the hotel was already packed for lunch, the Vintage and Veteran Car Club Rally arrived; among the vehicles was a Mercedes with an aero engine, a Ford steam car, Triumphs and motor bikes from 1916. The buffet lunch was provided for the drivers in the staff dining room, which meant we all had to eat outside sitting on the wall in the cold and infrequent sunshine.

Later I saw the rangers rushing out in search of a boy who had fallen off a cliff on the nearby Annette range. They searched through the night, returning at 4 am, but had failed to find him. When he was eventually located the following day, it took four hours to haul him up from where he had fallen. He was alive but battered. This really upset Dixie, the Maori pantry maid; a large woman with big lips and drooping eyes who talked loudly and swore like a trooper, her black frizzy hair always dishevelled. Poor Dixie, she just couldn't stop trembling.

It was early November and had been snowing steadily. Jane and I decided to carry our skis up to the Müller Hut on Mt Kitchnet, a 4,000 ft/1,219 m four hour climb. Full of enthusiasm we set off at 5 am, with four other enthusiasts following a precarious rocky ridge through deep snow, up and down smooth rock faces. Our four companions were roped together. Jane and I trudged behind, passing the skis to each other when it was too difficult to carry them. We eventually had to leave them behind to climb the remaining few hundred feet to the top, as the last ridge was unstable and dangerous. For safety we had to be belayed down on the rope. From there we easily skied down the precipitous slope to the hut, the other four making their way more slowly taking care not to slip on the hard surface.

We arrived back at the Hermitage, exhausted, after seven hours on the go. The snow hadn't really been worth the effort, though I thoroughly enjoyed the jaunt. Jane's face was really burnt from the filtered rays of sun, hiding behind white fluffy clouds. On the last leg, she slipped, and as her skis went flying, she fell awkwardly on the uneven path. Poor girl, she hurt her ankle and had a half-hour hobble back to the hotel.

One Thursday morning at 4.30 am, we set out for Christchurch in pouring rain to have the Mini's windscreen repaired and do some necessary shopping. Even though well wrapped up and not cold, the raindrops stung my eyes, making it hard to see the road. "Just our luck to choose a rainy day," I moaned, peering through the hole in the splintered glass.

In Christchurch we bought some knitting wool and material to make dresses. The staff had the use of a sewing machine and I had been taught how to make my own patterns at school and had always made many of my own clothes. Jane spent many of her idle moments knitting a pretty white cardigan.

I often disappeared to the garage lent to me by one of the rangers to fill in and repaint the scratches in Honey's paintwork as well as polishing and cleaning her while Max was repairing his motor bike. I had not played cars since leaving home.

One Monday morning, Max and I went up the valley on his precarious motorbike and drove out onto the glacier, at the foot of Mt Cook. Quite different to any in Europe, it was a mixture of shale and ice, 1,000 ft/304 m deep at one end and a mere 30 ft at the other. Above us the Hochstetter Icefall came tumbling down the rock face, a jagged curtain of blue ice glinting in the sunlight. In vain we went searching for ice caves, until on the way back we met one of the guides, on a conducted tour, who pointed them out to us. They were very small and apparently grow as the surface ice melts and the water carves the ice away. During the summer months the surface ice can melt at the rate of four to six inches per day. In the far distance we saw a lone chamois trotting down the hill – the New Zealand pioneers introduced them from their natural home in the European Alps – but as soon as he saw us crossing the wide stretch of flat stony ground, he disappeared among the rocks.

Because of the rain, we celebrated Guy Fawkes on November the 6th, a day late, with an enormous bonfire, barbecue and fireworks. I was one of three on cooking enormous quantities of sausages and chops. It seemed strange to be celebrating something so English on the other side of the world.

In one of my weekly letters home, I complained bitterly that I'd never worked so hard in my life. We hadn't had a day off for ten days. That was the week we had an invasion of twenty-one girls on a training course learning to be waitresses, housemaids and pantry workers. What an education! Their manners and language were most picturesque. The boys fled in horror.

A party was held for them the first evening. Dressed in short, tight skirts and sporting beatnik hairdos, they sat in the game's room swigging beer out of the bottle – I'd never seen that before – and stuffing the bottles and cigarettes down their bosoms. The reputed wolves among the boys went round kissing each one in turn. Most of us just stood and stared at the spectacle in amazement.

We often played darts in the evening. I had a wager with Long

John for whoever reached the highest score with six darts. Long John threw 105. I started badly, throwing five low numbers. To everyone's astonishment, including my own, I followed this up by an amazing treble 20. It won me a double gin.

My parents surprised me with a telegram on my birthday. It had been my brother Nigel's 21st the day before and all my friends joined me in singing happy birthday in the bar, which helped, as I felt I was missing out on the festivities on the other side of the world. The week leading up to Christmas was hectic, with parties every night and dancing into the early hours of the morning. To make it more special, a visiting vicar held a church service for all the guests and staff.

The celebrations kicked off with the staff cook's 21st birthday party, paid for by his parents, and for which we decorated the staff lounge. This was followed by a staff party on Christmas Eve and on the 25th the administration staff waited on us at tea (our evening meal). Tablecloths and menus adorned the normally bare tables. To raucous cheers, the assistant manager Barry landed a tray load of vegetables on the floor. He swore it was the fault of Bob, the objectionable carpenter; he had stuck his foot out and tripped him up. Dressed in a smock, Barry was alternately the tea-house slut and impeccable head waitress.

In my free time, I was still walking up the mountains or completing an oil painting of Mt Cook, so I missed the evening of limbo dancing, the craze of the time. Things hadn't livened up by midnight so I went to bed. However Jane enjoyed it. She was quite pickled at the time. Together with three others, she had managed to polish of a bottle of sherry during the afternoon while I was out. She was certainly having fun.

Towards the end of our planned three-month stay, the soul-destroying nature of the work finally got the better of us. Jane and I were used to getting up early and didn't mind that, nor turning down the beds in the evening. It was just doing nothing creative or satisfying during the working day- just an endless round of making beds, cleaning rooms and bathrooms, etc. At the Hermitage we lived in a closed community. Our only contact with the outside world was the radio and old magazines left by the hotel guests. Even though we enjoyed the company, the parties and the amenities of the natural park, it was time for change. We would soon be leaving New Zealand and wanted to make the most of our stay.

"I didn't expect you to leave so soon" exclaimed Mrs Jamieson when we told her, but she gracefully accepted our reasons.

"You fitted in well," she went on, "and I quite expected you to stay until the end of the season. I am especially grateful to you Jane for your nursing assistance. We shall miss you both and wish you well."

On the 5th of January 1963 we bid goodbye to the Hermitage. It was a frustrating start and it seemed we'd never get away. The previous evening Tom, the ranger, had managed to break a spark plug while adjusting a tappet which he could hear knocking - he worried it would give us problems. I rang him after breakfast.

"Have you managed to find a replacement?" I enquired.

"Yes," he replied and I heaved a sigh of relief. "But" he continued "I can't get them to fire on all four." Eventually it transpired that he had muddled the leads up.

I was fond of Tom, a great lover of nature and a good friend. Sadly for me, his future wife was already on board a ship bound for New Zealand. I admired his skills as a carpenter, he had made a traditional cradle that had a place of honour beside his double bed, in anticipation of having a family.

We said goodbye to the girls at morning tea and sat in the sun chatting to whoever was around until the car was ready. Peter, the gardener, gave us half a dozen eggs and some cheese towards our picnic. Max was wandering around as usual, not quite knowing what to do with himself. Fritz helped load the car and after much fuss and sad farewells we made our get-away.

It was a fine sunny day. We drove south between the valleys of the Lindus and Ahurri rivers, surrounded by dramatic tussock-covered mountains and up over the Omarama and Lindis pass. At an altitude of 3,186 ft/ 971 m, this is South Island's highest point on the State network. We had little reason to hurry, so we stopped to swim and cool off in the tempting waters of the fast running Ahurri River.

Clouds appeared on the horizon and on arrival in Queenstown, it was drizzling lightly. Queenstown was then a small-scale tripper's paradise. We peeped through the window of the staff dining room of the largest hotel, and decided that the Hermitage was definitely preferable. Lake Wakatipu beach was littered with paper and other junk left to blow in the wind. The Remarkables weren't nearly as 'remarkable' as on the postcards, nevertheless they were an attractive range running along an arm of land reaching out into the lake. We had been spoilt by the sheer magnificence of Mt Cook National Park.

Just as dusk was gathering, a party of teenagers arrived on the beach, armed with beer and a guitar, ready to party the evening away. They built a large fire and we wandered over to join them. Half the group only wanted to get drunk while the others wanted to sing and enjoy themselves. One of the boys was full of fun and a mine of information.

"When the white man came," he told me, "New Zealand had no animals, only birds, among them the Nautilus. You know, they were thought to be extinct but one was recently discovered in the Fiordland National Park."

I learnt that the lakes were devoid of fish and have since been stocked with rainbow trout from the USA, which do far better in the New Zealand waters, and that the fishing boats at Milford Sound were manned by two and went out for two weeks at a time to catch crayfish, their haul being worth up to £3,000.

Apparently there was still a lot of gold to be mined, but it was only profitable when sold to American tourists.

The scenery was reminiscent of the Scottish Highlands, until we turned off onto a dirt road winding through the trees towards Lake Te Anau. Here the hills were covered in bush, much as on the east coast of Australia. A small settlement had sprung up around the beach. Several batches and one or two shops and restaurants catered to the passing tourists.

On our way around the lake to rejoin the metalled road to Milford Sound, something sharp punctured the right front tyre.

"I knew we shouldn't have taken this short cut" I exclaimed, annoyed. But it didn't take long to change the wheel and in spite of the continual rain, we made good progress until as we were coming round a sharp bend onto a steep descent, the brakes failed. Reacting quickly and worried sick that Honey would soon be out of control, I quickly changed down a gear and pumped the brake pedal like mad, getting almost no response. The remainder of the downhill journey in first gear was hazardous and extremely stressful.

We drove past an impressive cascade of boiling water, tumbling down and down through the now lush tropical forest, and on into the dark, narrow and nerve-racking Homer Tunnel. It was three quarters of a mile long, cut at a steep angle through a wall of rock to emerge into the damp mist of Milford valley.

There is a saying in New Zealand: 'God made Milford Sound and then the Devil came along and added the sand-flies'. How true! That night, the endless rain and sand-flies nearly drove us mad, but after twelve hours of broken but much-needed sleep, we awoke to glorious sunshine. Feathery clouds were curling around the famous Mitre Peak and other steep hills that rise vertically from the sea and the valley. Mitre Peak, at 5,560 ft/1,692 m, just over a mile high, is the highest cliff in the world rising directly out of the sea. Its distinctive shape, like the mitre headwear of Christian bishops, gave it its name.

Milford Sound is an amazingly beautiful fiord, known in Maori as *Piopiotahi*, reaching some ten miles inland from the Tasman Sea. It has one of the world's most humid climates. We were lucky to have been blessed with such a beautiful day. During the two-hour launch trip along the Sound and back, Jane nattered incessantly with a Kiwi overlander she had just met, while I just enjoyed the calm waters, marvellous scenery and waterfalls that came cascading down from high above directly into the sea below.

After a thwarted attempt to build a fire and yet another meal of bread and cheese, we climbed up to the Bowen falls, which tumble vertically 500 ft into the sea. The forest trail was an eternally dank track marked by rails made of wood and rope. We clambered up and down wooden stepladders with only an occasional glimpse of the sky above.

After having the brakes repaired at a local garage, we set out for Christchurch, arriving two days later. Jane was delighted to find her boyfriend, Bob, was in Christchurch at the time. Together with his brother George and girlfriend Rosemary, as well a thin-lipped young man who was too full of himself for my liking, we went out on the town.

Next day we piled into George's car to motor back to the Hermitage. He was a safe driver but I would have been happier if he hadn't been constantly gazing into Lynn's eyes! She wasn't even his girlfriend, just one of the staff returning to work.

Jane had stayed behind in Christchurch with Bob, who had promised to deliver her to her uncle's farm. His wife Nan had died suddenly of a heart attack while we were working at the Hermitage and Jane had valiantly offered to help out.

Lunch was at the Pukaki Inn; a pleasant bar panelled with bark and beer barrels used as seats. Old prints of the McKenzie country adorned the walls. The waitress embarrassed me by yelling our order out to the kitchen for all the other diners to hear.

It was wonderful to see the Mt Cook range rising from the lake and to see the snow-capped peaks, as well as the hills we had so often climbed, and to round the bend into the Hooker Valley and once again see the Hermitage nestling against the hillside. It was like coming home. Several members of the off-duty staff welcomed us back and we immediately began to plan a trip up Footstool. At 6 pm that evening six of us set out: Warwick, David, Peter, Jim and Max. I was the only female.

The two-hour walk refreshed me. The moon rose from behind the Ball Pass, on the lower ridge of Mt. Cook, and we continued climbing the final ascent by moonlight. While debating where to sleep, the wind got up, so we retreated into a bivouac, just large enough for our six bodies lying side by side on the earthen floor, which we covered with a ground sheet. We had very little fuel for the primus, so we kept it for the morning tea, and ate just a little fruit before falling asleep.

No-one heard the alarm, but as thick fog obliterated everything, it didn't really matter. However we got under way at 6 am, and started trudging upwards through the snow. I climbed with Peter, Max and Jim for about an hour until we reached a shrund, a crevasse that forms on the upper portion of a glacier where a moving section falls away from the headwall. The others followed close behind. It was now snowing heavily and we were disinclined to continue on.

While fooling around, Warwick managed to fall into the shrund. Both Peter and David made valiant attempts to pull him out. In the end he had to cut steps in the compacted snow and climb out. Hungry, we glissaded back to the bivouac to tuck into as much food as we could tackle. Max boiled the kettle and made a hot jelly drink, which is delicious when not too concentrated. He also made a totally undrinkable billy of tea. Typically British, he had added far too many tea leaves.

At last, the sun came out and we returned to the valley.

Next day, we made a hurried decision to go to the Blue Lakes for a swim and a climb. Warwick, David and Peter planned to climb Rotten Tommy, otherwise known as Blackburn. Jim and I decided to go a different way up the Nun's Veil. The three boys never managed to get there as they were crossing the River Tasman by a different route.

Jim and I traversed the moraine and followed the Murchison downstream until we were able to cross it. The fast-flowing, thigh deep waters bowled me over. Fortunately we were roped together and after regaining my balance I reached the shore without too much trouble. Hurriedly we changed into dry clothes and made tracks to the hut at the foot of Rotten Tommy, now the nearest place to go.

It was when we inadvertently frightened a Paradise duck and her young that we realized the others hadn't made it across the river and had returned to the Hermitage. We ate a meagre supper and snuggled down on the hard bench under the only available blanket.

We set the alarm for 4.30 am and were glad to have done so, as the temperatures soared during the day and the trek took far longer than it should have - fifteen hours in total. We set off up the grassy slope, followed by a shingle slide and onto the ridge, roped together as I had little experience of rock climbing. It seemed very precarious to me, but stepping gingerly, avoiding as much as possible to glance downhill, I managed and didn't fall off into the abyss below. Slowly I gained confidence and improved, though at times I thought we'd never make it. My mouth was so dry and throat parched with thirst. We tried to melt some snow in the concentrated lemon juice Peter had prepared for us the previous day. It was better than nothing.

Stunning views surrounded us. We could see to the far end of the Tasman, Sefton and Sealey beyond, also to Pukaki and the range of mountains that extends to Tekapo. It was well worth all the pain of getting there.

The 1,000 ft/304 m shingle slide down was sheer exhilaration as we leapt from one mountain-boot clad foot to another, digging our heels in deeply to maintain balance. It is quite a technique, but once mastered was such fun. By the time we got back to the hut, it was already 9 pm. We built a small fire and drank some hot chocolate made with the powdered milk we found on a shelf. We had no food left. It didn't matter very much as we were too exhausted to eat or go any further. We slept soundly until 8 am.

It was a relief to ford the Murchison without mishap, though we were wet to the waist, but the Tasman was a different matter. We chose a part divided into four and by holding hands and more or less supporting one another to avoid falling over the hazardous boulders that can trip you up unexpectedly, we crossed the first two branches without much difficulty. The water was icy cold. Unconcerned, a duck went floating serenely past bobbing up and down on the double-backed waves.

Secured by rope, I set out first into the fast-flowing water, scared to death that the river would be too deep, which it was. I found myself running downstream trying to stay upright, being swept continuously off my feet, fighting to get across. The rope tightened around my waist and at last I found a foothold at the top of the rapids, some six feet from the opposite bank. I paused to get my breath and glanced back to see Jim standing with his hands out – the rope had bust. I froze, not daring to move.

Jim was yelling at me anxiously, "Get on with it. Move. Hurry, get out."

It took me several minutes to recover before I found enough courage to make headway. Swimming frantically, I finally reached the shore after having, once again, been knocked off my feet. Jim repeatedly tried throwing the rope across to me and when that failed, after long deliberation to pluck up courage, he set out to cross the river. He was taller and stronger than me and had no problem in reaching the other side. He dumped his pack on the ground and laid his head on my lap, shattered, until he had recovered. Then he grumbled at me for taking a photo, distracting him, but I just had to have something to remind me of that epic crossing.

To celebrate, we polished off a few remaining squares of chocolate that Jim had hidden away and sat on the roadside to await the Ball Hut bus or a lift. We were back at the Hermitage in time for a much-needed lunch.

Lynn, Jim's girlfriend, was in a strange mood. I wondered if she was annoyed with me for having been climbing with Jim. But I couldn't understand why she should, because he was younger than me and more like a brother. I had to repair the trousers I'd borrowed from him and was grateful for bunking down in their hut for the night.

I woke feeling sad. It was time to leave and as I couldn't manage to cadge a lift back to Christchurch, I took the bus. Peter, Jim and Lynn came to see me off. The bus stopped briefly at Pukaki and longer for lunch at Tekapo, where I sat on the steps of the Church of the Good Shepherd with an orange, totally absorbed by the sheer beauty of the place.

On top of the pass, we stopped again to read the plaque commemorating Robert O'Hara Burke, exhorting man to plant trees for future generations. Burke was an Irish soldier who had emigrated to Australia, where he became a policeman. Dissatisfied with the humdrum life, he became an explorer and he and William John Wills became the first white men to travel from Melbourne to the Gulf of Carpentaria, some 2,000 miles to the north.

Back in Christchurch, I walked from the bus depot to Usk Street to pick up the Mini and was back at the Butt's farm at Kaiapoi by 6 pm, where Jane was staying to help out. The next few days were spent slashing thistles, being generally useful and giving Honey a spring-clean.

My parents had written to say they were returning to Ceylon at the end of January to spend a month at Redcliffs, the house they had bought the previous year. To my great joy they sent me an air-ticket as a Christmas present and an invitation to join them. Travel by air was still in its infancy and a great adventure. I felt bad leaving Jane behind looking after her uncle, but I couldn't have missed the opportunity to return to that exotic island.

Mr Butt drove me to the airport and saw me off on the first leg of my flight to Colombo. South Island looked wonderful from the sky; the heavily-cultivated Canterbury plain with its fruit orchards, golden stretches of freshly-cut corn, ploughed fields and paddocks. The farms were neatly spaced with interconnecting roads. In contrast the hill country was bare of vegetation and topped by shingle slides similar to the Mt Cook region, though not so high. Away to the south I could just discern the snowy peaks of the Kiwi Alps. It clouded over as we headed north across the Cook Strait, dividing North and South Island, and flew on along the coast to Auckland.

The second leg of the journey in a long-haul TEAL jet was most exciting; it was so much larger than the propeller-driven planes I'd flown on before and so luxurious with a brilliant onboard service. As the plane soared into the sky above the scudding clouds, I gazed down at the vast expanse of the Tasman Sea below and remembered the excitement when the SS *Fairsea* hove to and rescued the two men, adrift on a ketch. It all seemed so long ago.

A blast of heat hit us as we emerged from the plane. What a contrast! George was there to meet me. It was good to see him again and to exchange news. After a walk on the crowded beach, he took me for a drive around the town. The Sydney streets, littered with old newspapers and sweet bags, struck me as being much dirtier than I remembered. Coming from the Indian continent the year before, I had not noticed it, but after the pristine cleanliness of New Zealand, I was shocked.

BOAC's Comet took off later that evening for Darwin. The de Havilland DH 106 Comet was the first production commercial jetliner and though it suffered many teething problems, by the 1960s the Comet 4 version was being used worldwide. It could carry up to eighty passengers, four abreast in comfortable, spacious seats with plenty of leg room. In those days travelling economy didn't mean you were stuffed in like sardines. It was an enjoyable experience.

The lights of Sydney scintillated in the gathering dusk as we rose higher and headed north over the harbour. I could pick out the bays, the bridge and all the main streets lit by brighter, whiter lights. After dinner served on a tray and a couple of hours' sleep, we were woken with a steaming cup of coffee. The aircraft was nearly empty so I had been able to stretch out over three seats.

A mechanical fault then delayed the flight for five hours. I was asked to share a room with a couple of friendly Ceylonese girls at the hotel in Darwin where the airline company put us up. They were on their way home. One was roughly 30 years old, a nationalized Australian, married to a Ceylonese doctor. They lived near Adelaide and after the first five years had become enamoured of the country. Life was definitely easier than in their native Ceylon. The other girl was a Tamil from Jaffna in the north, a schoolteacher and very forthright. She had fallen in love with life in Melbourne, where she had been studying for the past six months on a scholarship.

"Life is very difficult in Ceylon for political reasons" she explained. "Buddhism has become the national religion and only if you are a Buddhist have you any chance of gaining scholarships. The trouble is that I'm a Christian."

"No money can be taken out of the country," added the other girl, "so it is practically impossible for those wishing to emigrate."

Returning to the airport just as dawn was breaking, we were able to get some impression of this still rural city. Bungalows were perched on stilts with cars parked underneath, each dwelling set in an acre of garden. The ultra-modern and colourful churches stood out against the bright red soil and the trees. In the high humidity they drooped low over the numerous waterways.

I thrilled to the thrust of the aircraft on take-off as we rose almost vertically into the sky to fly at 520 mph (840 km h) at an altitude of 42,000 ft /13,000m. What a wonderful way to travel, like a giant bird in the sky. So much quicker than in a Mini! But even aircraft have their problems....

Because of further mechanical delays both in Singapore and Kuala Lumpur we finally landed five hours late in hot and humid Colombo. Nobody was there to meet me and I knew my parents didn't have a telephone. Luckily a member of the BOAC staff, concerned that I was travelling alone, delivered me directly to the train station to catch the afternoon express to Galle and subsequently on to Welligama.

Ceylonese trains had three classes – deluxe, comfortable and hard seats. They were bouncy and purposefully draughty – a perfect, natural air-conditioning. Sitting opposite me, a well-spoken Tamil from the north befriended me, brought me a cup of tea and organized an extension to my ticket for the last leg of my journey. He even found someone to carry my luggage onto the quay and summoned the stationmaster to find me a car with a trustworthy driver to deliver me to Redcliffs.

The month together with my parents and brother, Nigel, was over in a flash and all too soon I was back in New Zealand. Back to reality and back to work on the Butts' farm. It was getting colder, with some morning frost. I really missed the hot humid temperatures and shivered in spite of a thick jacket as I gazed longingly at the distant Alps, coated with recent snow glistening against a clear blue sky. In New Zealand it was already well into autumn and winter skiing was not far away.

It was the busy fruit-picking season and the trees were laden with pears and the last of the peaches. That meant an early morning start. Strong winds were responsible for the windfalls, known as wiggins. This meant losses for the farmer. They had to be gathered up first. It was also important to pick the peaches that hung over the road in danger of falling. Jane didn't like the high ladder so she picked from ground level while I spent many hours climbing up and down, up and down. With only two short tea breaks and half an hour for lunch, it was a long, strenuous day. The peaches, covered in a natural white protective coat, had to be handled delicately and placed without bruising in the cases. Then they had to be sprayed, stacked and covered in straw. The cases of pears weighed up to 40 lbs. No wonder we were tired after being on our feet all day. But we needed the money to pay for our onward journey.

Come evening, it was such a relief to put my feet up, relax and get on with my sewing as I had a suitcase full of oddments needing repairs and alterations.

For a change of scene we went to a service in Christchurch Cathedral and enjoyed watching the local girls flirting with the American sailors, on leave from a long spell of duty in Antarctica. It was customary for the locals to attend church and then go to the pictures but as the film didn't appeal, we went back to the farm. The previous evening the vicar and his wife, from Uncle John's parish in Amberley, had come on a goodwill visit. We chatted over tea and cakes until well after 10 pm. The conversation covered a wide range of subjects, so stimulating after nearly three weeks of sewing in the evenings and picking fruit all day.

Jane's boyfriend came over at the weekend to take her to the cricket. I felt their relationship didn't seem to be as happy as before. She tended to be a bit short-tempered and had been fighting with her Uncle John, probably because of the dull life she had been leading. He, meanwhile, was coping with grief and hadn't introduced her to anyone her own age. It had been all work and no play, followed by long dreary evenings. Such a contrast to the hectic social life at the Hermitage!

She had cheered up, since my return, with the realization that we would soon be moving on. Fortunately one of Uncle John's daughters, whose husband would be away in the UK for five months, had arranged to take over when we left. It was time to look ahead and move on.

CHAPTER ELEVEN

PACIFIC CROSSING

I was sorry to be leaving New Zealand with its emphasis on culture, its pleasant sleepy atmosphere, memories of the outdoor life at the Hermitage and the range of hills dividing east from west. They always looked so beautiful, especially on my way to work in the morning. However, should I have chosen to emigrate then I would have opted for Australia, for the opportunity and prosperity that was so evident, especially on arrival fresh from the decomposition of Ceylon.

We were due to sail on the 27th of March. The Mini had had to have a couple of new rings and valves fitted. The mechanic seemed to have taken great care, so hopefully all would be well for a while. To smarten things up, I gave the roof rack a coat of aluminium paint.

Stuffed with packages and suitcases, Honey was loaded onto the Lyttleton ferry. This was to avoid the long drive north to Wellington. Similar to a Cross Channel steamer, with numerous two-berth cabins, it carried eighty cars and took twelve hours, arriving early the following morning.

A distinctly arty couple, more of Jane's relations, welcomed us to their old farmhouse high on a hill over-looking the Cook Strait. They were endeavouring to modernize it but what a mess! The bathroom had no door and the entrance hall was used as a workshop. Still they were highly intellectual and interesting and took the trouble to show us around Wellington. What impressed me most, in their house, was an antique HMV gramophone, its horn hewn out of wood and it still worked.

Next day we boarded the *MS Oranje*, a Dutch ship, designed like a galleon with a third propeller for greater speed. She may have looked beautiful, but she rolled and vibrated horribly. Stabilizers were still a dream somewhere out in the future. In spite of this she was comfortable and everyone on board was so friendly, which helped to make the voyage across the Pacific one of the best holidays I'd ever had. The captain and crew were all Dutch, the cabin stewards and waiters Chinese.

It was a relief to be on board with nothing to do except relax – that was after Honey was safely stashed on the foredeck and we had finished filling in forms galore. This was followed by boat drill, rushing to get a book from the library before it closed, entering for the deck quoits' competition and excitedly running up and down deck umpteen times. This would be our home for the next six weeks and we wanted to know where everything was located.

We shared a spacious four-berth cabin with an elderly lady going to the UK for the first time. Poor old girl, she struggled to climb up and down the steep narrow companionway to the lower deck, and must have found our erratic timetable difficult to put up with, but she never complained. We had two portholes and two washbasins, as well as four cupboards, a table and a chair. This was much more comfortable than camping.

Life onboard was brilliant, though some people complained there wasn't enough to do, but we joined in all the activities and danced until the early hours of the morning. The food was good, though repetitive, especially the sweets, which only varied in name. We shared our table with three young Englishmen, wearing Castro-type beards, on the way to the States for a working holiday; a rough and ready but kindly Dutch couple going home; Ann, an English girl, returning from Malaya where she had been working for the British High Commission and who subsequently became a very good friend; and lastly Bruno, a Swiss citizen, jovial, rotund, lazy and fond of drink. Ours was a lively table!

The sea was reasonably calm for the first few days and we spent many a happy hour lounging in the sun beside the deep swimming pool. I attended keep fit classes most mornings. They were strenuous, especially the abdominals and I constantly complained of feeling stiff. Once we skipped flat out for a very long minute! Well that was an achievement. Even in a light Pacific swell, the deck came up to meet you abruptly or fell away leaving us floundering in mid-air, much to the amusement of our trainer.

"Come on, you can do it" he called out loudly, to be heard above the sound of wind and waves, as we chucked heavy balls about or endeavoured to slim our rotating hips. It was all about laughter and movement. In the afternoon we played ping pong, and competition deck quoits in which Jane came second even though she'd never played before.

Our little group consisted of Anne, Jane and I, Bruno and his friend Ernst. At first Bruno had his eye on Anne, then on me, but that proved depressing. He was jealous of my flirting with the other young men, so that didn't last. Jane eventually started going around with Dieter, a tall German and we became a multi-national gang – including Fred and Ro, Bruno and Betty, Herman and Anne, Werner and myself.

After sundown, entertainment was provided such as films, dancing and theme evenings. The costumes were spectacular on the Hawaiian evening; an elderly couple won first prize. She was so excited she jumped up and down hugging her husband like a teenager, squealing with delight. On another occasion for the Latin American Night, Jane and I dressed up as a bull. I was the rear end and sadly unable to see what was going on. Bill, an effeminate young man, was our slim, dark Matador and we stole the show by putting on a *corrida*, complete with red cape. The trophy was a much appreciated bottle of Italian *Spumanti*.

A military-style band kitted out in the national uniform - navy blue jackets and knee-length white skirts with neat zigzag hems - welcomed us to Suva, on the island of Fiji. Palm trees created a perfect natural backdrop. It was magical. Everyone was up on deck in anticipation, and amazingly, no formalities were required and we were free to go ashore almost immediately.

Jane and I wandered around the diminutive market and purchased a length of colourful cotton material each and a few souvenirs. The women were dark-skinned and buxom, their beaming smiles showing off beautiful even teeth, each face framed by a mop of tight and curly black hair.

"Why don't we catch the bus to Nausauri? It's only twelve miles inland and we have plenty of time" I suggested. "Come on let's go. It should be fun."

The rickety old bus was tightly packed with women and children going home with large baskets laden with fruit and vegetables, bought in the market. Some carried chickens in cages. We took it in turns to sit on the only available worn-leather seat.

It was a bumpy ride as the bus lurched along the uneven road, stopping periodically to let people off. We saw rice being harvested in the neatly-kept paddy fields and learned that a free train runs inland twice a week during the cane cutting season.

In the village of Nausauri, we bumped into some of our friends who had been sampling the national drink, kava. "It is non-alcoholic," or so Bruno said, "and it's made from the root of the pepper plant which after aging for three years is ground into a white powder and mixed with water."

The men were sitting cross-legged in groups at low tables under a canopy of palms, with a large enamel bowl, full to the brim, between them. They used smaller bowls, made from half a coconut, to scoop up the liquid. They made us welcome, even though we noticed that the 'tavern' was occupied by men only. To satisfy our curiosity, one man insisted that we taste the kava, which everyone thought a huge joke. It slightly numbed the tongue and lips, but was most refreshing and above all thirst quenching, far more so than water. Later we learnt that no women are ever allowed to share their drink.

The island was completely unspoilt and reminded me of Ceylon, only cleaner and tidier. It was hot and humid with tall palms and flowering trees. Dotted along the coast, the many attractive villas were surrounded by tropical gardens, but inland the houses were traditional, set on stilts and made with panels of lattice worked palms, allowing a natural air conditioning inside.

Another bus took us to the end of the road and a sleepy river. The ferry across was manned by an old man with a simple paddle. While waiting for the bus to turn round we chatted with an Indian schoolmaster who was obviously pleased to have someone to talk to.

"My family have lived here for several generations" he told us, typically nodding his head from side to side. "Indians particularly, followed by the European residents, outnumber the Fijians on the Island".

The ferry arrived back and the bus started filling up. It was time to go.

Two days later we docked in Honolulu on the island of Oteo, Hawaii. This modern American state had swallowed up the south sea island atmosphere. It was quite different to Fiji, surrounded by fertile plains. Volcanic hills rose sharply behind the city and disappeared into clouds that hung ominously low. In order to see as much as we could, we shared a hired Datsun with Ann for the day and drove all over the island.

Along the quiet coastal road we saw sandy beaches and curious rock formations covered in vegetation, with deep indentations scoured by frequent rain. We passed the impressive Mormon Temple, a low, symmetrical, white building surrounded by formal gardens, neat box hedges and red bushes. Disappointed that it was closed to non-members, we had to content ourselves viewing it from a distance.

Fields full of six-foot-high sugar cane and pineapples stretched for miles. It was harvesting time and large machines, with arms that reached far out over the pineapple crop, were used for harvesting. It reminded me of the much smaller hay baler on the farm back home. Sadly, the view the highest point was obscured by a light drizzle.

The city of Honolulu resembled an exclusive resort. Ten-storey buildings mingled with sumptuous private homes and flowering trees. Tall palms lined the streets, where large flashy cars, with high tail fins, crawled along driven by equally flashy young men. Luxury ocean-going yachts were moored stern first to the pier in the small harbour and beautiful people worshipped the sun on Waikiki Beach. Everything was incredibly expensive, from food to clothing. How we wished we could afford to buy the 'muumuus' made from brightly-coloured cotton materials. I could have happily spent a fortune, but we had to content ourselves with oohs and ahs and window shopping.

That evening, however, we did treat ourselves to an organized bus tour to two of the most exclusive nightclubs in town. The Royal Hawaiian was a gorgeous hotel on the sea front offering dancing on the patio lit by the full moon and a floor show featuring hula-hula girls with long black hair, grass skirts and swaying hips. It had the splendour and romance of the hotels portrayed in American films.

Unused to a life of sophistication, some of our party were completely out of their depth in such an opulent atmosphere. They were more at ease in the rustic Hawaiian village. The simple main building was made of wood and lined with reeds. The floor show was especially vivacious and down to earth; the highlight, a buxom indigenous woman entertained us with rowdy songs about the merits of the Islander's large 'opu', (stomach)and the foreigner's red 'opu' which had been burnt on Waikiki beach. Hers was certainly large, bouncing up and down, barely covered by a reed skirt. She had the audience doubled up with laughter.

After a night out on the town, Bruno and I ended up walking the four miles back to the ship, arriving at 5 am.

The final days at sea were unexpectedly cold and mainly overcast, not really my idea of the tropics, but it was exhilarating. The *Oranje* rode the crest of the giant waves valiantly, dancing in a sideways slip to avoid crashing too heavily into the deep trough ahead, the bow waves spewing a curtain of water to either side as she rose once more to teeter on top of the next roller. It was thrilling to watch from a vantage point on the forward deck, balancing skilfully from one leg to the other, hair flying and wet with spray. I loved it. All around, the Pacific Ocean reached to infinity. Nothing but sea and sky!

Ten days after leaving Wellington, we steamed into Acapulco, Mexico: a new country and a new continent. Not being the *Oranje's* usual port of call, it was discovered that the water around the new extended wharf was not deep enough for her to berth alongside. She would have to anchor offshore for the day. This led to an added complication. The Mini could not be off-loaded and a special raft would have to be constructed. It would have cost us £45 sterling and was unlikely to have been ready in time.

The Management magnanimously offered to take us for free to Balboa, on the Pacific side of the Panama Canal, but it would have been impossible to drive north through Central America at that time of the year. It was the rainy season and the as yet uncompleted Pan American Highway was a daunting venture to undertake in a Mini. It was finally agreed that we should continue on to Miami at the discounted price of ten pounds each. We realized that by the time we had driven south to Mexico City, it would cost us about the same as having the raft built, but we were going to see so much more for our money. The extra three thousand miles, added to our planned journey through Mexico and the United States of America, was also going to stretch our already tight budget.

Acapulco was a charming holiday destination with American/Indian characteristics and a Mediterranean flavour; it was as yet unspoilt by the many large expensive looking hotels overlooking the golden sands of the numerous beaches that encircled a sheltered bay.

The Mexicans seemed to resemble more closely the Tibetan peoples than the European or Asian races, plump with flattish faces and almond eyes. The women, enjoying the Good Friday holiday, ambled through the dusty streets, their black hair braided in plaits reaching to below the waist, children clinging shyly to their long colourful skirts.

Inside the cathedral, all the altars were covered in the purple cloth of mourning. We stood with the crowd, listening to the priest as he expounded on the crucifixion in almost incomprehensible Latin, and observed the people at prayer, fingering their rosaries, children fidgeting and a baby crying. The men sauntered in and out. Dogs lay in the aisle asleep, flicking the flies idly with their long tails or having an energetic scratch. Even a hen, clucking contentedly, pecked at the floor near the pulpit. The women contributed to the collection, helping themselves unselfconsciously to the change. Nobody stayed long, just a constant coming and going. All the doors remained wide open to let in the sea breeze.

Back out in the brilliant sunshine, we climbed a nearby hill to a prominent position overlooking the rooftops and the stunningly calm natural harbour. Water skiers, speed craft and fishing vessels jostled for space, somehow avoiding collisions with amazing dexterity. Proudly the *Oranje*, anchored out in the centre, towered above them and was the great attraction. Small boys were making the most of the occasion, diving for coins thrown overboard by passengers or crew still on board.

Down on the quayside we meandered through the market, which was full of tempting things to buy: handcrafted Mexican silver pendants, bracelets, earrings, woven baskets and enormous sombreros. In the square, men lay enjoying an afternoon siesta under a large shade tree. An eight-year-old boy playfully tickled the ear of his sleeping friend with a stalk of grass. Nearby, a slinky-hipped Adonis, all rippling muscles and dark glistening skin, posed for the photographers: his catch, a giant pacific-blue marlin, was hoisted up beside him for all to admire. It must have been at least eight feet (two and half metres) from the eye to the tip of the tail.

From Acapulco, we sailed south across the bay of Tehuantepec, along the coasts of Guatemala and Nicaragua to Panama, docking in port mid-afternoon. This left only a few hours of daylight to visit the city, though long enough to catch a rickety old bus into town and wander through the streets to soak up the atmosphere. Much like any other port, it was teaming with sailors, perhaps a predominance of black people and noticeably, few native Indians. A modern, unpretentious church boasted a sparkling, solid gold reredos, a legacy from the days of the Conquistadors when Panama City was the starting point of expeditions to destroy the Inca Empire in Peru. It was amazingly beautiful and unexpected.

All the young men in our group went out on the tiles that evening in search of fun but returned disappointed at the lack of girls. We had opted for an early night, weary after all the partying, and I wanted to be up early so as not to miss any of the exciting day ahead.

Through a sleepy haze, I dimly heard the deep-throated sound of the horn as the *Oranje* left the port at 5.30 am for the ten hour journey through the canal. Somehow, I managed to rouse myself and be on deck at 7 am, just as we entered the first lock, a double one. Once full of water, the connecting doors gradually opened and the *Oranje* inched forward into the second lock.

Leaning over the stern, Jane and I watched fascinated as the doors closed. We then ran excitedly to the forward deck. We didn't want to miss anything. Once again, the *Oranje* gradually rose on the incoming water to emerge onto Lake Miraflores. A third lock linked it to the Gatun Lake, eighty-five feet above sea level. The lakes were held in check by four dams, of which the Gatun Dam was one, at that time the 2nd largest earth dam in the world. A final set of locks, three of them this time, took us back down to sea level. Compared to those on the French canals, where I had spent many a summer holiday, these were colossal.

It was only after years of construction difficulties and loss of life due to tropical sickness that the Panama Canal was finally opened in January 1914, linking the Pacific Ocean with the Atlantic. It was an amazing achievement . The narrow isthmus, covered in tropical rain forest, is vital for the functioning of the canal. I later learned that this vast engineering project has actually helped to preserve the forest, as the forest provides the water required for its operation. Typically, clouds hung low and it was drizzling lightly until we reached the Caribbean Sea later in the day.

CHAPTER TWELVE

MEXICO

At dawn, two days later, the *Oranje* docked in Port Everglades, Miami in the USA. We disembarked, sad to leave our friends behind, yet anxious to be on our way at the start of a new adventure. As usual, we hung around endlessly, waiting for the Mini to be unloaded and then washed down scrupulously for agricultural safety. I did wonder what all the fuss was about and how she could possibly be a carrier of foot and mouth – after all, no cases had been reported in New Zealand when we left. Then we still had to meet the insurance representative, clear customs and pack our belongings away.

It was midday before we finally set out across a giant causeway towards the city centre. Werner, one of our gang, came with us as he had to hang around waiting for an afternoon flight to New York. An unbroken line of luxury hotels separated the long golden beach and ocean from the main thoroughfare. Each had its own private area fenced in, leaving access to tiny strips of sand for the general public; very unfair in my opinion.

A network of smaller causeways connected a myriad of islands. This was the residential area, in a sheltered lagoon, protected from the sea by a narrow strip of land and surrounded by the fabulous homes of the wealthy. Meticulously-tended gardens reached down to the water, each boasting a marlin fishing boat moored to a private jetty.

We stocked up with provisions for the journey ahead at an ultra-modern supermarket unlike anything we had ever seen. The doors slid open automatically and outsize metal prams were provided for shopping. The selection of pre-packed and tinned foods, stacked high on a maze of shelves, and the variety of fresh frozen foods was mind boggling. All things that we take for granted nowadays. Not only was the store open from 7 am until 9 pm, but open all day Sunday. Sunday opening was unheard of in the UK at that time.

Miami was vibrant and beautiful, but unpleasantly hot and humid and the noise of the traffic deafening. So with windows wide open to create a breeze, we immediately headed north on Highway 27, through the Everglades. This subtropical wilderness, the largest in the USA, was a network of wetlands and decaying trees, dripping with grey moss. I was unaware of the crocodiles lurking in the shallows and other exciting wildlife, so to me it was just a flat, uninteresting marshy swamp. Fortunately we were not too bothered by mosquitoes that first night.

On the second day we passed through citrus country. Orange trees stood in neat, evenly-spaced rows, covering acres of undulating land as far as the eye could see. Oranges were only sold by the half bushel, which according to the English dictionary means four pecks, the equivalent of 16 dry pints. In other words the sack was too bulky for us to carry, so we had to do without.

Florida, though sparsely populated, was being advertised as a retirement paradise and the Americans were slowly starting to build on the shores of the numerous lakes in the region. It was Sunday morning and we observed that the car parks in front of the many different denominational churches along our route were all full.

The highway continued on through the extensive Alpachee National Pine Forest and across the Central time zone line. Putting our watches back an hour seemed confusing after repeatedly putting them forward whilst crossing the Pacific.

I found the sixty-five mph speed limit frustrating – far too slow on the tarmac road. On top of that, the carburettor kept flooding and causing problems, one of the tyres developed a slow puncture and the exhaust was rattling so much it had to be secured temporarily with string. This did not bode well but we somehow made it to Tallahassee, where we stopped at a garage. Jane was soon in deep conversation with the proprietor.

"Besides running the automobile company," he told her proudly, "I grow peaches, beans, corn and fatten cattle. Ma'am, I live like a king in an air-conditioned house and drive an air-conditioned car. I earn $500 a month, of which $150 goes towards my daughters' upkeep. I employ black labour at $3 to $5 a day. You know ma'am, wages are low because 70% of these people lack enough intelligence to do anything other than menial jobs." This seemed to be the general attitude at the time and we just accepted it as a fact of life in America.

In fact, the Civil Rights Act that outlawed discrimination based on race, colour, religion, sex or national origin was not signed into law until July 2nd, 1964, a year later, and even then it took ages for change to happen. Attitudes take a long time to adjust.

Jane also asked about the best onward route to take.

"Go south to Panama City, ma'am and on along down the coast," he advised.

It turned out to be disappointing. The beaches were dominated by hotels and private homes. The bitterly cold water and the jellyfish, known locally as bluebottles, spoilt my plan to go swimming. But further along the coast, a long line of motels and gaudily-coloured adverts helped to make Pensacola and Alabama more picturesque. To our great delight, we found an idyllic spot to camp among the wayside tables and pine trees bordering the sea. It was good to be back on the road again, seeing new places and living out in the open. Nobody bothered us, nobody stood by and stared and for once we felt quite safe.

Just north of New Orleans, in Southern Louisiana, we drove across one of America's most astonishing bridges. It spanned Lake Pontchartrain from Mandeville to Metairie, a suburb of New Orleans. Stretching just over 26 miles (38.4 km), it was at that time the world's longest bridge over water and was first opened in 1956 as a two-lane highway.

In New Orleans, we parked the car in the Vieux Carré, the old quarter, and wandered the narrow streets between old buildings with frilly wrought-iron balustrades. We glimpsed intimate patios accessed through tall forbidding gates. Numerous restaurants had sprouted in the tree-shaded squares, each claiming to be the birthplace of Dixieland jazz. Even so the area was somewhat decrepit. It lacked the charm of Soho in London, though an obvious effort was being made to turn it into an artistic tourist attraction. For a fee, young artists offered visitors portrait drawings in charcoal. Penniless musicians livened up the street corners, strumming the blues. The original market had survived, run rather like a supermarket. And horror of horrors, women went out shopping wearing curlers in their hair like decorations. They didn't even wear scarves to hide them.

Seventy percent of the population was black. They mingled among the whites in the streets. Public transport and shops did not discriminate, but the buses full of children going home from school indicated that segregation was a reality. Flashy adverts and neon signs topped the four to five storey buildings that lined the wide avenues. Brightly coloured elongated vehicles made Honey look like a toy.

That night, we camped beside the wide, slow-flowing and muddy Mississippi. An earth dyke had been built in 1923 after disastrous floods had carried away some of the most beautiful plantation houses. The straggly trees provided shelter. It seemed an ideal spot.

It must have been nearly one in the morning when we were disturbed by the flashing headlights of a car repeatedly driving past flat out, revving loudly, pretending to run into us, yet veering away at the last minute. We feigned sleep, hoping the perpetrators would tire and go away. Earlier in the evening, a couple of black men had driven past along the top of the dyke, paused and driven on, reversed and then disappeared. Both Jane and I had inwardly felt apprehensive, but neither of us mentioned it.

"What shall we do?" I asked nervously during a lull.

"Shall we move or do you think they've gone away now?" Jane whispered hopefully.

With difficulty, we tried to relax and go back to sleep. Once again it was quiet and peaceful, the crickets chirping away and the river murmuring sleepily.

Ten minutes later, all hell broke loose. The young men were back again, this time venturing closer. They stopped their car, laughing loudly, drunkenly, tauntingly. Then away they sped, tyres squealing, deafeningly revving their engine.

Scared stiff, that incident in Pakistan etched sharply on our minds, we didn't hesitate to jump down and leaving the tent in situ. We climbed into the car and set off for somewhere safer. Just round the next bend in the river we came to a village. A caravan was parked under a solitary street light.

"Let's stop beside the caravan. They surely won't bother us here" I said with relief, happy with the thought of other people close by.

At that moment the door opened and a woman came out wrapped in a housecoat, her hair awry. "What are you doing here?" she asked huffily. After all, we had woken her up. Visibly shaken, Jane explained what had happened.

"Oh! You poor dears! Don't worry any more. You just go to sleep and stay until the morning."

Next day, while packing up, a man emerged from the caravan and sauntered over to talk to us.

"Ye guys okay? Where's ye headed for?" Curious about us and glad of the opportunity to have a chat, he went on to tell us that he had taken early retirement.

"We had a good life ma'am, but we workers went on strike demanding better pay. In our absence the staff took over and kept the firm afloat. Ma'am, we lost our case and when we returned to work, 250 men were fired. Ma'am, I was one of them. Life is different now and it isn't always easy to make ends meet."

The dyke disappointingly hid views of the Mississippi River from the narrow winding road. Only a few plantation houses remained. In their heyday they must have been beautiful, but they were now sadly neglected and in need of renovation, each one surrounded by an expanse of untended lawn.

This was rural sugar cane country, though rice was also cultivated. Yellow school buses collected and` returned the children directly to their homes. Wherever they stopped, so did the traffic while the children rushed haphazardly across the road without a glance one way or the other.

The monotonous landscape became increasingly built-up as we approached the industrial towns of Baton Rouge, Beaumont and then Houston, linked by a modern and as yet incomplete six-lane carriage way with slip roads on either side, flyovers and unders, circles and diamonds, all bringing the vehicles efficiently into the correct stream. It was amazing and so easy to follow the clear signs. Despite the heavy traffic, there were no hold-ups. This was the city where NASA had opened the first manned spacecraft centre the previous year, bringing with it more jobs and greater prosperity. Big cities held no attraction for either of us, so we just kept driving south. Besides sugar cane and rice, cotton was one of the predominant crops.

And so, on into Texas, still flat, increasingly arid and ever more sparsely populated. It reminded me of the Australian Outback, mile upon mile of scrub. Cattle roamed the prairies. Windmills and outsize billboards indicated the locations of isolated ranches, reached by rutted and dusty tracks. Beside the gates, resembling lone sentinels, tunnel-shaped letter boxes topped posts sticking out of the ground. Groups of oil drills purred, incessantly dipping and raising their metal beaks from the ground.

After the long day's drive the wayside park looked inviting. It was just perfect, with shady trees and a stream running by. Wearing light sandals, I ventured through the barbed wire fence into the scrub in search of fire wood.

"Ma'am, you can't go there," drawled a tall Texan cowboy towering above me. He had just driven into the park.

"Why not?" I asked, taken aback.

"It's the rattlesnake mating season and if you disturb them, you could easily get bitten. That's why I wear these tall boots, you know." They were quite fancy, sporting two inch heels and spurs and the leather decorated with twirls.

He climbed over the fence and vanished into the bush. He reappeared shortly with enough wood for a large fire, which he proceeded to saw into logs suitable for the barbecue. What a character! He even had an interior sprung mattress in the back of his pickup. He obviously liked a bit of modern comfort.

As usual we were up at daybreak, 5.30 am, sometime before the Texan emerged. The long straight highway stretched away to low lying hills on the distant horizon, to Laredo and the Mexican border.

I couldn't believe it. Formalities were almost nonexistent, just stamps all over our tourist cards and proof of ownership for the Mini, and on across the new International Toll Bridge. It spanned a mere trickle of water in the wide bed of the Rio Grande.

Nuevo Laredo was another world. Real foods in the market! None of those prepackaged goods, uniform vegetables and mushy industrial bread; there were tomatoes, cucumbers, sweet potatoes in all shapes and sizes, tropical fruits – varieties we'd never seen before - and of course the baskets, jewellery, scarves and other indigenous handiwork on sale for the American tourist. Small shops sold exciting, unhygienic food. For lunch, we bought and ate a delicious ready-made cactus salad with goat's cheese and melon. It was scrumptious.

And was it hot! A sweltering 106 degrees in the shade as we set off across two hundred miles of sandy desert, unable to find respite even with the windows wide open. Only tall cacti and spindly palm trees, sprouting dazzling white blooms, relieved the monotony.

Imperceptibly we climbed and at the top of the pass, Honey boiled over, protesting vehemently. She too was feeling the heat. The radiator needed a top-up but of course we had to wait until it had cooled down, and there was no shade. To make matters worse, the petrol had started flooding again. This time, a Mexican truck driver came to the rescue and tied a piece of nylon thread in the float regulator, which helped for a while, but by evening, the same thing happened again.

Road repairs abounded, with many irksome diversions along dusty, corrugated side-tracks. These had to be negotiated carefully to avoid getting bogged down in the sand. Intermittent petrol stations, painted green and bearing such names as 'la Gloria', served as stores, stocking everything but the kitchen sink even though they were the only sign of habitation in the lonely landscape. Late afternoon we took a break for a prominently-advertised thirst-quenching Coca Cola. At least here we could enjoy a bit of shade and relief from the relentless heat of the sun. Later that evening we treated ourselves to supper at a lean-to café: egg, mincemeat and hot chili sauce dished up with tortillas while we watched a rollicking Western, in Spanish, on TV. There was enough action for Jane, who didn't speak Spanish, to get the gist of the story and enjoy it.

It rained during the night, settling the dust and giving some relief from the intense heat. Monterrey was the first large Mexican town we came to. It had attractive buildings and parks, and looked sparkling clean after the downpour. The stalls in the market were just being unfolded and stocked with goods brought in by truck. In the stately old cathedral, early morning mass was being sung. The women's voices resonated divinely in the vast nave. A multi-coloured shaft of light shone down on the main altar from the stained glass window above, a spiritual moment of great beauty.

Interspersed with stretches of hilly or flat untended scrubland, fertile valleys filled with citrus groves, sugar cane and flax replaced the harsh desert. We drove on into mountainous country with tortuous roads lined with flame trees in bloom, vivid magenta, highlighted by a deep blue sky. Orange groves and papaya trees clung to the steep hill sides. Maize was cultivated on almost inaccessible terraces. The village houses were made of mud and woven reeds, some round, others rectangular in shape. A few 'campesinos' sat idly, sipping coca cola at a local café or going about their business, yet the women were conspicuously absent.

In Tamazunchale, we ambled around the market taking lots of photographs, determined for a change to take enough. In the days before digital cameras, to reflect different aspects of the journey, it was necessary to choose the subject carefully so as not to run out of film, which was expensive both to buy and to develop. This was a centre for the Aztecs and Otomies. Colourful cloths, earrings and shawls were on sale, displayed on the pavement. The women sat patiently beside their wares, dressed in long skirts with shawls wrapped around their shoulders, often with a baby strapped tightly to their back with another length of cloth. The men wore Texan-type hats and carried cloth shoulder bags. We bought *tortillas* - flat, unleavened bread, coated with or without chillies – and sipped at the fermented brew somebody offered us. Neither Jane nor I liked the bitter taste.

The road climbed to 8,600 ft/2,621 m into the Sierra Madre Oriental, which curves all the way south from the border, the backbone of Northern Mexico, separating east and west. Honey made it over the pass without giving us any trouble. A haze lay like a blanket all around and masked the view; to compensate, it was refreshingly cooler,

Next stop: Ciudad Manté. A sleepy stream had been dammed to provide a swimming pool for the villagers.

"Let's take a break and have a swim to cool off," suggested Jane. She was finding the high temperatures difficult to cope with and had been complaining bitterly. We plunged in, happy to get some exercise without melting in the heat; such a relief from sitting long hours in the car. The guardian came over to chat to us, clearly worried about two girls travelling alone.

"We live simple lives," he told us. "Many children cannot read or write. They have to work in the fields or look after the animals. The government understands and hasn't made education obligatory." Both Jane and I enjoyed meeting people and learning about the lives they led. The indigenous Indians struck us as intelligent and good-looking, always friendly and willing to talk.

The following day we unexpectedly happened upon the ancient Indian city of Teotihuacan, which means 'where men become Gods'. It was an influential centre that had, in its heyday at the beginning of the Christian era, a population of some 175,000 people consisting mainly of priests, warriors and artisans. It was now in the early stages of being recovered from oblivion; the excavation and reconstruction was an ongoing project. A handful of tourists wandered along the wide avenue, known as the Way of the Dead, which stretched south for two kilometres across the buried city. It started in the main square, where the victims of human sacrifice had been herded together at the foot of the 63 m high pyramid temple to the sun.

We toiled up the steep narrow steps to the summit of the Sun

Temple, intent on the next tread, fearful of falling. You certainly needed a good head for heights. From the upper platform, we gazed down on the Way of the Dead and the smaller Pyramid of the Moon, and away on the distant horizon, the Sierra of Patlachique. I felt deeply for those overcome with awe and dread, forced to lay their heads on the block at the top for the *coup de grâce* so that their sacrificial blood could flow down a central channel, to appease the gods.

Inching my way down again, on all fours and sideways, trying hard not look below, was a nightmare. A mere glance made me feel quite sick and dizzy.

South of Tehuacan it was once again flat and rocky. The multi-purpose maguey or agave, a bluey-green cactus needing little water, was cultivated in neat straight lines for use as cloth spun from the fibre, as paper, as roof tiles or for medicinal purposes. A thirst-quenching, milky-coloured drink with a low alcoholic content called *pulque* was extracted from the juicy heart. It could also be distilled to make tequila.

It was tempting to drive to the Yucatan to see the Maya temples, but by this time we were feeling jaded. Since leaving Miami, we had covered three thousand miles in only ten days. It was time to take a break and rest before heading north. To save money we opted for a small family-run hotel on the outskirts of Mexico City. We planned to stay for three nights, but found it too much trouble to drive in and out, especially as in-town parking was non-existent, so we moved to the more convenient and swish 'San Francisco' in town.

On the Wednesday morning, we decided to start by getting the car serviced before going to the bank to collect the money that had been ordered previously. We hadn't realized that it was May 1st and Labour Day. Everything in Mexico was closed. The people, in a festive mood, were out parading through the streets, with their Union flags, manifesting allegiance to the President; each group, preceded by a battery of drums, headed for the main square in front of the Presidential Palace, to hear the speeches. It was to be a long day. The crowds started assembling at 7 am, the parade started at 10 am and continued through until 3 pm. This was followed by dancing in the streets until late into the night.

We wandered around tasting some of the strange concoctions offered for sale before sitting on some steps to eat our sandwiches. A couple of traffic police approached and offered us a Coca Cola to drink and enquired about our travels.

"Why are you so reticent to talk to us? Don't you trust us?" one of them asked.

"It is our duty to be courteous to foreigners. We have been trained to do so," added his fellow officer. "Where are you staying?"

Once they realized we were English and not US citizens they cooled down and left us in peace. It was only much later that we understood that American girls were a possible means of entry, through marriage, into the promised land of the United States.

Mexico City was a strange mixture of old and new, a blending of Spanish and Indian cultures, skyscrapers and modern shops rubbing shoulders with massive baroque churches, sinking precariously at odd angles.

In the evening we went to the theatre of the *Bellas Artes* to see the folk dancing. The programme presented tribal dances from the time of Moctezuma, through the Spanish conquest, the revolutions and regional dances up to present-day Christmas celebrations. Included was a brilliant performance of hunters, stalking a deer with a bow and arrow as it is still practised in the Central American jungle. The death of the stag was extremely poignant, bringing tears to my eyes as it took me back to the reality of stalking in the Highlands of Scotland with my father. They are such majestic beasts.

During the interval, the fire curtain was rolled down. Made from New York Tiffany glass, it depicted the two highest Mexican mountains: the snow covered Popocatepetl, 17,906 ft/5,458 m, an active volcano and the linked Ixtaccihuatl (pronounced Ista-si-hua-tl), meaning the sleeping woman, surrounded by a myriad of Mexican plants and birds. In the darkened theatre, coloured lights played on the curtain, transporting us impressively from dawn to dusk.

On the Thursday morning we headed for the bank once again, to find it heavily guarded by several on-duty policemen. The money had not arrived. Even though I produced a confirmation letter from the Westminster Bank in the UK to prove that it had been sent in good time, it was nowhere to be found. A telegram was dispatched immediately, but we continued to draw a blank. This was worrying, as we were running short of funds.

To save money, we checked out of the San Francisco Hotel and drove sixty miles south via Ameca, from where we had a distant view of Popocatepetl, and on to Cuautla, known as the city of Hot Springs. Here we spent a wonderful relaxing day sunbathing and swimming in the sulphuric waters of the Agua Hedionda Spa, translated as 'stinky water'; still a favourite resort for modern Mexicans. The spring which originates from the melting snows of the Popocatepetl and Ixtaccihuatl volcanoes has been known since antiquity for its healing properties. The decaying minerals cause radioactivity and are considered to be an important source of mineral-therapy, beneficial for the skin and respiratory system.

It started to rain as we headed back towards Mexico City. On the way, we asked permission to camp in a field near some houses. These kind people offered us the use of their sitting room for the night. Gratefully we accepted. Such generosity, unheard of back home, still surprised us.

On Saturday, the money still hadn't arrived so we went sightseeing: first to the National Palace, an imposing building festooned with flags, famous for Diego Rivera's superb frescoes celebrating Mexican history and depicting Indian art. He helped establish Mexican mural art at the beginning of the 20th Century.

Next we visited the Sanctuary of Our Lady of Guadeloupe, patroness of the Americas. Legend tells us that four hundred years ago, San Juan Diego, a young convert, experienced four visions of the Virgin Mary on Tepeyac hill. She asked for a sanctuary to be erected on the site. As a sign she told him to pick the roses that flowered miraculously in the middle of winter, where none had ever grown before. He carried them to the Bishop and when the roses were removed from his mantle, an engraved image of the Virgin appeared. The cloth, an object of deep devotion and veneration, is still preserved as a backdrop to the high altar in the magnificent Basilica.

From the vast square, we could see the chapel on Tepeyac hill. A smaller building, alongside the Basilica, leaned precariously away to the right. Mexico City had originally been built on an island in the middle of a lake. To allow for expansion, the water has been pumped out over the years causing the earth to shrink. This accounted for the drunken-looking state of most of the large churches.

Inspite of a light drizzle, the villagers had come, wearing their ceremonial dress, to dance in honour of the Virgin. The women were draped in blue shawls and long blue dresses, the men in panel-like blue skirts to match with a white frilly boarder, bells on their ankles and a feather headdress. Passers-by threw pesos at their feet and these were then offered in the church. Pilgrims advanced on their knees or crawled across the square with deep devotion, all the way to the foot of the altar. Others shuffled along silently praying and turning the beads of their rosaries.

We headed south to Puebla, arriving early the following morning, the 5th May. *Cinco de Mayo* is a regional holiday commemorating the victory of the Mexican militia over the French army in 1862, a decisive battle during the revolution for Independence, though not the last. The schoolchildren from miles around, all dressed immaculately, often in oversized garments, were gathering in the square in preparation for the parade. Each school had its own distinct uniform and was preceded by young drummers and trumpeters creating a cacophony of sound. Bringing up the rear came the army, complete with bayonets and tanks. We had a grandstand view from the white stone steps of the gaudily decorated church, its façade a mass of colourful mosaic motifs. People threw confetti from the rooftops and horsemen, wearing large white hats and tight black trousers decorated with brass buttons, paraded on beautifully-groomed horses, often with a young girl riding side saddle behind decked out in a long flowing dress and a high Spanish mantilla.

In the company of a group of Central American medical students, we spent the evening watching the battle of the flowers and dancing in the streets. Boys and girls wandered around the square carrying armfuls of flowers which they offered to whoever took their fancy; a great way of making contact with your peers in those days before mobile phones.

It was back to Mexico City the next morning. The money

still hadn't arrived. Another telegram was dispatched requesting confirmation of receipt. This was beginning to be a serious matter. Feeling utterly dejected and not knowing what else to do, we drove out to a nearby National Park, El Desierto de los Leones, to spend the next 24 hours sheltering under the trees from the intermittent rain. Here we experienced the bleak reality that we had only a few pesos left – the equivalent of eight pence, half a loaf of bread and a packet of soup for supper; so far from home and seemingly powerless to do anything about it. I spent the afternoon writing a four-page letter to my parents, relating our exploits since our arrival in Mexico City. Meanwhile Jane was sleeping off the 'battle of the flowers' curled up in her sleeping bag under the picnic table, to avoid getting wet.

In times of real trouble, the fighting spirit somehow bubbles up. It helped that the sun was chasing the clouds away and once again, we set off ready to do battle. The Bank was turned upside down, but the money still could not be found. I insisted on seeing the Director and told him to telephone. He promised to send a telex. We had repeated interviews with the managers, who in the end, out of pity when we complained we were getting very hungry, took us out to lunch to a really nice restaurant; a four-course meal and wine. It tasted scrumptious. We hadn't had so much to eat in days and our hosts were good company and most interested in our adventures.

Back at the bank that afternoon, a confirmation that the money had been sent had arrived and mysteriously it was discovered, filed away under another initial. 'Surely it must have been there all the time', I thought, but no hard feelings; we'd had a good lunch. – Smiles all round, laughter, warm handshakes, elation and relief. At last, we were no longer penniless in a foreign country and free to move on. The nightmare had lasted a whole week, but it was finally over.

Some weeks later, a forwarded letter arrived from the bank in UK, apologizing profusely and explaining that the problem had arisen with intermediary agency. They had made a hash of transferring the money to Mexico City.

In pouring rain we headed north through Torreon, hugging the eastern side of the Madre Sierra Occidental, and on through rich agricultural country. Tractors were in use in the well-tilled fields. The corn harvest was in full swing and in the vineyards, plump purple grapes were nearly ready to pick. No wonder people seemed to be better off.

Unbeknown to us, Parral, in Concho Indian territory some two hundred miles south of Chihuahua on the border with the USA, was once a bustling centre for silver mining and famous for its *dulces de leche*, candies made from cooked milk, nuts and fruits. We just hurried on, always hoping to find more sulphur springs to indulge in, taking a break in the frequent, mainly small industrial towns, to buy food in the colourful markets. The profusion of vegetables was so tempting. The only way to cook them was to throw them all in the saucepan together and make a delicious vegetable hotpot. It must have been the green peppers that made it so unexpectedly spicy for the palette.

The scenery changed frequently and we passed through cattle country, similar to the Australian Outback, except that it turned green during the annual rainy season. And then, leaving the proximity of the Sierra Madre behind, the weather improved and we found ourselves once again in semi-arid desert. At one point, after climbing through a range of barren rocks, ninety miles of road stretched away ahead of us, as straight as an arrow, not a bend in sight. Here and there small dwellings dotted the desolate landscape; only the fleshy succulent stems of tall prickly cacti stood proudly defiant of a harsh reality. An occasional lone

Mexican and his horse sheltered from the burning sun on the shady side of a solitary palm tree.

Our last day in Mexico was spent relaxing at the tourist camp in Chihuahua, making the most of the swimming pool and regaining some of the tan we had lost over the last three weeks. The 1,200 mile drive from Mexico City had taken a week and we had been camping wild, wherever we found a secluded spot. Ahead lay many more hours of driving. No wonder we were beginning to look forward to going home and were planning to take the first ship across the Atlantic in September.

CHAPTER THIRTEEN

THE USA

The border controls back into the States were as already experienced, tedious and time consuming. The form-filling seemed never-ending. Then the customs officer insisted we unpack all the contents of the car, but we had so much stuff that half way through he impatiently told us to stop and repack. Much to my disgust, he threw away a small bag of potatoes he had found. We didn't realize that fresh fruit and vegetables could not be imported into the country. Finally Honey had to be sprayed as a potential carrier of foot and mouth disease.

At last we were free to head north into Arizona, via Las Cruces to the unusually named town of 'Truth and Consequences', a resort with hot sulphur baths. We had really been looking forward to this, but it was after 5 pm when we arrived and the baths were already closed. "Just our luck", I commented, disappointed.

A few miles further on, we came to Elephant Butte, a long, narrow reservoir. The blue water lapping along the shoreline looked so tempting. I just had to jump in for a quick dip. It had been a long hot day; first dealing with customs and then there had been no respite from the hot relentless sun. We hadn't even been able to find sufficient shade for a midday siesta.

"Let's stay here for the night. It's an ideal spot." said Jane, glad to get out of the car and stretch her legs.

"Come in for a swim. It's so refreshing" I said. But she couldn't be bothered, she was quite happy to dip her toes in the water, prepare some food, relax and enjoy the view.

Next day on the way to Albuquerque, we made a detour into Isabella Pueblo, a typical Indian village where the inhabitants lived in a similar style to the Mexicans, except that they all had large automobiles outside their front doors. The American Indian had grown dependent on tourism and no longer tilled the fields nor took his cattle to pasture. Instead he thrived on parading around in brightly-coloured traditional costume, performing dances and selling handicraft.

Albuquerque was unusually quiet and slow-moving after the bustle of most American cities, a really pleasant town in which to take a break. A few sturdy trees gave shade to an elderly couple and a young mother minding a mischievous child in the peaceful plaza. At an exhibition celebrating the music and ceremony of the indigenous people, we learnt about the changing customs and introduction of different religious denominations that occurred when the Europeans came into the State of New Mexico. Apparently the ancient ancestral beliefs, the so-called superstition and black magic, remained endemic among the Indian folk.

The Blue Water Lake, another reservoir, was also a perfect place to spend the night alongside other campers who had come with their launches to go fishing. After dark the twinkling lights, spread out across the lake, mirrored the starry vault above.

Nature has blessed the American Southwest with grandiose phenomena and vast vistas unlike anything we had encountered elsewhere. The highway crossed through the Indian town of Gallup, and along the rim of the aptly named Painted Desert we saw astonishing views of the eroded hills, splashed with red and grey horizontal strata and topped by green vegetation. This adjoined the Petrified Forest National Park, which was not quite what we expected. No trees, just logs lying in disarray, deposited by fast running streams eons ago. They had lain below drifting sands and sediment containing volcanic ash. Groundwater full of minerals had seeped into the wood to form quartz crystals that gradually replaced the normally bio-degradable organic matter. The resulting petrified stone looked wonderful when polished and therefore, sadly, was subject to theft.

We took another break from the long hours of driving to explore Meteor Crater, created by the impact of a meteor at least 23,000 years ago. The hole is 570 feet deep and three quarters of a mile in diameter, the perimeter 150 feet above the surrounding ground. The museum displayed the various types of rock and minerals found in this and similar craters elsewhere in the world. In a dark room, a mysterious mauve light highlighted amazing colours normally invisible to the naked eye.

We walked down into the bowl of the crater, the towering sandy sides eerily shutting out all but the blue sky high above. Back at the surface we enjoyed a grandstand view from the lookout platform. Here, recorded lectures explained all about the crater, the native people of the region and the timber industry vaguely discernable on the horizon, just beyond the never-ending desert. We learnt the reason there were no cattle to be seen; they had gone to the more temperate climate of the hills for their summer holiday.

We arrived at the Grand Canyon campsite around midday, which gave us the whole afternoon to use the showers and the washing machines and to give the Mini a much-needed clean-up. It was just wonderful to wash off the dust and not feel that everything you touched was grubby. The facilities on the American campsites were luxurious. Back in Europe, it was cold showers and open-air tubs in which to do your washing or wash the dishes. If you wanted hot water you had to boil a kettle.

It was a lonely two-and-a-half mile walk to the rim of the canyon, though we did meet one or two Indians clad in vivid blue dresses - a bright splash of colour in the otherwise monotonous brown of the desert.

What a spectacular sight awaited us! Sharp shadows enhanced the colours and drama of the rock formations, eroded over time by winds, water and weather, exposing the different strata of rock. There were dozens of conical towers, softened by the soil and stones slowly falling away to form green grass skirts between the horizontal cliffs. The Kaibab trail, used mainly by pack mules, disappeared down into the abyss. Lush green bushes marked the passage of a stream as it meandered across a plateau just below. It then disappeared into a rocky crevice cascading down to join the mighty Colorado River.

As we set off down the seven and half miles of the Kaibab trail, a string of mules and donkeys passed, carrying sacks of rubbish up from the ranch at the bottom. Perched precariously on the outer-most edge of the narrow path, they plodded up slowly, steam belching from their nostrils. Here and there placards explained about the rock, its age and composition making the descent a fascinating experience. As we dropped steeply down, the climate changed and the temperature rose until it was as hot as the Mexican desert. At least it was cooler in the lee of the sheer vertical cliffs. Lizards darted among the rocks, while squirrels edged dangerously close in the hope of some tempting morsel. The many deer watched immobile from a distance.

A group of boys had booked into the Phantom Ranch for the night, but they never turned up, which meant we could have a cabin to ourselves and get a good night's rest. Was I glad to be warm again! The previous night on the camp site at the top, I'd shivered miserably from the cold.

We enjoyed the rest of the afternoon in the cool waters of the pool, chatting to other hikers. A hearty meal was served to all the guests seated together around a communal table. Jane fell into deep conversation with Colin Fletcher, a writer, who was tramping the Canyon from end to end on a lone jaunt. He was resting his blisters at the ranch and had completed a couple of articles which he asked Jane to comment on. She was quite chuffed. Meanwhile I chatted with some of the many American and Canadian students taking time out to explore the continent. Everyone we had met in America was so friendly and happy to exchange news and views.

Because of the midday heat and the eleven-mile return hike to the top of the Canyon up the Bright Angel Trail, I suggested we make a 5 am start, but Jane was not too keen. She said she was tired. It must have been all that talking! So we ate a copious breakfast at the Ranch and then set out at 7.45 am. The first seven miles were easy going, but the remaining five to the summit were tough. Jane really struggled and as there was no available water from this point until the top, we just had to keep going. It would not have been wise to linger along the way as dehydration would have set in.

Not surprisingly, the following day, our legs were so stiff and painful that we were quite happy to be sitting in the car once again. We had certainly not been having enough exercise, but this was something I couldn't persuade Jane to do, and I found it boring to go walking on my own. I was so glad we had made it to the bottom of the Canyon and back again – an exhilarating experience, well worth the effort, and the weather had been superb.

We continued north to Zion Park, another recreation area, complete with museum and a fifteen mile-long scenic drive through a spectacular wide canyon. Either side the reddish-coloured Navaho sandstone cliffs rose, almost vertically, as much as 2,624 ft/800 m; fashioned by a river, glaciers and sand dunes that had hardened into limestone. Leaving Honey in the car park, we followed a nature trial for about half a mile, while reading the pamphlet provided that gave detailed descriptions of the plants to be encountered along the way. This was a fun, informative way to go walking and we were becoming well versed in geology, tracking and fossil hunting.

Keen to explore some more, I handed Jane the car keys and asked her to meet me later in the day at the other end of the trail I planned to follow. Years later, she told me how thrilled she had been to be trusted to drive the car, even if only briefly in the park. I left her reading and chatting to an English couple we had met, and set off to the summit of Lady Mountain. At 2,116 m/6945 ft, it was the highest peak in the park. The well-marked trail climbed 815 m/2,675 ft in just under two miles. It was fascinating and quite a challenge. Where it was really steep, chains were provided to haul your way up, or to assist you on the way down. Two really difficult stretches even had ladders.

The bird's eye view from the peak was breathtaking. The

canyon was filled with green trees drawing nourishment from the Virgin River, which meandered between towering cliffs and disappeared towards the distant Temple Mountains. The round trip took me three and a half hours. Clambering about in the midday heat was not ideal but I felt great after the exercise. Was I glad I had not encouraged Jane to go with me against her will. She would have hated it.

The Valley of Fire falls gently away towards Lake Mead, the largest reservoir in the USA, which fills with the melt water from the Colorado, Wyoming and Utah Rocky Mountains. It was yet another of nature's not-to-be-missed grandiose panoramas, framed by a strange rock formation that at sunset resembled flickering flames rising from the sand. These radiated enough heat to keep us warm through the normally chilly desert night.

Dispensing with the canvas cover, for once we were able to sleep out under the stars on top of the Mini. Adjacent to the camp site barbecue, we even found a neat pile of firewood left for our convenience. At least it ensured that campers didn't destroy the vegetation.

Next day we stopped briefly in Las Vegas, which was just a small town in those days. It was decorated with bright lights and garish billboards, a glorified funfair. This was 'civilization' in the middle of nowhere. Much too expensive for us, but we did take a look around the flashy air-conditioned 24 hour casino, which was full of slot machines and hunched, harassed people desperately trying again and again to win the jackpot. Levers were pulled down relentlessly, wheels whirred and just sometimes there was a cascade of coins, followed by whoops of joy. We just couldn't resist giving it a go. We agreed to spend just one dollar to try our luck, but as we took it in turns to pull the lever and watch colourful discs spin, discouragement set in. By the time we had lost 40 cents of that precious dollar, which we could ill afford to do, we called it a day. It all seemed so artificial and a waste of time and effort. We infinitely preferred the freedom and naturalness of the wide open spaces.

As we ventured out from the cool interior, the heat hit like a roaring furnace. It was so difficult for the body to adapt to the abrupt changes in temperature and the Americans certainly liked to keep their public buildings and homes stone cold.

The roadside was plastered with warning signs. 'You are entering the desert... Check your fuel gauge... Be sure to carry enough water.' We laughed about it. To us it was obvious, having just crossed 2,000 miles of desert since leaving Mexico City. Brightly coloured placards broke the tedium of desolate wasteland advertising frequent gas stations. Water cans were placed at convenient intervals as car radiators all too often boiled dry. Wayside parks provided restrooms and picnic tables but the young trees that had been recently planted gave little shade. They were tended to by the road maintenance men who arrived at some point during the day to set the water pump going, to fill the storage tank and water the trees.

Two hundred and eighty miles of sweltering desert still lay ahead of us. The car engine, as had been the trend all week, continued to over-heat. All we could do was stop and wait for the radiator to cool down enough to take the lid off and let the steam out before topping up with water again. When finally the sun sank towards the horizon it mercifully cooled down.

It was still cool in the morning of the 22nd May as we drove through the sprawling suburbs and into downtown Los Angeles. Expertly negotiating the flyovers and unders of the multi-lane highway teeming with aggressive large cars, we ended up at the main post office; a feat to be proud of in a diminutive Mini. The trucks towered above us; Honey was only the height of their tyres. The cars were two or three times as long. The Americans loved us, tooting their horns and waving us along. This was great fun, but you had to concentrate. Jane was becoming a brilliant navigator and we now rarely took a wrong turning.

As always, it was a treat to have news from home, but my father hadn't been well for some time and was still under the weather.

"Don't worry. It is quite normal to feel that way when taking drugs or antibiotics. You know, hospitalized patients always react that way" remarked Jane, the nurse, in a matter-of-fact way, to cheer me up. Well, it wasn't that easy, as it had now been several months with the same disquieting news. However we had to keep going, which left little time to dwell on something we couldn't do anything about.

At the time my brother had a lithesome girlfriend called Lorraine. Her married sister and husband Mike lived with their pretty little daughter in a magnificent villa in South Laguna, some fifty miles south of Los Angeles. They had invited us to visit on the way by. This was a great opportunity to spend time with an American family.

South Laguna was a seaside resort and artist community on a narrow strip of land separating the golden sandy beaches of the Pacific Ocean from the hills and canyons of the San Joaquin Hills, a truly idyllic place. Four busy days passed in a flash. We were taken out to dine on hot chilli con carne at a Mexican restaurant, went sailing with Mike and revelled in the sun and waves crashing on the beach.

One of the highlights was a visit to Knott's Berry Farm, a collection of wooden homes and stores rescued from the dereliction of the ghost towns of the Wild West and turned into a tourist attraction, it was a popular and crowded Sunday venue. It was a glimpse into history and a way of life long gone. Originally the restaurant sold chicken dinners and boysenberry pies made from its own boysenberry preserve. Subsequently the small family business mushroomed into a thriving enterprise, riding on the preserve's incredible popularity. A boysenberry is a cross between a European raspberry and a common blackberry. It looks like an overgrown, deep maroon raspberry and bears the name of its creator, Rudolph Boysen.

Another highlight was Disneyland, an expensive and novel attraction featuring a monorail on which to ride around the perimeter. This just couldn't be missed. It was like sitting in London underground train, only it was silently gliding along several meters above ground with amazing views. In the beautifully laid-out shopping centre we gazed longingly at the tantalizing things for sale. But never knowing when unexpected expenses could pop up, we quickly put temptation aside and went for a ride in the Tunnel of Love - or was it Horrors? The open air cars shot into the dark. Spider's webs hung down eerily brushing past my face. Rustles and screeches pierced the silence. As we hurtled round blind corners, strange shapes sprang out menacingly from dimly-lit caves. A deafening sound of cascading rocks and water…just as we thought it would never end, the car emerged once more into blinding sunlight.

Back on the road, we drove north past the sumptuous residences of Hollywood set in large gardens providing plenty of privacy, a mixture of modern, Spanish and Victorian styles, and onto the Cabrillo Highway, the winding coastal road to San Francisco. At that time it was a sparsely-inhabited area of green rolling hills that tumbled down to grey sandy beaches lapped by the Pacific Ocean.

This was cattle-breeding country, mainly Herefords and enormous beasts by UK standards where animals were still raised on smallholdings in the traditional way. Farming was very different in America. The cattle were bred by one farmer, fattened to 750 lbs weight by another, then pen-fattened to 950 lbs for market. This conveyor-belt process took a mere eighteen months compared to the four years normally required to mature an animal.

That morning we had a puncture and had to set to and change the wheel. We now had it down to a fine art. While I loosened the nuts, Jane got out the jack and hoisted the car up. We exchanged wheels and once the spare was in place and the nuts on, Jane let the jack down and I tightened them up. With everything neatly stowed, we were soon on our way again.

A visit to the Hearst family home, run by the California National Park, made a convenient break. A small bus delivered us up a steep twisty lane to the 'Enchanted Peak' where a media mogul and multimillionaire, William Hearst, had tried to imitate grand living European-style. He had imported a great number of antiques from abandoned monasteries, such as heavily-carved ceilings and choir stalls to use as panelling. The rooms had been designed to match the ceiling. A huge refectory table with baronial chairs adorned his dining room. Regardless of origin, age or style, everything was mixed up together with all modern conveniences. To my mind, this was sacrilege, a real 'hotchpotch', but for people in the New World it was a wonderful opportunity to experience their rich European heritage.

The garden was a mass of flowers and shrubs set amid dozens of ornate pillars rising out of the ground like stalactites and leading to an Olympic-size swimming pool surrounded by Roman arches to provide shade. The focal point was a delicate statue of Venus rising from the waves.

It grew cold and cloudy and the onward journey, which should have been a delightful scenic drive, became a chore of tiresome curves. Was I glad when we finally reached San Jose, a quiet residential town on the outskirts of San Francisco, where we stayed with Jane's friends, the Listons.

After a day of rest they took us to see the sights, including the university campus, where to our amazement all the students had their own large car, if not two. In the Japanese Tea Garden, we sampled delicately-scented jasmine tea served with cookies that foretold the future. We ate fresh shrimp cocktail on the quayside and visited Chinatown, full of typical restaurants and shops selling oriental jewellery, cane and bamboo furniture. We even rode on the famous cable car up Hyde Street. From the top we had a magnificent view of the Golden Gate Bridge.

"It was opened in 1937 and took four years to construct. At the time, it had the world's longest span of 4,200 feet," Mrs Liston explained. "With a record of only eleven lives lost and ten of those in the last phase when the safety net broke. You know, the San Francisco Chronicle referred rudely to the Bridge as the '35 million dollar steel harp'."

Always curious, Jane asked, "Why was it painted orange?"

"Orange vermilion is a warm colour consistent with the warm colours of the surrounding land masses and easily discernible in spite of the frequent fogs rolling in from the ocean. It took its name from the Golden Gate Strait, the entrance to San Francisco Bay from the Pacific."

Wider than Sydney harbour, the surroundings were less inhabited and fewer craft plied the water. From the bridge we could see the lighthouse on Alcatraz Island, the oldest on the West Coast. The island, surrounded by dangerous currents, was first used by the military before becoming a secure federal prison in use until 1963. I felt for the inmates, who must have gazed across the narrow strip water with little hope of escape.

Our route took us north across the bridge into redwood country. I had never imagined that so many trees could have such an enormous girth and height. The world's largest, the Lost Monarch, was 320 ft high and 26 ft in diameter. It would take six people holding hands to encircle it. It was even possible to drive a car through an archway at the base of one such tree. The ground was richly carpeted with ferns and moss and somehow the sun managed to cast rippling shadows through the trunks stretching away into a mysterious dark mass.

Route 99 snaked its way through the wooded glens and lush farming valleys of Oregon County. I loved the spaciousness and the Scandinavian architecture of the farmhouses and barns. The Mini hummed along and suddenly we realized we had covered three hundred miles. Our normal average was two hundred, whether it took two or three hours or all day.

We took a break in Portland to see the forestry building, constructed entirely of redwood timber, the largest log cabin in the world, built in 1905 especially to house an exhibition. Photographs of the different species of fir trees, as well as satellite industries using wood, were on display.

Also in Portland, we visited the Sanctuary of Our Sorrowful Mother, a Roman Catholic shrine set in a quiet botanical gardens and run by the Order of Friar's Servants of Mary, commonly known as the Servite Fathers. Our Lady's Grotto, a rock cave, had been carved into the base of a 110 ft cliff with a life-size marble replica of Michelangelo's Pieta featured in the centre. The plaza above was reached by escalator. Father Miller met us there and explained: "Over there is the Chapel of Mary. The thirty-four carved figures represent the Seven Sorrows of

Mary. They are the work of Professor Heider of Pietralba in Italy and took four years to carve."

Father Miller walked us through the manicured garden, pointing out the different shrubs, flowers and trees. The roses were a blaze of colour with so many specimens in bloom; such a peaceful place for contemplation and meditation.

"I write poetry and books" he told us, happy to show off his fluent knowledge of several European languages as we returned to the Plaza. "Look, what a wonderful view we have of Columbia River Valley and Mount Hood on the horizon."

He left us at the souvenir shop, where I bought a small booklet of his beautifully-written and inspiring poems.

Unfortunately it wasn't worth our stopping off in Seattle to visit the Space Needle, as it was bucketing down with rain and continued to do so all the way to Vancouver.

During the last thirty miles before reaching the border, the road narrowed and the countryside took on the unkempt look of no-man's land. In stark contrast, we suddenly came upon the lonely Customs Offices on the border with Canada, separated by an Archway of Peace and set amid a parkland of flowers.

The Canadians didn't want to give us the immigrant visas we requested and pleaded for. Non-immigrant visas meant we would not be allowed to work, and we really needed to top up our now dwindling resources. Seeing our desperation, the kindly customs officer who accompanied us to the door tried to comfort us, and with a bright smile he said: "I'm quite sure you girls will have no difficulty in obtaining work".

CHAPTER FOURTEEN

CANADA, AND HOME

For several days, Vancouver remained shrouded in cloud and constant drizzle. We spent the first night at the YWCA and then rented a room in Robson Street. The landlady, Mrs R, was a gushing woman, full of charm; that was as long as you let her run your life. For days she wouldn't speak to us, and then for no apparent reason she would be all over us. Maybe we were just too independent for her liking. Her dark spooky house was plastered with 'DON'T DO' notices and we rarely met the other tenants, who were all elderly women.

Whenever the doorbell rang Mrs R. would open it a crack and especially if the person standing there was male, ask sharply, "What do you want? Oh! Just wait a minute." Then she would promptly slam the door in the face of the astonished visitor.

One day, fed up with the situation, Jane announced that we were leaving because we couldn't afford the rent.

"Good! Besides, I wouldn't have kept you on anyway," she snapped, even though she knew Jane had already found a job.

Finding work in Vancouver had been deadly. We traipsed from one agency to another, ending up at Office Overload. Here we underwent a gruelling examination as to our circumstances before being granted 'Unemployment' cards from the Employment Exchange.

In three weeks, I only managed to do three days' work as a typist. Meanwhile Jane did nothing. This wasn't going to get us anywhere and we were becoming very downhearted. In desperation she went to the General Hospital. A few days later, after a further telephone call, she was given a job as nurse in the nursery of the Maternity Department. She was a registered sick children's nurse, but British qualifications weren't recognized in British Columbia. This was the case all over North America, where each state refused to recognize the qualifications from another. Working hours were from 7 am to 5.30 pm on a shift basis, so that Jane never knew whether she would be free at the weekend. Living so far from Downtown, she would have to be up at 5.30 in the morning, which wasn't ideal. So we moved to a more conveniently situated but rather dreary basement flat in Dunbar, overlooking Downtown and West Vancouver. A much happier situation, especially as we spent a lot time during the day or evening watching TV in our landlady, Mrs Weatherby's, sitting room. She was such a friendly woman and I was even allowed to take her big, bouncy mongrel dog for lots of walks, which kept the pair of us out of mischief.

Stanley Park was just a few blocks down the road. Jane and I would walk down to the Lost Lagoon in the evening to feed the ducks and swans and enjoy the dancing fountain with its twinkling lights which changed colour and reflected in the water at night. Tennis enthusiasts filled the numerous courts at their disposal. One weekend we visited the zoo, which housed polar bears, penguins, seals and a large variety of birds. It was possible to escape the bustle of the city along the many narrow trails across the thousand-acre park and find quiet woodland dells and beaver lakes hidden away among the tall redwood trees. From the totem pole at Prospect Point we had a brilliant view of Vancouver Island.

The Weatherbys were really kind and welcoming. They took us to a Chinese restaurant and to the Yacht Club and even helped me get a job at the Yacht Club for a PIYA event. It lasted seven days, working a twelve-hour day, and it was good fun; sometimes hectic and at others quiet enough to have time to read a couple of books. Many Americans had come up from Seattle for the long-distance race around Vancouver Island, which was covered at record speed despite the rain and no doubt due to the strong winds. Earning $1.50 per hour, my take-home pay was $130. What a relief. Those first three weeks in Vancouver we had been very broke until some money arrived from the UK and we managed to earn some more.

I had been browsing through the advertisements in the newspaper and unintentionally rang Avon, a door-to-door cosmetic sales company. The result was a black bag brimful of sample cosmetics and a 'beat'. But what a depressing job! Starting at one end of a long street full of identical houses, with front doors at the top of a steep flight of steps, I plodded up and down all day. Many doors remained closed and when opened, I was greeted with a brief "What do you want? Oh, no thank you", and the door shut in my face. All this for so few orders and then, because we decided to leave before the goods arrived from Montreal, I was unable to deliver the merchandise. The net result of my endeavour was a bag full of sample cosmetics and the firm resolution that I would never ever do that again.

Temping as a typist was almost impossible, so I had resorted to picking strawberries, while they lasted. It was better than doing nothing and I took a few to Mrs Weatherby at the end of the day.

On one occasion, the dog and I climbed through the low cloud to the top of Grouse Mountain following the steep path up under the chair lift – a 2,000 ft hike. We saw the Cleveland Dam where the city's water is stored and gazed at the famous Capilano Canyon, which had cut a deep, narrow gorge into the grey rock. The halfway point was marked by a skier's village of log huts and a camp site. Although unclear, the view from the top was fantastic. Vancouver had such a wonderful setting, so close to the sea and the mountains; the best of both worlds. As we prepared to leave, a large St Bernard dog flopped over towards us, his long tongue hanging out, terrifying my normally bouncy companion into a quivering wimp.

It was the beginning of July and we had been in Vancouver for a month. We both loved it, but I was getting restless with nothing to do and not being able to earn any money. Jane was happy enough in her job, but frustrated with the lack of authority she was allowed to exercise. She soon agreed with me that with no other work available, it would be better to move on, complete our journey and if we had time left to try our luck in Eastern Canada. We made a snap decision.

The hospital matron wasn't very pleased. The boat tickets we had ordered for the Atlantic crossing weren't ready and would have to be picked up in Montreal. The photos I had taken in to be developed had been lost. To make things worse, parking places were unavailable anywhere near the offices I had to visit. It was one of those frustrating days. Still we managed to clear up our mess, vacate the flat and pack the car ready for departure.

Waving goodbye to the Weatherbys, we set off via Langley, Hope and Princeton towards the interior of British Columbia. It rained most of the day. A damp haze obliterated the scenery and the dripping trees looked somewhat forlorn. But although we had liked living in Vancouver, nothing managed to spoil our delight at being on the road again, away from the city streets festooned with unsightly hanging electricity wires, noisy cars and hard pavements.

Beside us a river came rushing, jumping its joyous way down the hillside. Sometimes a deer strayed across the road and at the campsite a large sign warned: 'Beware of bears at night'. Not that we saw one, but it was important to leave nothing lying around.

The timid morning sun soon dispersed the damp of the previous day as we continued on through the Okanagan fruit country. Delicious cherries were plentiful, and oh so cheap. This was followed by fields of ripe golden corn surrounding neat wooden homesteads, protected from the harsh world by a towering range of dark green mountains clothed from top to bottom in cedar trees. Feathery clouds scudded across the sky casting dark shadows down in the valley.

We loved Western Canada. The Rockies were scenically outstanding and many areas had been preserved as National Parks. Among them was Mt Revelstoke, home of the world's only inland temperate rain forest and a photographer's paradise. The steep rugged mountains provided protection for stands of old-growth cedars and hemlock, as well an essential habitat for threatened species such as caribou, mountain goat and grizzly bear.

Here we purchased a licence granting entry to all Canadian National Parks and motored on into the adjoining Glacier National Park. In the horizontal rays of the setting sun, the scintillating glacier, a vast cascade of ice-blue blocks, towered impressively above us, reaching far away into the mountains. A stream bubbled up from the moraine at its base, merrily skipping along as it curved and sped away towards the south-flowing Columbia River and the distant Pacific Ocean. A few lone trees gave shade to a picnic area. The campsite-to-be was still only a pipe dream, but in those days rules and regulations didn't prevent us from camping wild.

As dusk fell, mosquitoes started buzzing and to avoid being bitten, it wasn't long before we clambered up on the roof rack, closing the netting tightly at either end. I awoke in the middle of the night to the sound of a veritable army of those spiteful insects dead set on attack. I peeped out through the flap horrified. We were surrounded. How sad that such a magnificent place could be so spoilt, I thought as I drifted back to sleep.

A wide, newly-completed highway took us over Roger's Pass. The mountains, covered in the last vestiges of dirty winter snow, continued to tower above to as much as 11,000 ft/3,358 m. As the day progressed, the traffic thickened. We passed through the small settlement of Field. Its claim to fame was nothing more than a dilapidated hotel, a small grocery store and several wooden houses that had once been used by the road gangs and park keepers. The Mini showed signs of boiling over yet again, so we left her beside a rushing torrent to cool off and continued on foot to a lookout, to see the entrance into the Connaught Tunnel.

Here the trains disappeared inside the mountain to climb or descend in a figure of eight, thus reducing the steepness of the gradient required. The frequent avalanches had caused considerable human and financial cost, so the engineers finally opted to cut a tunnel through the mountain and under Roger's Pass. The missing link of the transcontinental railway line was finally completed in 1885.

After topping up Honey's radiator once again, we headed for Lake Louise, an unbelievable expanse of milky-turquoise water contained within a bowl of high peaks. The lake was fed by a glacier at the far end. A trail around the perimeter led through the pine trees to the Mt Fairview lookout. It was closed, but undeterred, we scrambled along as far as we could. Giant boulders frequently barred the way. They had to be circumnavigated and at one point we climbed upstream to a narrower place and waded across. The hillsides were carpeted in flowers. Yellow striped chipmunks tamely hopped around. We even saw a couple of marmots scampering away.

At the top end of Lake Louise, the enormous hotel built for the influx of tourists arriving by train looked like a barracks. It was softened by the surrounding lush gardens with intricate paths meandering along the shoreline. In unexpected contrast, the interior was lavishly decorated in Victorian style. It would have been so comfortable to stay overnight...

Camping in the Rockies was not much fun. Come dusk, those bothersome mosquitoes were on the rampage again. I had always thought that mosquitoes belonged to tropical climes.

On the way into Banff, we saw a young eleven-pointer stag feeding unperturbed beside the highway. We just had to stop to take a photograph to capture the moment. Later we fleetingly glimpsed a fox as it sidled into the forest.

Banff was a tranquil and typically touristic town, surrounded by tree-covered towering mountains. The spacious layout reminded me of Canberra in Australia. Long John, one of the young men we met at the Hermitage in New Zealand, had told us that he had worked at the Banff Springs Hotel. Keen to find out about working conditions, we talked to one of the maids. She told us that the season was from May to September but jobs were hard to come by at the beginning of the season; by July, no problem.

"Oh I love it here," she exclaimed. "I'm a university student and this supplements my income. We earn $75 per month, working a six-day week in shifts of eight hours. Working conditions are good. We live in dormitories with three to nineteen others and our dining room is in the basement."

We soon realized that life and conditions at the Hermitage had been far superior, and neither of us wanted to apply for a job here.

"Let's go for a dip in the hot springs", I suggested, keen for another dip in the hot waters. It was just wonderful to relax in 90 degrees Fahrenheit, while the tip of my nose stayed cool at only 60 degrees.

Jasper, the last of the national parks we visited, was reached via a scenic route of more mountain peaks framed by the dense foliage of trees. Wide rivers tumbled frothing over rocks and flowing through sunlit valleys. On the cold side of the valley, glaciers cascaded down the bare mountains. Melted winter snow revealed large tracts of scree. Abundant turquoise lakes lay hidden in the forest. You had to experience this incredible gift of nature to really appreciate it.

Waterfowl Lake Camp allowed little privacy. It was full to capacity. I cooked porridge for breakfast in the cookhouse and watched fascinated as one woman made pancakes. "Here, why not try it out for yourself. It's so easy" she said. She smiled and handed me the remaining half a packet of pancake mix.

A couple of fisherman packing up to head for home gave us a loaf of bread, a can of milk and some tomatoes. "I wonder if we look poor and hungry," Jane commented. Perhaps they realized we hadn't made provision and that there were no shops within a hundred and fifty mile radius.

One of the activities we enjoyed most while travelling through the Canadian Rockies was the wonderful walks, a great antidote to the hours spent driving. It took us a good sixty minutes to reach the lakes in the lee of Mt Chephron, walking along a narrow, winding and muddy track meandering through the pine forest. Serenaded by songbirds, we were constantly on the lookout for wildlife. The milky-cold glacial waters lapped the logs that lay haphazardly on the shore; so peaceful and timeless.

That day we saw an elk and mountain goats grazing, completely ignoring the humans who stopped to take photographs. A big brown bear ambled hopefully from car to car. Windows remained tightly shut. Everywhere notices warned of the danger of feeding greedy bears which can suddenly become quite aggressive.

Apparently the Athabasca Glacier, one of the six principal 'toes' of the Columbia ice field, has lost a shocking 25% of its volume since we visited in the early 1960s. We were lucky to have seen it then.

The Mini struggled, in first gear, up the steeply graded road of the 5,751 ft/1,753 m Athabasca Pass. I worried constantly we wouldn't make it, but thankfully we did. And what a view! Far below canoeists were paddling along a fast-flowing torrent towards the Athabasca River. Waterfalls tumbled into narrow canyons, turbulently cascading on into the torrent beneath, finally making their way to the distant plains.

We dropped down to Jasper, a town with no purpose other than tourism. Railway yards lined one side of the main street, a few small shops and a laundry on the other.

Behind us the Rocky Mountains receded into the distance, as did the continuous stretches of pines. Spindly deciduous trees started to predominate until these too disappeared from the scene. The undulating hills flattened out as we hit the Stony Plains and eventually the Prairies.

We took a break in Edmonton, just long enough to go to church, as it was Sunday, and continued on East into Saskatchewan. Storms threatened all around and occasional showers drenched the roads. At one point hailstones as large as marbles fell with a clatter and were gone as suddenly as they had arrived, followed by more torrential rain.

That night we camped on a picnic ground just east of Maymount. Unsightly litter had been left lying around, but we made do as here we could build a fire and use the water pump. In the dead of night, a torch shining in my face disturbed my sleep. Silently, a Canadian Mountie had arrived. I noticed his pensive look, but without a word he disappeared as he had come and let us be.

Jane loved the prairies. They reminded her of Norfolk. I just couldn't appreciate how she found them attractive. Besides, it was raining so hard, it was a miracle she could see anything. To me they were monotonous and never ending. I was in a hurry, as so little time remained and we still had a lot to see. Worst of all, the mosquitoes were a menace every night.

Canada was full of surprises as her people were so diverse. At one of the roadside parks near Winnipeg, a party of Mennonite girls, dressed in long print dresses with gathered skirts and pretty aprons, stopped to use the 'ladies'. Demure white caps covered their long braided hair. It was hard to believe that modern girls still dressed this way.

In Kenora, the Mini went into a garage for a service. I was very impressed because the mechanics managed to change the oil without dismantling the sump guard. This was the very first time. So far it had always been such a performance. The only extra was a new flicker cover on the front right-hand side.

What a relief when at last the scenery changed. Ontario was hilly, sometimes rocky or tree covered, interspersed with numerous lakes. The sun was shining again, lifting my spirits. Fluffy clouds scudded across the blue sky.

However, large and forbidding 'No Camping' signs adorned every roadside stop. Camping wild was obviously not allowed. Funds were running low and we couldn't really afford to stay at an official camp site. Disgusted, we kept on driving until we reached a town called Sunshine, just twenty miles north of Fort William. The road surfaces had deteriorated considerably and over the last thirty miles had been under construction; flying gravel, dust and corrugation. Tired and grumpy, we eventually parked the car on a lay-by and hoped for the best.

During the night a truck stopped. Was it a nature-stop or was the driver picking something up? Funny how we only woke up when a vehicle stopped, masking the constant drone of passing traffic.

"I don't think he noticed us," whispered Jane and we drifted back to sleep.

Our first glimpse of Lake Superior was in Fort William. It seemed incredible that this lake was one hundred and fifty miles wide and approximately four hundred miles long. It had looked like an enormous inland sea when viewed in my geography book at school, and the reality of its size only hit as we started to drive along the shoreline. Four hundred miles of the Trans-Canada highway followed the perimeter, with only three fair-sized towns between Port Arthur and Sault Ste Marie, each with fewer than 4,000 inhabitants at the time. We had expected to pass into a new time zone, but for some reason it didn't happen.

One morning, I managed to get Honey firmly stuck in the mud trying to climb up a steep bank out of a disused gravel quarry where we had hidden ourselves for the night. Unable to budge her, we set about trying to remove the loose earth from underneath. As if on cue, two good-looking American men with obvious Germanic features arrived on the scene. They climbed out of their Mercedes and came to the rescue. Together with Jane they pushed and rocked the little car, with me at the wheel, until she was back on terra firma. Impressed that we had travelled all around the world in our precocious little Mini, they just had to immortalize the moment with a photograph.

"Follow me, I'll get you there," offered the kindly driver of a pickup who guided us along a maze of streets through Sault Ste Marie to the Post Office. We didn't have a 'Poste Restante' arrangement, but we needed to post our weekly letter home so the folks would have some inkling of where we had got to.

All across the open countryside, farmers were busy cutting the grass to make hay. The wide expanse of farmland was interspersed with rivers and woodland. Abruptly the scenery changed to desert and in the environs of Sudbury numerous large factories sprouted among the barren volcanic eruptions. Before long it was back to the farmland.

Another 'No camping' sign didn't deter us from once again parking on a wayside stop for the night, just hoping that all would be well. No sooner had we climbed into our sleeping bags than a car towing a boat pulled in, with a policeman on his tail.

"You know your rear lights aren't working," the officer admonished the driver. "You'll just have to leave the boat behind and go and find a replacement."

"Oops. That was a near one" I whispered as the police car disappeared, having taken no notice of us.

"Wake up. Wake up." Jane was digging me in the ribs. "A bear has been swimming across the river and it's foraging in the rubbish bins."

I grunted and turned over, not interested in the slightest. I hated being woken up. "You know what, it was only an Alsatian," she admitted with a giggle when I enquired about it the following morning.

This conversation was followed by one of our rare tiffs, because Jane wouldn't join me in the river for a swim. 'Little spoilsport,' I grumbled under my breath as I negotiated the sharp stones and eased myself into the brown water of the Ottawa River. At least I felt refreshed and cleaner afterwards.

That day an eclipse occurred. It was quite eerie. We couldn't make out through the thin layer of cloud whether it was partial, total or if only a sliver of the sun remained. It grew very dark in mid-afternoon, the birds stopped singing and all the vehicles were driving with headlights on. It was as if dusk had fallen too soon.

The farmland seemed to stretch right into Ottawa city centre, especially as the Research Farm was part of the city itself. It was Sunday morning and the streets were empty. A scenic drive took us along tree-lined boulevards, through squares and down pretty streets with pleasant homes. Unexpectedly, from nowhere, a battalion of guards appeared dressed in ceremonial red and wearing busbies. Excited, we quickly parked the car and together with several other tourists followed them as they marched towards Parliament Square for the changing of the guard.

Canada's Parliament buildings resembled their counterparts in London. The nearby Mall was amazingly traffic–free, so on the spur of the moment, we decided to have lunch in one of the cafés before motoring on to Montreal.

The next few days were spent with my half-sister Peggie, her husband Hein and their three adorable kids. Their bungalow was surrounded by a neat garden in a typical suburban area not far from the city centre. Peggie had jet black hair, just like my father, and had spent her eighteenth birthday with us over in the UK. It was wonderful to see her again and spend a few days in a family atmosphere.

First we booked our passage home for the 9th of August. This left us just over two weeks to travel south to New York and back. Then we sorted through and packed our surplus possessions and cleaned up the now travel-weary Mini. Once this was done, we spent some glorious hours relaxing, sunbathing in the garden and exploring Montreal.

The next port of call was Burlington in Vermont, USA, where my other half-sister, Peggerty, lived with her then four children. I never questioned the fact that they had similar names. Peggerty was very different; blonde, typically American like her mother and ten years older than me. She was responsible for the school run, driving one of those yellow school buses, brimful of noisy kids, around the neighbourhood. She too I had met only once previously, also when she had come to spend a month's holiday with the family in the South of France. Once the strangeness wore off, we had a great time playing with her five children, swimming in nearby Lake Champlain and barbecuing on Mt Philo. Despite its fancy name, it was only a hump with good views of the surrounding countryside. At the local disco, Jane and I died laughing at the local youth doing the 'shimmy', the craze of the early sixties. In contrast to the normal American decorum, it struck me as a surprisingly suggestive dance.

Further south in Boston, unable to find a suitable camp site we treated ourselves to a night at the YWCA. Professor Ted Kubtz, who I had met in London before leaving, took us sailing off Marblehead. The weather wasn't the best but that didn't bother me, I just loved to be out at sea. The wind dropped away altogether and we had to paddle some of the way back. Slowly the breeze got up again and up went the sails. We were finally making good progress, weaving in and out of all the other boats and just coming into harbour, when a sudden gust caused the yacht to veer and we very nearly smashed into another boat coming up alongside. Only Ted's quick reactions dropping the jib and steering off course saved us from collision.

At that moment the heavens opened. All around large drops of water danced on the surface of the sea. It was impossible to see where we were headed. Everyone and everything was drenched. Within five minutes the squall passed and in the ensuing calm, it was as if nothing had happened except that we were all wet through. Later that evening Ted drove us out of town to a typical New England hotel for a delicious dinner of local lobster.

Saturday morning was a non-working day, so driving along the uncluttered streets into New York, past Harlem and downtown to Manhattan was relatively easy. The Empire State Building was a must, so we queued for the elevator, amazed at the crowds, especially to get from the 86th to the 102nd floor. The red marble tiles of the entrance hall and the Seven Wonders of World depicted on the wall impressed me more than the view at the top.

Like trees in a forest, the fabled skyscrapers were shrouded in mist. In fact my first impression of New York had been of dirt and noise. I felt hemmed in by the tall buildings all around me. However a three-hour boat ride round Manhattan in brilliant sunshine with a postcard vista of skyscrapers and sailing close to the Statue of Liberty helped me to see things from a different perspective.

We stayed two nights with Peggerty's mother and stepfather, who was in the sharkskin business. We learnt that the fins were a delicacy used in Chinese cooking and he insisted on sending us to a restaurant in Chinatown. For some reason they didn't want to accompany us.

"Mr Stanley Wu will look after you royally" they said, and he did.

From among the many strange named delicacies he suggested, we tasted sharkskin soup and sweet and sour pork, dishes we had never heard of before. Mr Wu even showed us the view from his modern apartment, carefully leaving the door ajar to preserve our collective reputations, using a chair to make sure it didn't close inadvertently.

"It costs $50 per week to rent a room here and that's $200 a month. On the other hand it costs $3,000 to buy a place, but then you pay $100 per month maintenance. It's expensive," explained Mr Wu. To me, Chinatown in New York was less colourful than in San Francisco but nevertheless had its own particular charm.

New York was a whirlwind of impressions and unlike any other city we had visited in America, an amalgamation of different ethnic peoples. I was awed by man's achievement in creating such a place and cramming so much into it. Somehow a picture formed in my mind, consolidated by a documentary film we saw in the UN building, of what America was striving to achieve in this world. It showed that by harnessing the energy of the sun, wind and earth to create power, much could be done to alleviate the people of the world from a life of drudgery. It was a very forward-looking vision back in 1963.

I loved the blue stained-glass windows of St Patrick's Cathedral. The famous Waldorf Hotel was teeming with people and definitely lacked the dignity of the Savoy in London. We learnt that Manhattan Island is solid rock, which had allowed the skyscrapers to be built safely. Wall Street was a man-made canyon cutting through soaring buildings reaching for the sky. In contrast the houses on Long Island appeared quite squat, still surrounded by bushes and empty spaces. And in the middle of the city, the long narrow Central Park with green trees, lawns, sheltered playgrounds for the children and winding walkways was an oasis of tranquillity.

We had lost the front number plate in Italy two years previously. It had never been a problem, but here in New York people would comment and ask, "Where you guys from?" Our battered, travel-worn blue Mini was quite a novelty. Dwarfed by long American vehicles and giant trucks, she looked just like a toy car. Driving through downtown, a truck driver drew up beside Honey at the traffic lights. He looked down from his lofty perch and called down to Jane, "Can I give you gals a lift?"

A few blocks further on at an intersection, the police cop on duty, grinning with amusement, stopped all other traffic, dropped down on bended knee and beckoned us forward, as if encouraging a tiny child by saying, "Come along now".

I had packed my typewriter in a trunk, together with other things not needed on the short journey to New York, and left it at Peggie's house in Montreal, ready for the homeward journey. I recorded only a bare outline of our final experiences and my last letter home was written from Long Island.

Jane remembers that we sailed on the *Carinthia* from Montreal, via Greenock to Liverpool arriving on the 16th of August 1963, just three weeks short of two years since we left home. The dancing lessons were the highlight of those five days at sea. One of the officers, who insisted he was under orders, frequently asked Jane to dance with him as he thought she knew the steps.

Best of all, our parents were there on the quayside in Liverpool to welcome us home. Honey had travelled freight and would not be unloaded until later in the day. Jane's father was deeply disappointed, as he wanted to have a good look at the car; he was really interested to see how she had fared. As usual my parents were in a hurry and whisked me away. Jane and I barely had time to say goodbye - as Jane said later, it was an abrupt arrival/departure.

To my parents, more concerned about what I was going to do in the future, it was the journey that never was and within a short space of time I was dispatched to London to find a job. For Jane and me, it had been the adventure of lifetime. Not only had we driven our faithful little Mini right round the world and brought her home in working order, but we had seen, done and learnt so much. We had met so many wonderful kind people and our guardian angels had seen us through the worst experiences.

I now realize how privileged we were to cross continents without any restrictions, to visit places of interest, cathedrals, mosques and monuments without prior bookings or battling with tour groups. Western-style hotels and fast food chains had not yet proliferated in far-flung places. Two girls travelling alone in a Mini were a novelty, and people took delight in helping us.

POSTCRIPT

I never saw Honey again. She had been a good and faithful friend, our home for two years, and I missed her. She was retrieved from the *Carinthia* by one of my father's employees and the shiny new Mini Cooper that replaced her never touched my heart in the same way.

Now, fifty years on, Jane and I have remained good friends even though we see each other infrequently. In the intervening years we spent one fabulous winter together running a chalet in Zermatt, Switzerland. Jane worked for IBM and Wang International as a Support and Educational rep and travelled widely on business. She eventually married an ex-Jesuit priest and went to live in Boston in the USA. Meanwhile I became the first British female helicopter pilot. I married an architect and after seven challenging years in the Middle East, when Dubai and Oman were mere desert outposts, we came to live in Andorra with our four children.

APPENDIX

Notes on motoring and camping

A **Green card** to cover third party insurance was required in France and Italy.

An **International driving permit**, including a passport-size photograph, was needed for Greece and Turkey. Third party insurance was not compulsory but advisable.

A **Carnet de passage** was issued by the motoring organization upon receipt of a banker's guarantee, for 100% of the value of the car.

An **International certificate for motor vehicles** was required for Iran, Pakistan and India.

The **price of petrol** varied between two and five shillings per gallon (one imperial gallon = four & half litres).

Camping
France and Italy: official sites in every town and village.

Greece: only nine official sites.

Turkey: in Istanbul and Ankara.

Iran: no official sites but safe to camp anywhere.

Pakistan: no official sites but the picnic areas were adequate.

India: almost impossible to find an undisturbed place.